THE ESSENTIAL REINHOLD NIEBUHR

THE ESSENTIAL REINHOLD NIEBUHR

Selected Essays and Addresses

EDITED AND INTRODUCED BY
ROBERT McAFEE BROWN

Yale University Press
New Haven and London

Designed by Nancy Ovedovitz and set in Trump Medieval type by The Composing Room of Michigan, Inc. Printed in the United States of America by Vail-Ballou Press, Binghamton, N.Y.

Library of Congress Cataloging-in-Publication Data

Niebuhr, Reinhold, 1892–1971.
    The essential Reinhold Niebuhr.
    Includes index.
    1. Theology—Addresses, essays, lectures. 2. Social ethics—Addresses, essays, lectures. I. Brown, Robert McAfee, 1920–
II. Title.
BR85.N62 1986   230   85–22798

ISBN 0–300–03464–4 (cloth)
        0–300–04001–6 (pbk.)

The paper in this book meets the guidelines for permanence and durability of the Committee on Production Guidelines for Book Longevity of the Council on Library Resources.

10   9   8   7

Acknowledgment is made for permission to quote from the following: Reinhold Niebuhr, excerpts from *The Children of Light and the Children of Darkness.* Copyright © 1944 Charles Scribner's Sons; copyright renewed © 1972 Ursula Keppel-Compton Niebuhr. New foreword copyright © 1960 Reinhold Niebuhr. Reprinted with the permission of Charles Scribner's Sons.

CONTENTS

PART V
THE POSSIBILITIES AND LIMITATIONS
OF OUR KNOWING

ACKNOWLEDGMENTS

Grateful thanks are given to Charles Scribner's Sons for permission to reprint the essays in this volume from the books cited below.

"Optimism, Pessimism, and Religious Faith" was originally the Ware Lecture, given before the American Unitarian Association and published as a two-part essay in *Christianity and Power Politics* (1940).

"The Power and Weakness of God" and "Humour and Faith" were sermonic essays (sermons delivered several times and later expanded into essay form) in *Discerning the Signs of the Times* (1946). The sermon "The Providence of God" was originally preached at Union Theological Seminary in 1952, and "The Wheat and the Tares" was preached at Union in 1960. (Niebuhr preached an earlier version of "The Wheat and the Tares" one summer to the farming community at Heath, Massachusetts, winning over his congregation with the opening comment, "This sermon may be good theology, but it's certainly bad agriculture.") The prayers are chosen from among those offered by Niebuhr during services of worship he conducted at Union and elsewhere over many years. The sermons and prayers are from *Justice and Mercy* (1974), edited by Ursula M. Niebuhr and published by Harper & Row.

"The Assurance of Grace" is from one of Niebuhr's early books, *Reflections on the End of an Era* (1934), and is included here as a reminder that the reality of grace was not a late discovery, but informed the whole of Niebuhr's writing, coming to a crescendo at the end of the Gifford Lectures: "Thus wisdom about our destiny is dependent upon a humble recognition of the limits of our knowledge and our power. Our most reliable understanding is the fruit of 'grace' in which faith completes our ignorance without pretending to possess its certainties as knowledge; and in which contrition mitigates our pride without destroying our hope" (*The Nature and Destiny of Man*, II, p. 321).

"The Christian Church in a Secular Age" was the address given by Niebuhr at the Life and Work Conference (a precursor of the World Council of Churches) at Oxford in 1937; it was published in *The Student World* and reprinted in *Christianity and Power Politics* (1940). "The Christian Witness in the Social and National Order" was an address at the first world assembly of the World Council of Churches in Amsterdam in 1948, and is reprinted from *Christian Realism and Political Problems* (1953). It first appeared in *The Chaplain* in December 1948. "Why the Christian Church Is Not Pacifist" was written during the early part of World War II, first published by the SCM Press in Great Britain, and included in *Christianity and Power Politics* (1940).

"Augustine's Political Realism," originally delivered as the Frances Carroll Memorial Lecture at Columbia University, appeared in *Christian Realism and Political Problems* (1953), as did "Love and Law in Protestantism and Catholicism," which was first published in *The Journal of Religious Thought* in Spring-Summer 1952. "The Children of Light and the Children of Darkness" consists of portions of the foreword and the whole of chapter 1 of *The Children of Light and the Children of Darkness* (1944), originally delivered as the West Lectures at Stanford University. "The Relations of Christians and Jews in Western Civilization" is reprinted from *Pious and Secular America* (1958). It was originally a paper delivered at a joint meeting of the faculties of Union Theological and Jewish Theological seminaries (located on opposite corners of Broadway and 122d Street in New York City), and has become a benchmark in Protestant rethinking about conversion of Jews to Christianity.

"Ideology and the Scientific Method" originally appeared in *Christian Realism and Political Problems* (1953), and illustrates Niebuhr's challenge to rival epistemologies; "Coherence, Incoherence, and Christian Faith," appearing originally in *The Journal of Religion* in July 1951 and reprinted in *Christian Realism and Political Problems* (1953), continues the discussion with a statement of Niebuhr's own position. "Mystery and Meaning," reprinted from *Discerning the Signs of the Times* (1946), develops a favorite theological theme of Niebuhr's, on which he preached and wrote many times. Other reflections on the same theme, with the same title, can be found in *Beyond Tragedy* (1937) and *Pious and Secular America* (1958).

"A View of Life from the Sidelines" was written in 1967 but never published during Niebuhr's lifetime. It was edited for the present volume and published in *The Christian Century* in the December 19–26, 1984, issue, as part of the centennial celebration of the magazine.

INTRODUCTION

One of Reinhold Niebuhr's early books, a journal of reflections written during the time he was a pastor in Detroit, was entitled *Leaves from the Notebook of a Tamed Cynic*. Another early book, published after he joined the faculty of Union Theological Seminary as a professor of Christian ethics, was entitled *Reflections on the End of an Era*. By combining elements from the two titles, we can describe the standpoint represented by the essays in this volume. They are the reflections of a pessimistic optimist.

The conjunction of the adjective *pessimistic* with the noun *optimist* may initially sound like doubletalk, particularly if one has not read Niebuhr, but the words are carefully chosen to reflect his own perspective. In the same way that the title of his early book qualifies the noun *cynic* with the adjective *tamed*, an attempt to characterize his mature thought must employ a seeming contradiction. There is an ultimate optimism in Niebuhr's thought that is often overlooked, especially by his critics: we are recipients of undeserved grace, which means that there are indeterminate possibilities for good on the human scene. A passage in the second volume of *The Nature and Destiny of Man* provides the locus classicus for such an assertion:

> There are no limits to be set in history for the achievement of more universal brotherhood, for the development of more perfect and more inclusive mutual relations. All the characteristic hopes and aspirations of Renaissance and Enlightenment, of both secular and Christian liberalism are right at least in this, that they understand that side of the Christian doctrine which regards the *agape* of the Kingdom of God as a resource for infinite development towards a more perfect brotherhood in history. . . . The freedom of man makes it impossible to set any limits of race, sex, or social condition upon the brotherhood which may be achieved in history.[1]

1. *The Nature and Destiny of Man*, II (New York: Charles Scribner's Sons, 1943), 85.

But such a sentiment always needs to be qualified to avoid sentimentality, so Niebuhr adopted a provisional pessimism as well; as
the following essays demonstrate, no one has ever catalogued more
tellingly than Niebuhr our ongoing capacity to abuse and turn to evil
every fresh possibility for good. The doctrine of original sin, he observed in *Man's Nature and His Communities*, is the one empirically
verifiable doctrine of Christian faith.

This mixture of grace and sin, in both individuals and cultures,
works as a potentially redemptive rather than an inevitably destructive ingredient in our political life, to take but one example. Niebuhr's most incisive epigram shows why: "Man's capacity for justice
makes democracy possible; but man's inclination to injustice makes
democracy necessary" (*The Children of Light and the Children of
Darkness* [New York: Scribner's, 1944], ix). We can use power creatively in the service of justice, and that is our glory. But we can also
abuse power destructively in the service of self (either the individual
self or the individual self's projection in the life of a nation), and that
is our demonry. Consequently, we need built-in safeguards to assure
that no individual and no group accumulates too much power.
Niebuhr saw a recognition of both sides of our condition in the
checks and balances built into the United States Constitution between the legislative, executive and judicial branches of government,
enabling each to ride watchdog on the other two so that no one
branch can engulf the others. The Constitution, as Niebuhr often
said (citing Lord Bryce), was the product of people who believed in
original sin. Our capacity for justice makes democracy possible—
hence the vast powers given to each branch of government. But our
inclination to injustice makes democracy necessary—hence the safeguards against a single branch gaining inordinate power over the
others. Pessimistic optimism.

Because Niebuhr had an incisive ability to ferret out the shortcomings and pretensions of any human claim or system of thought, a
talent for finding "sin lurking at the door" (Gen. 4:7)—any door—he
was often perceived as an almost unqualified pessimist. As will be
apparent in the pages that follow, however, the pessimism, if per-
vasive, is provisional; and the optimism, if not omnipresent, is ultimate. Even divine judgment, which Niebuhr discerned so clearly and
which seems to justify a pessimistic stance on the part of its discern-
ers, can be an ultimate source of hope, for it reminds us that human

sin is only the penultimate reality, and that when sin has been judged and defeated, the very judgment provides the seedbed in which mercy and grace can be sown and take root in human life. To be sure, temptations to pretension and pride are tares growing alongside the new wheat, and the struggle between them will continue generation after generation. And while we are perplexed by this, Niebuhr reminds us, following St. Paul, that we are "perplexed but not unto despair" (2 Cor. 4:8).

The substantive word is *optimist* and the modifier is *pessimistic*, not the other way around. Niebuhr is not an optimistic pessimist but a pessimistic optimist. The first essay in this volume serves to clarify this matter further.

With that secured, the word *reflections* can be dealt with more briefly. The book that originally bore the word was a collection of essays on a variety of topics rather than a single, sustained theological argument. While Niebuhr wrote a number of volumes of "sustained theological argument," such as *Moral Man and Immoral Society, An Interpretation of Christian Ethics, Faith and History,* and, most notably, *The Nature and Destiny of Man,* he also published many books that brought together originally unrelated essays, such as the books from which selections were made for this volume. The essays here might be called reflections as well, since they treat many topics in brief rather than extended compass.

Niebuhr's resources in this sort of writing were always two: (1) the particular heritage of the Christian faith that he had appropriated, drawing especially on the Hebrew prophets, Jesus, Paul, the Reformers, and Kierkegaard; and (2) a viewpoint in scrutinizing the world around him not only in the light of this faith, but also with the tools of social science, political philosophy, and history that he acquired during his adult life. He was writing not so much for the ages as for the moment, and we must be careful not to assume that a particular analysis, eminently valid for the time in which it was written, is necessarily valid for another time. But along with that caveat, it is worth noting that the amount of Niebuhr's thought that transfers from one age to the next is impressive. The essays that follow have been chosen to exhibit the enduring, and not just the ephemeral, in Niebuhr's thought.

Reflections has another meaning, not necessarily one that Niebuhr himself intended, but one that can be creatively applied to him. His reflections are not only a record of his own musings, but a mirror of the times on which he was musing. While a mirror reflects our world, it does so in reverse, so that we perceive not simply that which is already familiar, but that which must now be viewed in a different way. It was preeminently a characteristic of Reinhold Niebuhr that he reflected the world around him in ways that were different from most of his contemporaries. His was almost always a minority report on the state of things, for he viewed the world from the perspective of the Christian faith, a perspective not shared by most commentators of his time. Niebuhr had no illusions that he could prove that his perspective was truer than those of his contemporaries, but he frequently observed that at least the profundities of Biblical faith made more sense out of more facts—allowing always for a healthy residue of mystery—than the secular perspectives with whose proponents he did frequent battle.

An account of Reinhold Niebuhr's life has been provided in Richard Fox, *Reinhold Niebuhr: A Biography* (New York: Pantheon, 1986); Paul Merkley, *Reinhold Niebuhr: A Political Account* (Montreal: McGill-Queens University Press, 1975); and June Bingham, *Courage to Change: An Introduction to the Life and Thought of Reinhold Niebuhr* (New York: Scribner's, 1972). Helpful interpretive material is available in Charles W. Kegley, ed., *Reinhold Niebuhr: His Religious, Social, and Political Thought,* 2d ed. (New York: Pilgrim Press, 1984). D. B. Robertson has compiled an invaluable reference work in *Reinhold Niebuhr's Works: A Bibliography* (Boston: G. K. Hall, 1979). Such resources will enable a new generation of readers to situate Niebuhr clearly within the events and ideas of his time and to enrich their appreciation of his writings. The following paragraphs seek to do the same in the briefest possible fashion.

Niebuhr was born on June 21, 1892, in Wright City, Missouri, the son of Gustav and Lydia Niebuhr. His father was a minister of the German Evangelical Synod, and Niebuhr grew up as a "child of the manse." His siblings included Helmut Richard, likewise a distinguished theologian and ethicist; Hulda, a practitioner (and later professor) in Christian education; and Walter, who worked as a journalist, filmmaker, and businessman rather than in the ecclesiastical arena.

After going to Elmhurst College, a small denominational high school in Illinois, and Eden Seminary, Niebuhr spent two years at Yale Divinity School, where he received an M.A., before serving for thirteen years as pastor of a middle-class parish in Detroit. He had inherited the liberal optimism of the "social gospel" of the time, but his parish experience and his excursions into political life led him to feel that such an attitude did not sufficiently measure the reality of evil and sin in the world. It was the autocratic practices of Henry Ford, he often said, that drove him back to the prophetic faith of the Bible, with its emphasis on sin and judgment as well as on grace, and forced him to confront the reality of systemic evil. His increasing recognition that even good intentions can serve socially disastrous ends received strong documentation in his *Moral Man and Immoral Society*. This book, which raised a furious storm of controversy, placed him in the public spotlight as a keen social and theological analyst, shortly after he became professor of Christian ethics at Union Theological Seminary in New York City, a position he held until retirement. (In a late book, *Man's Nature and His Communities*, Niebuhr commented ruefully, as his recognition of the pervasiveness of human sin deepened, that the thesis of the early book could have been more accurately communicated by the title *The Not So Moral Man in His Less Moral Communities*.)

While serving as mentor to many generations of theological students, Niebuhr matured in his own views during his four decades of teaching. His increasing recognition of the inadequacies of theological liberalism led him to articulate a position usually called neo-orthodoxy, although this is a term that Niebuhr himself disliked. Neo-orthodoxy represented a recovery of the classical Christian heritage. In Niebuhr's case, this meant giving special attention to such figures as the Hebrew prophets, Jesus and Paul, Augustine, the Protestant Reformers and Kierkegaard at their best—hence *orthodoxy*—but without the rigidity, exclusiveness, and archaic world view that characterized post-Biblical Christianity at its worst— hence *neo-*.

Too facile a use of this term to describe Niebuhr does him a disservice, however, for he was never the captive of any school, and his insights continued to grow and change throughout his career. Indeed, as a few of the essays published here demonstrate, some of his choicest polemics (not always directly on target) were reserved for the Swiss theologian, Karl Barth, usually designated as Europe's leading neo-orthodox theologian; and for all his fulminations against theological liberalism, Niebuhr always exhibited openness to change and to an experiential starting point—a position that characterizes liberalism at its best.

We do Niebuhr no injustice, however, by positioning him within what he often called Biblical prophetic faith, a position with many implications for social analysis, and one that acknowledges the transcendent God of Amos, Isaiah, Jeremiah, Ezekiel, Jesus, and Paul. Throughout his life, Niebuhr was increasingly able to affirm the Biblical message of the justice and mercy of God, aided by the insights of Biblical criticism—another of the positive legacies of the liberalism he otherwise found wanting, a legacy that enabled him in his mature years to be relevant rather than obscurantist.

Politically, the Biblical realism Niebuhr rediscovered went hand in glove with his early espousal of socialism and a strong critique of capitalism. The socialist affirmation was gradually mitigated and then increasingly rejected, because Niebuhr recognized the theological and philosophical inadequacies in Marxism as well as the historical betrayals of socialism that emerged in Stalinism. He came to an increasing appreciation of what could be accomplished within the New Deal capitalism of Franklin Roosevelt, but he also observed historical betrayals in Western capitalism. His enduring stance alongside the Hebrew prophets was clearly manifested in that he found all political and social constructs wanting when measured against the yardstick of divine justice. Such constructs were in constant need of an inner critique that he never failed to supply, even though some were clearly better than others—which, in a world of ambiguity, may be the best one can hope for.

Niebuhr's method can be described, in the parlance of his day, as dialectical, involving the simultaneous affirmation of what initially seem to be contrary propositions. Love as an "impossible possibility" was one such early expression in *An Interpretation of Christian Ethics*. By this he meant that love is the ultimate norm for all human activity, hovering over every situation as a possibility of achievement, and yet impossible in the sense that it can never be fully achieved in any human situation. Rather than destroying the relevance of love, such a recognition establishes it even more fully, for love always remains both as a judgment on the adequacy of every partial achievement and as a challenge toward fuller approximation in the future.

Perhaps the clearest example of a Niebuhrian dialectical position is the opening sentence of the second volume of his most profound work, the Gifford Lectures delivered at the University of Edinburgh in 1939, published as *The Nature and Destiny of Man*. Niebuhr began the second set of lectures with the claim, "Man is, and yet is not, involved in the flux of nature and time." Those who take the trouble to parse this statement theologically will discover that it makes perfectly good descriptive sense. We *are* "involved in the flux of nature and time"; we are born, we live, we eat, we make love, we die. But it is also true that we are *not* "involved in the flux of nature and time" completely, for we transcend, in part at least, that very flux; we not only die but we know that we will die, we reflect on the fact, and we dread our own death. By the gifts of memory and anticipation, we stand in some sense above our mortality and survey it. Birds and humans both sing, Niebuhr reflected, but birds do not write histories of bird music. That we stand at a unique "juncture of nature and spirit," neither dimension of which can be collapsed into the other, is what distinguishes us from the rest of creation.

For Niebuhr, one of the indirect vindications of the Christian faith is that it "makes more sense out of more facts" than does any other faith. This thesis is nowhere more clearly illustrated than in the point under discussion. Naturalism, as Niebuhr argued in the Gifford Lectures, tries to "reduce" humanity to the flux of nature and to find a full explanatory principle there; idealism, on the other hand, assumes that humanity can achieve a full emancipation from the world of nature and inhabit the realm of pure mind. Neither position is dialectical enough. The Judeo-Christian tradition insists, by way of contrast, that we have not been adequately described or assessed until it has been noted that we are an indissoluble unity of nature and spirit. Such a dialectical assertion may not be as immediately tidy as its alternatives, but it is ultimately truer to the facts of our experience. We are, and yet are not, involved in the flux of nature and time.

Working from such perspectives, Niebuhr became one of the leaders and inspirers—and critics—of his generation, not only among theologians, but among politicians, economists, and social analysts as well. A steady stream of editorials, essays, articles, and books emerged from his study. He wrote for both religious and secular publications, traveled widely, lectured incessantly, preached more weekends than not, and kept a pragmatic approach to issues that allowed him to explore many options and to change positions when the facts dictated a need to do so. Having been a pacifist during his "social gospel" years, he came in the late 1930s to espouse the necessity—a tragic necessity, as he acknowledged—of increasing U.S. involvement in the war in Europe, lest what he called the synthetic barbarism of Hitler's Nazi ideology engulf the world. He served on countless committees to that end, and helped to found a journal, *Christianity and Crisis*, intended to combat the isolationism of the United States and of American churches. Throughout his mature years he was active on the American political scene, moving finally from the Socialist to the Liberal party in New York, sometimes serving as a consultant of the State Department and other governmental agencies.

Niebuhr was active in the church to a degree often overlooked by both supporters and critics, not only as a member of the faculty of an interdenominational seminary preparing students for Christian ministry (a post he never forsook despite a number of offers from universities), but as a truly great preacher whose vigorous delivery and prophetic insights kept him in constant demand on the university chapel circuit, often to the detriment of his health. He was also a participant in ecumenical activities of the worldwide church, speaking at the Life and Work Conference at Oxford in 1937, and at the initial world assembly of the World Council of Churches at Amsterdam in 1948.

So great were Niebuhr's intellectual and critical gifts that from a distance (and even, on occasion, up close) he often appeared formidable, if not frightening. Never one to suffer fools gladly, he could engage in polemics before which even the mighty had ample reason to cringe. And yet, as generations of students and friends will testify, his manner in individual relations was supportive. In class, his usual comment, "That's a very good question," before responding to a student's query, was conducive to dialogue rather than intimidation.

His faculty apartment at Union Seminary was the location of weekly "at homes" for several decades. The human side of Niebuhr emerged on such occasions, in exchanges with his wife, Ursula M.

Keppel-Compton, a brilliant Oxford divinity graduate who taught religion at Barnard College during most of the New York years; and in stories about their children, Christopher and Elisabeth, whose presence not only gladdened Niebuhr's heart, but provided him with endless examples of his dialectical view of the complexity of human existence. It was Ursula Niebuhr's inspired decision to include a generous sampling of her husband's prayers in *Justice and Mercy* (a book of Niebuhr's sermons that she edited after his death), a collection that reveals dimensions of Niebuhr's personal faith in God, and his love of the world God has created, that would otherwise have remained unknown to all but his closest friends.

In 1952, Niebuhr suffered a severe stroke that impaired his left hand and side, had some effect on his speech, and diminished his previously capacious energy for the rest of his life. Even operating on less than full strength, Niebuhr was more than the equivalent of most people at their physical best, and after a time of enforced leisure, as he called it, he returned to writing and teaching on a more limited basis until his retirement in 1960. He died in Stockbridge, Massachusetts, where he and his wife had moved, on June 1, 1971.

For half a century, Niebuhr exercised a decisive impact on the thinking of his contemporaries, responding to the transitions from crisis to crisis through which they were living: World War I and its disillusioning aftermath, the Great Depression, the buildup of U.S. isolationism, World War II and its disillusioning aftermath, the advent of the nuclear age and the possibility that it would have no aftermath at all, and the Vietnam tragedy, an example of American imperialism toward the end of Niebuhr's life that he particularly deplored. A *New Yorker* cartoon he would have appreciated shows Adam and Eve being driven out of the Garden of Eden by an angel with a flaming sword; Adam is commenting to Eve, "My dear, we live in an age of transition."

Recalling that one of Niebuhr's favorite words, *crisis*, means not only "critical time," but also "judgment," we find in Niebuhr's message a judgment against all pretensions to premature or overly simple solutions, and yet an acknowledgment that beyond judgment there is always a message of mercy, and thus of hope, for the contrite. Niebuhr recognized the ongoingness of tragedy as perceptively as anyone of his era, but he also saw, as many of his contemporaries failed to see, that (as the title of perhaps his finest book of sermonic essays suggests) there are always possibilities *Beyond Tragedy*.

Relating the events of tragedy and those beyond tragedy is a never-ending, ever-changing task. Not everything that Niebuhr wrote for his age automatically speaks to our age. While the word of the gospel is "the same, yesterday, today, and forever" (Heb. 13:8), and the resources of divine grace and mercy are always available, the way we appropriate those resources, and, more important, what actions we engage in as a result of the appropriation, may vary dramatically in different historical situations. To make honest use of Niebuhr in our own time, we must remember what he never forgot, that the gospel speaks different words to different times, and even different words to different participants in the same times. A clear example is found in Niebuhr's World Council speech in Amsterdam in 1948, at a time when the world was only beginning to rebuild after the devastation of World War II.

> Must we not remind those who are weak and defrauded and despised that God will avenge the cruelties from which they suffer, but will also not hear the cruel resentment which corrupts their hearts?
>
> Must we not say to the rich and secure classes of society that their vaunted devotion to the laws and structures of society which guarantees their privileges is tainted with self-interest? . . .
>
> Against those who make the state sacrosanct, we must insist that the state is always tempted to set its majesty in rebellious opposition to the divine majesty. To those who fear the extension of the state for the regulation of modern economic life, we must point out that their fears are frequently prompted not by a concern for justice but by a jealous desire to maintain their own power. (See below, pp. 98–99)

The fact that there are different messages for different constituencies is of signal important as we move from Niebuhr's actual impact on his own era to his potential impact on ours. We need to learn from him that proximate judgments about contemporary events must never be carved in stone, not even—or especially—if they are Niebuhr's judgments. In the early days of the U.S. labor movement, Niebuhr observed, almost any action in the self-interest of labor was simultaneously a blow for social justice, so great were the disparities between the relative power of labor and management. Niebuhr could say, in Biblical parlance, that labor "had a righteousness not her own." But such an estimate, while true in the early days of the labor movement, was certainly not true by the 1950s or 1960s, when labor had achieved enough power that its self-sought ends were not necessarily congruent with the common good at all. (Perhaps in the 1980s, when the power of labor unions has waned, yet another appraisal is needed.)

To take another example, Niebuhr wrote many things, both supportive and critical, about socialism. In the process, he became increasingly disillusioned by the way Russian communism had gradually succumbed to the brutalities of Stalinism; his later writings, such as *The Irony of American History*, are full of warnings and denunciations of the aberrant unfolding of the left in Russia. Latter-day advocates of anticommunist ideology in the United States have focused on such statements, hailing Niebuhr, astonishingly enough, as a precursor of the new conservatism.

But they have listened to Niebuhr with only one ear. Having summoned him by selective quotation as a spokesman for their own brand of anticommunism, they have not heard his full message: that the patent evils of Stalinism, which must be denounced, are latently (and sometimes not so latently) present in other systems of government, including our own, and must be denounced there as well. Americans today would not so wildly affirm the public perception of Russia as the empire of evil, with its implicit assumption that we are the empire of good, if they had listened to Niebuhr's reminders of our own national sins and shortcomings.

"We must fight their falsehood with our truth," he often said about such one-sided activities, "but we must also fight the falsehood in our truth." It is the failure to recognize that sin is not the exclusive monopoly of the enemy, and that virtue is not the exclusive possession of the "righteous," that makes many current Christian right-wing claims so un-Niebuhrian. Niebuhr's recognition of ambiguity does not mean retreating into a Hegelian universe where all cows are black at midnight, for there are still choices to be made. But the choices are not (as many contemporary right wing anticommunists insist) between pure virtue and absolute vice, but between differing combinations of vice and virtue, some of which are less demonic than others. Niebuhr's most important contribution to our own time may be his reminder that one clear sign of the presence of virtue is an unwillingness to claim it too absolutely as one's own possession.

It remains curious (and painful) to those who knew Niebuhr and whose thought was shaped by his that many in the new generation ignore this part of his message and use him to support extreme conservative positions he would almost surely have opposed. Niebuhr himself furnishes the best refutation of such co-optation. In his last book, *Man's Nature and His Communities*, he surveys changes in his own thought during a long lifetime and concludes: "[It is] my strong conviction that *a realist conception of human nature should be made the servant of an ethic of progressive justice and should not be made into a bastion of conservatism, particularly a conservatism which defends unjust privileges.* I might define this conviction as the guiding principle throughout my mature life of the relation of religious responsibility to political affairs."[2]

Although I have suggested that none of Niebuhr's political comments should be carved in stone, this is one quotation for which an exception might be made, as a way of safeguarding Niebuhr's own estimate of "the guiding principle throughout [his] mature life of the relation of religious responsibility to political affairs" against unjustified usurpation.

It remains only to comment on the rationale for selecting the present group of essays. Faced with an embarrassment of riches—hundreds of articles came from Niebuhr's ever-flowing pen—I worked with Ursula Niebuhr and with John Ryden at Yale University Press to develop some initial guidelines. Few if any essays currently in print would be included, and the book would not be merely a collection of "fugitive pieces" that had somehow escaped inclusion in other collections of Niebuhr's essays.[3] This translated into a decision to choose essays that Niebuhr or his wife had included in books now unavailable.[4]

2. *Man's Nature and His Communities* (New York: Charles Scribner's Sons, 1965), 24–25; italics mine.

3. Attention should be called to three excellent collections: D. B. Robertson, ed., *Love and Justice* (Philadelphia: Westminster, 1957); D. B. Robertson, ed., *Essays in Applied Christianity* (New York: Meridian, 1959); and Ronald Stone, ed., *Faith and Politics* (New York: Braziller, 1968). All of these works center on Niebuhr's political writings.

4. This category included *Does Civilization Need Religion?*; *Reflections on the End of an Era*; *Christian Realism and Political Problems*; *Discerning the Signs of the Times*; *Pious and Secular America*; *Justice and Mercy* (posthumous); *The Self and Dramas of History*; and *Man's Nature and His Communities*. Since the first title contains very dated material, and the last two are works of sustained argument rather

The principle employed in the final selection is subject to misunderstanding if an immediate qualification is not introduced. The principle: preference is given to the theological rather than the political essays. The qualification: there is no way, if one wishes to be faithful to Niebuhr, of drawing a true line between the two categories. One cannot imagine Niebuhr writing nonpolitical theology or nontheological politics; the connections, if not always explicit, are implicit in every article. However, in most essays there is a tilt—toward Augustine instead of Richard Nixon (let us say), or toward defining the church's task in a secular age rather than reflecting on attempts to create the New Deal—that suggests a way of distinguishing the enduring from the ephemeral. That which endures in Niebuhr gives us splendid resources for making our own judgments about contemporary analogues to Richard Nixon or for reflecting on current attempts to dismantle the New Deal. There are many ways of betraying Niebuhr in this endeavor, but immersion in his thought, as represented in the essays chosen for inclusion, should at least make such betrayal more difficult.

While I take final responsibility for the selection and arrangement of the essays, I gratefully acknowledge assistance from a number of Niebuhr's friends, and students of his thought, whose responses to a query about the most enduring essays helped to inform my final choices. These include: John C. Bennett, Richard W. Fox, Franklin I. Gamwell, Richard Harries, Charles W. Kegley, John H. Leith, Robin Loven, Martin E. Marty, Nathan A. Scott, Jr., and William J. Wolf.

Special thanks are due to Ursula M. Niebuhr, who gave unstintingly of time and advice from the moment the idea for the volume surfaced. As Niebuhr himself indicates in the introduction to *Man's Nature and His Communities*—a volume which he virtually concedes should have been published as a joint work—theirs was a lifetime of collaboration, theologically as well as personally; Ursula Niebuhr's editing of the sermons and prayers in *Justice and Mercy* (published posthumously) is an enduring tribute to the sensitiveness of their relationship. I am also grateful to Niebuhr's son, Christopher, for help in tracking down some elusive references.

---

than individual essays, the selections have been drawn from the other five titles. The two exceptions to this rubric are "The Children of Light and the Children of Darkness," from *The Children of Light and the Children of Darkness*, and "A View of Life from the Sidelines," from *The Christian Century*.

The essays appear in virtually their original form, with only the following changes: correcting typographical and punctuation errors; inserting Biblical references where needed to identify quotations or allusions; recasting direct quotations that Niebuhr had incorrectly cited from memory; and subdividing inordinately long paragraphs. I have also introduced section headings within the essays to help readers not immediately at home with Niebuhr's sometimes complicated style to keep pace with the argument. My initial inclination to recast the essays in inclusive language, in order to enhance communication with a new generation, was decisively overruled; readers for whom sexist language is a barrier to communication are urged to remember that Niebuhr wrote before the issue had surfaced.

Because Niebuhr quoted from various versions of the Bible, usually without attributing the version, I saw no need to provide the name of the translation used. In the few cases where a version is mentioned, it is Niebuhr's own reference. Similarly, I have not sought to make spelling practice consistent from chapter to chapter, since these essays come from different volumes and were published both in the United States and in Great Britain.

Reinhold Niebuhr was not only my teacher and theological mentor; along with his wife and children, he was a close personal friend. He and John Bennett had more influence than anyone on my theological development and my increasing personal commitment to the Christian faith. That is a debt one can never truly repay, but it will be the modest beginning of repayment if the present volume makes some of Niebuhr's enduring insights available to a new generation of thinkers.

During the summer of 1943, in the tiny village church in Heath, Massachusetts, where Niebuhr worshipped and occasionally preached in the summer, he offered a prayer hastily written on the back of an envelope. It has survived and has achieved considerable fame through its adoption by Alcoholics Anonymous. It goes: "God give us grace to accept with serenity the things that cannot be changed, courage to change the things that should be changed, and the wisdom to distinguish the one from the other." That kind of wisdom is another part of Niebuhr's legacy to successive generations. ...ays tilt, as he did, in the direction of courageous change ...erene acceptance.

—Robert McAfee Brown

I
PESSIMISTIC OPTIMISM

1

Optimism, Pessimism, and Religious Faith

Human vitality has two primary sources, animal impulse and confidence in the meaningfulness of human existence. The more human consciousness arises to full self-consciousness and to a complete recognition of the total forces of the universe in which it finds itself, the more it requires not only animal vitality but confidence in the meaningfulness of its world to maintain a healthy will-to-live. This confidence in the meaningfulness of life is not something which results from a sophisticated analysis of the forces and factors which surround the human enterprise. It is something which is assumed in every healthy life. It is primary religion. Men may be quite unable to define the meaning of life, and yet live by a simple trust that it has meaning. This primary religion is the basic optimism of all vital and wholesome human life.

PRIMITIVE RELIGION

In primitive life the meaning of existence is revealed in the relation of the individual to his group. Life achieves meaning through its organic relation to a social enterprise. This loyalty usually results in some form of totemistic religion which gives a mythical and symbolic expression of the feeling that the value and meaning of the social group really represents absolute meaning. Such totemistic religion remains, in spite of all further elaborations, a permanent source of optimism of some people in all ages and all cultures, who refuse to ask ultimate questions about the relation of the value of their social group to some ultimate source of meaning. Some men achieve a very considerable happiness in their devotion to their family or their com-

3

munity or nation without asking any further questions about life's meaning. When national loyalty is reconstructed into an all-absorbing religion, as in modern Germany, we may witness the recrudescence of primitive religion in the modern period on a large scale.

In spite of the comparative satisfaction of many people, both primitive and modern, in a little cosmos, it is inevitable that men should seek to relate their group to a larger source of meaning just as surely as they must relate themselves to the life of the group. Thus animism is as primordial as totemism in the history of religion. In other words, men tried to bring the world of nature into their universe of meaning from the very beginning, and sought to relate their little cosmos to a larger cosmos. The gradual identification of nature gods with the gods of tribes and cities in the religions of early civilization shows how quickly the social cosmos was related to the larger universe, revealed in the world of nature, and a common center and source of meaning was attributed to both of them.

But the simple faith and optimism of primitive man did not exist long without being challenged. The world is not only a cosmos but a chaos. Every universe of meaning is constantly threatened by meaninglessness. Its harmonies are disturbed by discords. Its self-sufficiency is challenged by larger and more inclusive worlds. The more men think the more they are tempted to pessimism because their thought surveys the worlds which lie beyond their little cosmos, and analyzes the chaos, death, destruction and misery which seem to deny their faith in the harmony and meaningfulness of their existence in it. All profound religion is an effort to answer the challenge of pessimism. It seeks a center of meaning in life which is able to include the totality of existence, and which is able to interpret the chaos as something which only provisionally threatens its cosmos and can ultimately be brought under its dominion.

In the Jewish-Christian tradition this problem of pessimism and optimism is solved by faith in a transcendent God who is at once the creator of the world (source of its meaning) and judge of the world (i. e. goal of its perfection). It was this faith in a transcendent God which made it possible for Hebraic religion to escape both the parochial identification of God and the nation and the pantheistic identification of God and the imperfections of historical existence. It provided, in other words, for both the universalism and the perfectionism which are implied in every vital ethics. It is interesting to note that the process of divorcing God from the nation was a matter of both spiritual insight and actual experience. If the early prophets had not said, as Amos, "Are ye not as the children of the Ethiopians unto me, saith the Lord" (Amos 9:7), faith in the God of Israel might have perished with the captivity of Judah. But it was the exile which brought this process to a triumphant conclusion. A second Isaiah could build on the spiritual insights of an Amos, and could declare a God who gave meaning to existence quite independent of the vicissitudes of a nation, which had been the chief source of all meaning to the pious Jew.

In the same manner, faith in a transcendent God made it possible to affirm confidence in a meaningful existence even though the world was full of sorrow and evil. Some of the sorrow and misery was attributed to human sin. It was because man sinned that thorns and thistles grew in his field and he was forced to earn his bread by the sweat of his brow. The myth of the fall may solve the problem of evil too easily by attributing all inadequacies of nature to the imperfections of man, but it contains one element of truth found in all profound religion, and that is that it reduces man's pride and presumption in judging the justice of the universe by making him conscious of his own sin and imperfection and suggesting that at least some of the evil from which he suffers is a price of the freedom which makes it possible for him to sin.

It is to be noted that in Hebraic religion the transcendent God is never an escape from the chaos of this world. This world is not meaningless, and it is not necessary to escape from it to another supramundane world in order to preserve an ultimate optimism. For prophetic Judaism, existence in this world is intensely meaningful, though the ultimate center of meaning transcends the world. It knows nothing of the distinction between pure form and concrete existence, or between a virtuous reason and a sinful body. It rejoices in the physical creation. "Lord, how manifold are thy works. In wisdom hast thou made them all" (Ps. 104:24). When the Psalmist faces the fact of death he does not have recourse to hope in immortality to save his optimism. He rather finds the glory of God exalted by the brevity of man. "For a thousand years in thy sight are but as yesterday when it is past and as a watch in the night" (Ps. 90:4). The threat of death to the meaning of life is destroyed by faith in a purpose which transcends the generations and by the thought that death is in some sense a just retribution for human evil. "For we are consumed by thine anger and by thy wrath we are troubled. Thou has set our iniquities before thee and our secret sins in the light of thy countenance" (Ps. 90:8).

The prophetic religion from which Christianity took its rise is therefore not an other-worldly religion. It is thoroughly this-worldly, though it has nothing in common with the secularized this-world-liness of modern culture which finds meaning only in the historical process and knows nothing of a source of existence which transcends the process. Unfortunately, as this religion was philosophically elaborated in Greco-Roman thought, it borrowed something from and was corrupted by Neo-Platonic dualism. Reason always has difficulty with an adequate view of transcendence and immanence. It inclines either to reduce it to a complete dualism or to a complete monism. As a result it expresses a world view which is either too pessimistic or too optimistic to do justice to all the facts of life. An adequate religion is always an ultimate optimism which has entertained all the facts which lead to pessimism. Its optimism is based upon a faith in a transcendent center of meaning which is never fully expressed in any partial value and is never exhausted in any concrete historical reality. But though it is not exhausted in any such reality it is incarnated there. Like the human personality in the human body, it lives in and through the body, but transcends it.

The other-worldliness of classical Christian orthodoxy came to a full expression in the Middle Ages. Though its sense of sin was sometimes morbid, and though it sometimes degenerated into a cult of death, it is not correct to attribute complete other-worldliness to the Middle Ages. Medieval Catholicism was sufficiently this-worldly to attempt the construction of a papal empire which would, through its universalism, transcend all the partial and parochial values of nationalism. It was sufficiently this-worldly even to give a religious sanction to the feudal structure of society, and to fall into the most grievous and the most perennial sin of religion: the sin of using the transcendent reference to absolutize rather than to criticize the partial achievements of history.

THE RELIGION OF MODERN CULTURE

Our modern culture has acquired its most significant characteristics in its conscious and unconscious reaction to medieval culture. Its scientific discoveries made it impatient with the mythical errors of medieval religion. But it failed to realize that mythical descriptions of reality, though always inexact in describing detailed and historical fact, have the virtue of giving men a sense of depth in life. Pure science is always secular and horizontal in its references, and cannot express the vertical tendencies in culture which refer to the ultimate source of meaning in life. Modern culture substituted for the dualism and pessimism of medieval culture a simple naturalistic monism and optimism. It conceived history in dynamic terms and found it easy to identify change with progress, and to ascribe divine attributes to nature. It discovered in the "laws of nature" the very guarantee of the meaningfulness of the universe which it is the business of religion to find.

The religious attitude toward nature and its laws is evident in all of eighteenth-century literature. Holbach becomes religiously lyrical in addressing nature: "O Nature, sovereign of all being," he cries, "and ye her adorable daughters, virtue, reason, truth, remain forever our revered protectors. It is to you belong the praises of the human race." The identification of nature, virtue, reason and truth is a perfect example of the superficiality of this new mythology. The old mythology is sloughed off for being inexact, and a new mythology is created which is supposedly scientific but which ceases to be scientific as soon as it achieves mythical-religious proportions. Its laws are not laws at all, but projections of human ideals ("liberty, property and equality"). Its inability to discriminate between "nature as the entire system of things with the aggregate of all their properties" and "things as they would be without human intervention" (J. S. Mill) reveals that it has no recognition for the problem of depth and height in life. Human ideals are uncritically read into the natural process.

The religion of modern culture is, in other words, a superficial religion which has discovered a meaningful world without having discovered the perils to meaning in death, sin and catastrophe. History has an immediate, an obvious, meaning because it spells progress. Progress is guaranteed by increasing intelligence because human sin is attributed to ignorance which will be removed by a proper pedagogy. It is surprising how little modern culture has qualified the optimism upon this point, first clearly stated by Condorcet. There is no recognition in it of the perils to anarchy which reside in human egoism, particularly collective egoism. The naturalistic optimism is revealed not only in its confidence in natural and rational processes, but in its identification of physical comfort with final bliss. Thus Priestley could declare: "Men will make their situation in the world abundantly more easy and comfortable; they will probably prolong their existence in it and grow daily more happy, each in himself, and more able and, I believe, more disposed to communicate happiness to others. Thus whatever the beginning of the world, the end will be paradisaical, beyond what our imaginations can conceive."[1] Thus an uncritical this-worldliness is substituted for the untenable other-worldliness of medievalism, and men become confused by a superficial optimism in the very moment when they celebrate their emancipation from a morbid pessimism.

Though there is a horde of moderns who still live by and in this kind of uncritical naturalism and optimism, it could not long claim the credulity of the more critical spirits. The simple identification of human ideals with the forces of nature inevitably gave way to a humanistic dualism in which a sharp distinction was drawn between the human and the natural world. No better definition of this dualism is given than that found in Huxley's famous Romanes lecture on Evolution and Ethics, in which he declared: "The cosmic process has no sort of relation to moral ends; the imitation of it by man is inconsistent with the first principles of ethics. . . . The ethical progress of society depends not on imitating the cosmic process, still less in running away from it, but in combating it." This kind of dualism is more realistic than the older type of naturalism, and it frees human moral life from slavish dependence upon the "laws of nature." Its general effect is to express optimism in terms of a human world of meaning and to relegate the world of nature to a realm of meaninglessness.

Thus the optimism of pure naturalism degenerates into a fairly consistent pessimism, slightly relieved by a confidence in the meaningfulness of human life, even when its values must be maintained in defiance of nature's caprices. Bertrand Russell's now justly famous *Free Man's Worship* is a perfect and moving expression of this pessimism. "Brief and powerless is man's life. On him and all his race the slow sure doom sinks pitiless and dark. Blind to good and evil, om-

1. *Essay on the First Principles of Government*, 4.

nipotent matter rolls on its relentless way. For man, condemned today to lose his dearest, tomorrow himself to pass through the gates of darkness, it remains only to cherish ere yet the blow falls, the lofty thoughts that ennoble his little day, proudly defiant of the irresistible forces which tolerate for a moment his knowledge and his condemnation, to sustain alone a weary and unyielding atlas, the world that his own ideals have fashioned despite the trampling march of unconscious power." It must be said in favor of this view that if human life and human ideals are the only source of meaning in existence, it is more realistic to regard the world of nature as a "trampling march of unconscious power" than to imagine that it exists only to support human purposes. In terms of realism sophisticated pessimism is preferable to the naïve optimism of the moderns.

Yet this pessimism is not completely realistic. The world of nature is after all not as inimical to the human enterprise as this view assumes. "Nature, the homely nurse, does all she can to make her foster child, her inmate man, forget the glories he has known and that imperial palace whence he came." The paradoxes of classical religion, in which God is known to be revealed in the beneficences of nature even though it is recognized that the processes of nature do not exhaust the final meaning of existence, are more realistic than this dualism. Furthermore, it leads to an unjustified human pride. Man celebrating himself as a "weary and unyielding atlas" is a slightly ludicrous object of worship. Inevitably this remnant of optimism finally yields to the prevailing pessimism until, as Joseph Wood Krutch confesses in his *Modern Temper*, "now we know that man is petty."

If anything further were required to complete the self-destruction of modern optimism we have it in the tragic events of modern history. They have negated practically every presupposition upon which modern culture was built. History does not move forward without catastrophe, happiness is not guaranteed by the multiplication of physical comforts, social harmony is not easily created by more intelligence, and human nature is not as good or as harmless as had been supposed. We are thus living in a period in which either the optimism of yesterday has given way to despair, or in which some of the less sophisticated moderns try desperately to avoid the abyss of despair by holding to credos which all of the facts have disproved.

THE MARXIAN ALTERNATIVE

Long before the disintegration of modern optimism, the liberal culture in which it lies embedded was challenged by a new mythology which grew out of the experiences of those who had been disinherited by the injustices of modern industrial civilization, and who therefore knew from their own experience that the liberal picture of human nature and human history was not true. The Marxian mythology, whatever its ultimate optimism, is thoroughgoing in its pessimism when it analyzes the facts of contemporary history and of human nature in the contemporary environment. Human ideals are but the rationalizations of human interest. And human history is a series of class conflicts between people of varying and contradictory interests. This series of conflicts will end in the final destruction of our present social system.

In this Marxian mythology some of the old paradoxes of Jewish mythology reappear. Marx gives us a secularized version of Jewish prophecy, though it is not nearly as secularized as the liberal mythology. Its view of history is less simple, and its view of human nature is more true, than that of liberalism. Though it denies God as the center and source of life's meaning more explicitly than liberal naturalism, it implicitly avows a divine support for human purposes, more particularly for the very specific purposes of those who intend to guide history toward a classless society. In the words of Max Eastman, the Marxian world "is made of matter, but this matter performs the essential functions of spirit, that of going where the believer wants it to go by a 'self-active' dialectical movement which constitutes its 'essence.'" Here we have again the Jewish hope for a redeemed world, not above history but at the end of history. Here also is the idea of the Jewish prophets that history is constituted of the judgments as well as the mercies of God. The provisional pessimism is relieved by various types of optimistic faith and hope.

The chaos of the moment does not drive the Marxian to despair as it does the disappointed liberal. He sees meaning in this chaos, as the Jewish prophets of the exile discovered meaning in the vicissitudes of their nation. God uses the wrath of man to praise him, and the destruction of capitalism is but the necessary prelude to the construction of an ideal society. In some of its aspects the Marxian mythology of history is a profoundly religious one. For it, life is not a simple harmony but a chaos which has the possibilities of harmony within it. Human nature is not immediately good, but it contains potentialities for co-operative living under the proper environment. In other respects the Marxian mythology is quite primitive, however, and in others, again, it is too much the child of secular modernism to escape its errors of superficiality.

It is primitive in its glorification of a particular social group. The Marxian conception of a Messianic class is a kind of primitive totemism. There are, of course, solid justifications for regarding the victims of injustice in modern society as a fateful class. Experience has given them eyes to see what keener eyes do not see. Nevertheless, the Marxian identification of the fate of a class with the future of civilization itself is akin to the pre-prophetic messianism of Judaism; and it is not dissimilar to the modern tribalism, propagated, for instance, by the Nazis. I do not mean to imply that it is not more legitimate to ascribe universal values to the objectives of the working class than to endow a particular (Aryan) race with divine significance. Nevertheless, in each case the individual rescues life from meaninglessness by attachment and religious loyalty to a partial human community.

The religious significance of this type of optimism is clearly revealed in an article by Rebecca Pitts in *The New Masses* in which it is declared: "The loss of religious faith is good only if we can put in its place a faith in life so real and driving that it endows men's acts with an equal validity. . . . Of course there is only one solution—the solution which the bourgeoisie rejects as worse than the total annihilation of modern society. . . . Men become sincere and incorruptible as they identify their aims with those of the working class as a whole."[2]

This is a new kind of patriotism, and one may well believe that it has possibilities which the older patriotic loyalties lacked. It will contribute more to the destruction of an unjust social system and the building of a new one than the loyalties which express themselves in futile conflicts between various races and nations. But it is not free of the demonic pretensions which express themselves whenever a partial human value is given absolute significance by religious emotion. If it should be finally proved, as well it may, that the working class is an important but not a sole instrument of a new society, the opti-

2. "Something to Believe In," *The New Masses*, March 13, 1934.

mism of those whose whole universe of meaning is contained in the life of one class will degenerate into pessimism again.

Perhaps more important than the primitivism of Marxian religion is its secularized naturalism. Its high ideals of a just society are to be completely realized in history. It does not see that the highest ideals of justice, love and brotherhood are concepts of the human spirit when spirit completely transcends the infirmities of the flesh and the frustrations of history. They must be approximated but they will never be fully realized. Marxianism is, in short, another form of utopianism. We have had utopian solutions to the problem of pessimism throughout history. They point to a future when the chaos of the world will be overcome and life will become a complete harmony and a fulfilled meaning. They save optimism not by faith but by hope. Life is not regarded as meaningful as it exists, with all its sad disappointments; but significance is imparted to it by what it will be.

There is an element of truth in this utopianism, as there is truth in every sober hope. Some of the chaos of human existence can be overcome. It is possible to have a society in which there will be security for every one rather than insecurity for the many. No doubt the proper education and experience can reduce human egoism and can beguile it into less socially harmful expressions. But this kingdom of God upon earth where every one will give according to his ability and take according to his need, this anarchistic millennium of communist dreams, what is that but a confused naturalistic version of a religious hope? The optimism which is based upon it may outlast one five-year plan and possibly two or three. But after many five-year plans have come and gone and it is discovered that strong men still tend to exploit the weak, and that shrewd men still take advantage of the simple, and that no society can guarantee the satisfaction of all legitimate desires, and that no social arrangement is proof against the misery which we bring upon each other by our sin—what will become of this optimism? We might have a society in which greed is practically abolished, and yet men would suffer from injustice in such a society, as, for instance, some monks suffered from the cruel tyranny of their abbots in the monasteries of the Middle Ages.

An optimism which depends upon the hope of the complete realization of our highest ideals in history is bound to suffer ultimate disillusionment. All such optimistic illusions have resulted in such a fate throughout history. Always there comes a period when scoffers will arise to say, "Since the fathers have fallen asleep, all things continue as they were from the beginning of creation" (2 Pet. 3:4). The beauty and meaning of human life are partially revealed in ideals and aspirations which transcend all possibilities of achievement in history. They may be approximated and each approximation may lead to further visions. But the hope of their complete fulfillment arises from a confusion of spirit and nature, and a failure to realize that life in each moment of history moves not only forward but upward, and that the vertical movement must be expressed no matter how far the horizontal movement on the plane of history is carried. Marxism may represent a more realistic politics than eighteenth-century democratic idealism. But as a religion it will end just where the latter ended. Its optimism will sink ultimately into despair.

THE JEWISH-CHRISTIAN ALTERNATIVE

The optimism of historic Hebraism and of classical Christianity (except where the latter has been vitiated by a too thorough dualism) is much more robust and satisfying than the modern substitutes which have run their course. While modern optimism was in its prime it could sneer at the pessimism of historic religion because the illusions of the former prevented it from recognizing the tragic realities of life and history which the latter had incorporated into its universe of meaning. Now that these illusions have been dispelled, it is possible to recognize again that historic religion has a note of provisional pessimism in its optimism, for the simple reason that it takes cognizance of more of the facts of human existence.

The view of life and the world in classical religion of the Jewish and Christian tradition can be stated in rough outline, though it is impossible in such an outline to do justice to the differences and contradictions which have appeared in the long history of Jewish and Christian thought. In this view human life is meaningful even though its existence in a world of nature, which is not completely sympathetic to the human enterprise, is not fully explained. The world of nature is not completely interpreted in terms of human values or ideals, as in naïve naturalism, nor is it simply a dark abyss or a "trampling march of unconscious power" which man defies and against which he rebels. Man and nature are reconciled by faith in a center and source of meaning which transcends both man and nature.

It is not assumed that God's purposes can be fully measured by any measuring rod of human ideals. In one of the greatest books of religious poetry, the book of Job, man questions the justice of God in terms of human standards, but is finally overwhelmed by the majesty and mystery of existence, and Job confesses contritely, "I have uttered that I understood not; things too wonderful for me which I knew not—wherefore I abhor myself and repent in dust and ashes" (Job 42:6). Something of that idea, i.e., that the world is intensely meaningful, even though its meaning transcends human comprehension, runs as one strain through all profound religion. "To know that there is meaning but not to know the meaning," declares the modern J. Middleton Murry, "that is bliss." That word is in the spirit of classical religion. It expresses a trust in life even when the immediate facts of life seem to outrage our conception of what life ought to be: "Though he slay me yet will I trust him" (Job 13:15).

The transcendent God, most adequately pictured in the mythos of a creator God, is, though clothed in mystery, not the God of deism. His purposes are relevant and related to the human enterprise, and the highest human virtues give us some glimpses of His purposes. He is a God of justice and love. His majesty is no more certain than His moral perfection. The difficulty of bringing God's omnipotence into consistent relation with his goodness has engaged all ages of religious thought. But the most adequate religion solves its problems in paradoxes rather than schemes of consistency, and has never wavered in believing that God is both the ground of our existence and the ultimate pinnacle of perfection toward which existence tends. Therefore, the highest human excellencies are clues to the character of God.

Faith in a moral perfection which transcends human perfection is the basis of the note of contrition in all great religion. Man does not feel himself an outraged innocent in the evil world. Indeed, he accepts some of the evil which befalls him in the world as a just punishment for his sin. While traditional religion usually overstates the case at this point and makes human sin responsible for all the imperfections of nature, it remains true nevertheless that this insight actually incorporates a good deal of what might be regarded as chaos into the universe of meaning.

It can be seen that love is the law of life, even when people do not live by the law of love. When that law is broken the consequences are death and destruction. For the religious man the tortures and agonies through which our generation is going and through which other generations will probably go, represent the inevitable judgment upon a civilization which violated the law of brotherhood and has destroyed itself by these violations. Chaos and death may suggest meaninglessness to the proud man, but to the contrite man they are revelations of the consequences of human sin; and if they cannot be completely comprehended in those terms they may still be regarded as a part of the meaning of life which has not been fully disclosed to man. They may thus be accepted with gratitude, and the believer is able to say, "The Lord hath given, the Lord hath taken away, praised be the name of the Lord" (Job 1:21), or, in the words of Francis of Assisi, "Praised be my Lord for our sister the death of the body from which no man escapeth."

To believe in a meaningful existence which has its center and source beyond itself makes it possible to preserve moral vitality, because the world as it exists is not regarded as perfect even though it is meaningful. Hebraic thought has always had greater ethical vigor than that of the Greeks; and Christian thought, where it has been most vital ethically, has borrowed heavily from Jewish thought. Purely rationalistic interpretations of life and existence easily make one of two mistakes. They either result in idealistic or pantheistic sanctifications of historic reality, in which the given is appreciated too uncritically to allow for a protest against its imperfections, or they degenerate into dualism, in which the world of concrete reality is relegated to the realm of the unredeemed and unredeemable. In the best Jewish-Christian thought, which conceives of God as both the creator and the judge of the world, evil must be overcome even while it is recognized that evil is part of the inevitable mystery of existence. There is no disposition to declare that all "partial evil is universal good." In fact there is always a devil in classical religious mythology, and the devil is a symbol of the belief that evil is regarded as an actual rebellion against God. Of course this realism is always balanced by an ultimate optimism, because it is never believed that the devil can seriously threaten the rule of God.

There have been times when Christian orthodoxy was too dualistic and pessimistic to take the moral and social tasks of society seriously. Against its complete pessimism the thought of the eighteenth century and of modernity in general was a necessary corrective. But it must never be forgotten that the pessimism against which modernity rebelled was but a corruption of a world view which was critical of the moral achievements of historic man because it viewed them from a high perspective. Only in a religion in which there is a true sense of transcendence can we find the resource to convict every historical achievement of incompleteness, and to prevent the sanctification of the relative values of any age or any era.

The qualified optimism of an adequate religion will never satisfy the immature minds who have found some superficial harmony in the world in which the evils and threats to meaning are not taken into account. Nor will it satisfy those who think that every ill from which man suffers can be eliminated in some proximate future. It will nerve men to exhaust all their resources in building a better world, in overcoming human strife, in mitigating the fury of man's injustice to man, and in establishing a society in which some minimal security for all can be achieved. But in an adequate religion there will be a recognition of the fact that nothing accomplished along the horizontal line of history can eliminate the depth of life which is revealed at every point of history. Let man stand at any point in history, even in a society which has realized his present dreams of justice, and if he surveys the human problem profoundly he will see that every perfection which he has achieved points beyond itself to a greater perfection, and that this greater perfection throws light upon his sins and imperfections. He will feel in that tension between what is and what ought to be the very glory of life, and will come to know that the perfection which eludes him is not only a human possibility and impossibility, but a divine fact.

"Religion," declares Whitehead, "is a vision of something which stands beyond, behind and within the passing flux of things, something which is real and yet waiting to be realized; something which is a remote possibility and yet the greatest of present facts; something that gives meaning to all that passes and yet eludes apprehension; something whose possession is the final good and yet is beyond all reach; something which is the ultimate ideal and yet the hopeless quest."[3]

These paradoxes are in the spirit of great religion. The mystery of life is comprehended in meaning, though no human statement of the meaning can fully resolve the mystery. The tragedy of life is recog-

3. A. N. Whitehead, *Science and the Modern World*, 267.

nized, but faith prevents tragedy from being pure tragedy. Perplexity remains, but there is no perplexity unto despair. Evil is neither accepted as inevitable nor regarded as a proof of the meaninglessness of life. Gratitude and contrition are mingled, which means that life is both appreciated and challenged. To such faith the generations are bound to return after they have pursued the mirages in the desert to which they are tempted from time to time by the illusions of particular eras.

II
GOD'S JUSTICE AND MERCY

2

≡

THE POWER AND WEAKNESS OF GOD

And when they had platted a crown of thorns, they put it upon his head, and a reed in his right hand: and they bowed the knee before him, and mocked him, saying, Hail, King of the Jews! And they spit upon him, and took the reed, and smote him on the head. And after that they had mocked him, they took the robe off him, and put his own raiment on him, and led him away to crucify him. . . . And they that passed by reviled him, wagging their heads, And saying, Thou that destroyest the temple, and buildest it in three days, save thyself. If thou be the Son of God, come down from the cross. Likewise also the chief priests mocking him, with the scribes and elders, said, He saved others; himself he cannot save. If he be King of Israel, let him come down from the cross. . . . The thieves also, which were crucified with him, cast the same in his teeth.

Matt. 27:29–31, 39–42, 44.

They mocked and derided him. The chief priest and scribes, the soldiers and passersby, and even the thieves, were all agreed in regarding the royal and divine pretensions of this Messiah as ridiculous. He was dying upon the cross. Could anything disprove and invalidate the Messianic claim more irrefutably than this ignominious death? He was weak and powerless. He had saved others but could not save himself. If he were any kind of king he ought to have the power to get down from the cross.

All this mockery and derision is the natural and inevitable response to the absurdity of weakness and suffering in a royal and divine figure. Common sense assumes that the most significant and necessary attribute of both royalty and divinity is power. The judgments of priests and soldiers, of passersby, and thieves may vary on other matters. But they are naturally unanimous in their derision of the royal and divine claims of a Messiah upon the cross.

21

THE PARADOX OF POWER AND WEAKNESS

The Christian faith has made this absurdity of a suffering Messiah into the very keystone of its arch of faith. It therefore allows the records to report the derision of the onlookers at Calvary. It feels that the mockery helps to measure the profundity of the revelation upon the cross. If common sense could comprehend this absurdity, that would be proof that there was no depth of revelation in it. A faith which understands the scandal of the cross also has some appreciation of the negative support which mockery gives to the sublimity of the truth apprehended by faith. In the words of a modern literary critic: "The image of Christ crucified is, of all Christian images, the one that in itself contains the full paradox of human doubt and human faith, the focal point of the temporal and the eternal, at which the eternal is at once most essentially challenged and most essentially triumphant."[1]

What is involved in the apprehension of Christian faith that a crucified Christ is the "focal point between the temporal and the eternal," the most luminous symbol of the divine in the historical, the best "handle" by which to grasp the meaning of the divine mystery, is its understanding of the paradox of the power and the weakness of God. The crux of the cross is its revelation of the fact that the final power of God over man is derived from the self-imposed weakness of his love. This self-imposed weakness does not derogate from the majesty of God. His mercy is the final dimension of His majesty. This is the Christian answer to the final problem of human existence. The worship of God is reverence toward the mysterious source and end of all of life's vitalities; and toward the mysterious source and end of all goodness. A truly "holy" God must be both powerful and good. Impotent or limited goodness is not divine. It can not be worshipped. Its weakness arouses pity rather than worship; and faith is distracted by thought of the power against which this goodness must contend.

But power without goodness cannot be worshipped either. It may be feared, or possibly defied; but reverence must be withheld. Bertrand Russell suggested in his *Free Man's Worship* that the highest religion is for man to "sustain for a moment the world which his own ideals have builded against the trampling march of unconscious power." But such defiance is only one step from despair. If the ulti-

---

1. Kathleen Raine, "John Donne and Baroque Doubt," *Horizon*, June 1945.

mate source of all of life's vitalities is the evil of "unconscious power," the sense of futility must finally overcome the attitude of noble defiance.

Faith has never been willing to be embarrassed on this issue by the consistencies of the philosophers. Even before the revelation of the cross, the "holiness" of God has always been conceived as implying both majesty and goodness, both power and love. Yet the two attributes of God stand, at least partly, in contradiction to each other. If God is all-powerful He must be the creator of evil as well as of good. All the suffering of the world would seem to be finally attributed to Him. If the suffering is due to disharmonies in the order of the world, which God has not mastered, and to recalcitrant forces which He has not subdued, the goodness of God becomes more sharply defined; but His power is called into question. This rational contradiction lies at the heart of faith's apprehension of the holiness of God. It is never completely resolved. The significance of the revelation in Christ is that the intellectual embarrassment is overcome. The mockery of the absurdity of the weakness of God is cheerfully accepted as a tribute to the truth of the revelation. And all the ages of faith have found in the crucified Lord a luminous point which "makes sense" of the eternal mystery by defying the conclusions of common sense.

THE POWER OF GOD

One reason why the Christian faith is able to resolve the seeming conflict between the idea of the divine power and the divine goodness is that it does not allow that conflict to be absolute. It does not accept the idea that power is of itself evil; and that the source of all power must therefore be lacking in holiness. One of the attributes of holiness is undoubtedly majesty. The Apostles' Creed begins with the credo: "I believe in God the Father Almighty, Maker of heaven and earth." The closing ascription in our Lord's prayer is: "For thine is the . . . power and the glory forever." In a majestic passage in Deutero-Isaiah, God is made to utter the most sweeping claims of power: "I form the light, and create darkness; I make peace, and create evil. I the Lord do all these things" (Isa. 45:7).

The power of God is conceived in biblical faith, primarily in twofold terms: It is the power of the creator of the world and the power of judgment which sets a final bound to the evil in the world. The divine power brings forth all the myriad forms of life on the one hand, and maintains order and harmony among them on the other. Human history by reason of human freedom had the capacity to defy the order which God has set for His creation; but there are limits to this defiance. He "bringeth the princes to nothing; he maketh the judges of the earth as vanity" (Isa. 40:23).

The acceptance of the goodness of power in the Christian faith is intimately related to its whole "nonspiritual" interpretation of life. It never abstracts the spiritual and ideal form from the dynamic stuff of life, to call the one good and the other evil. The created world as such is good; and all forms of creation represent various strategies of power. Life is power; but all created power points beyond itself to an ultimate source. The fact that life is power is not the cause of the evil in it; and the power of the creator is not a contradiction, but an aspect of His holiness.

Furthermore, the power of God as judge is holy. God is the ultimate source of that indestructible order in the world against which man's pride and self-will beat in vain. Here the Christian faith, drawing its conceptions of divine justice from the teachings of the Old Testament prophets, reveals similarities with the interpretations of the Greek tragedies, in which the power of Zeus is conceived of as the final order and power which ultimately defeats all lesser majesties and forces which are arrayed against it. All lesser sources of power, which seek proudly to usurp the position of Zeus, are finally brought low. Greek tragedy is not quite sure whether the "jealousy" of Zeus is really a source of justice; because it is not certain whether the vitalities and ambitions of the heroes of history, who defy Zeus, may not be noble and heroic and whether the jealousy of Zeus is not an unjustified egotism. There is, in other words, no consistency in dealing with the world as a unity and harmony. Sometimes Zeus is the divine protector of the ultimate harmony and order of the world. And sometimes those who defy him are the necessary heroic protagonists of the various powers and values of the world.

In the Bible, particularly in Hebraic prophetism, there is no question about this point. The nations, judges, and princes of the world are all in partial defiance of the divine creator and judge of the world; and the terrible character of His wrath is a justified judgment upon the various idolatries of history. For all lesser gods are false gods. Only the real God, who is the final source and end of all existence, deserves the unqualified worship which the lesser gods claim for themselves.

We have had ample proof in our own day of the efficacy of power in setting the outer limits of order in the world. We have lived through a great war in which the idolatrous pretensions of a "master race" have been defeated by power. These pretensions clothed themselves in the majesties of power and had to be defeated by power. The human instruments by which the defeat of tyranny was encompassed were of course themselves tainted with some of the evil against which they fought. There are no perfect human instruments of either the divine power or the divine mercy. But we cannot escape the responsibilities of power by preoccupation with these corruptions. Life is power. Power is not evil of itself; but evil incarnates itself in power and cannot finally be defeated without the use of power.

There are always highly "spiritualized" forms of faith which assume that the only hope of virtue among us is to disavow power, and that a virtue which is as impotent as it is good, will, by that impotence, achieve the spiritual power to defeat evil. There is an ultimate truth in this contention at which we must look presently. Immediately it is not true. In any immediate situation neither man nor God can defeat a powerful defiance of the order of the world without using power to set the limits of that defiance. There is no purely spiritual method of preserving minimal justice and order in a world, for the world is not purely spiritual. Power is the basis of justice in history as it is of order in the entire natural world. To declare the omnipotence of God is to insist that the ultimate power which maintains the order of the world is superior to all subordinate powers and majesties which tend to create anarchy by making themselves the premature and inadequate centers of order in the world.

THE "POWERLESS" CHRIST

Yet, despite the certainty of biblical faith that God is all-powerful, it looks upon the crucified Messiah as the final revelation of the divine character and the divine purpose. This divine representative was so powerless that he could not save himself, and he died an ignominious death. One reason why his claims to Messianic authority were rejected by the leaders of the Jews was because they expected a Messiah who would combine perfect power and perfect goodness. That was the meaning of the hope of a "shepherd king" which informed the Messianic expectations not only of Hebraic prophets but of Egyptian and Babylonian prophets before them. Always in human history the same power which maintained order in the world also introduced injustice into the order by reason of the selfish use which the king made of his power. How could history finally culminate in a reign of perfect righteousness except by a divine king who would combine justice with absolute power? This was the expectation. The expectation was doomed to disappointment. Perfect power and goodness can be united only in God, where the contest of life with life is transcended and where the possession of power does not lead to its misuse in the struggle for existence.

In human history disinterested power is never as disinterested as it claims to be. It always insinuates something of the special interests of a participant in the struggle of life into the pretended position of disinterested preservation of justice. Thus the so-called democratic nations were good enough to preserve a measure of justice against tyranny in recent conflicts. But the idea, which they have written into the Charter of the United Nations, that there are "peace-loving" nations who can be absolutely distinguished from the peace-breaking ones, obviously does not bear close inspection. The peace of the coming centuries will be less than a perfect or stable peace because Russia, Britain, and America will compound their concern for justice with a concern for their own prestige and power. Every "shepherd king" of history is more king and less shepherd than he pretends. That is as true, in an ultimate sense, of democratic centers of power as of tyrannical ones, though the former are prevented by wisely constructed social checks upon their power from following the logic of selfish power to its final conclusion.

For this reason the revelation of the divine goodness in history must be powerless. The Christ is led as a lamb to the slaughter. He cannot save himself from the cross. No human cause or interest gains a triumph through him; all human interests and causes are revealed as practically in contradiction to the divine goodness because "all seek their own." The best law of his day (Roman law) and the best religion of his day (Hebraic monotheism) are implicated in the crucifixion, though the latter expected to be the righteous victor who would gain a triumph over its unrighteous foes in the coming of the Messiah. Christ is thus doubly an offense to the common sense of mankind. He possesses no royal trappings of power and no divine symbols of omnipotence. He is an offense also because he convicts the righteous as well as the unrighteous by his impotent goodness. Therefore the Christian faith regards this scene at the cross as an ultimate point of illumination on the character of man and of God.

It was inevitable that this ultimate illumination should be mistaken again and again in human history for proximate forms of moral illumination and thus lead to pacifist illusions. According to such interpretations, the goodness of Christ is a form of powerless goodness which can be emulated by the mere disavowal of power. In such interpretations the tragic culmination of the cross is obscured. It is assumed that powerless goodness achieves the spiritual influence to overcome all forms of evil clothed with other than spiritual forms of power. It is made an instrument of one historical cause in conflict with other historical causes. It becomes the tool of an interested position in society; and a bogus promise of historical success is given to it. Powerless goodness ends upon the cross. It gives no certainty of victory to comparatively righteous causes in conflict with comparatively unrighteous ones. It can only throw a divine illumination upon the whole meaning of history and convict both the righteous and the unrighteous in their struggles. Men may indeed emulate the powerless goodness of Christ; and some of his followers ought indeed to do so. But they ought to know what they are doing. They are not able by this strategy to guarantee a victory for any historical cause, however comparatively virtuous. They can only set up a sign and symbol of the Kingdom of God, of a Kingdom of perfect righteousness and peace which transcends all the struggles of history.

This aspect of the revelatory mission of Christ is expressed in the Christian creeds by the distinction between God the Father and God the Son, between the "Father Almighty, Maker of heaven and earth," and His "only begotten Son" who "was crucified dead and buried." The distinction is between the divine power which underlies all creation and the divine as it appears powerless in history. Most of the efforts to reduce this distinction to nice metaphysical points of discrimination, and to indicate just how much of the divine omnipotence or omniscience the historical revealer of God carried with him into history, are meaningless or even confusing. The truth which is revealed in Christ must be apprehended in faith. Faith, as far as it uses our natural endowments, draws on poetic and imaginative capacities

rather than rational ones. The point of the Christian story is that we
see a clue to the character of God in the character and the drama of
Christ; and we have some understanding of the fact that the similarity of love between God and Christ is partly revealed by the dis-
similarity of power in the historical and trans-historical. The divine
goodness is a part of the divine majesty and power; but it can appear
in history only in powerless, rather than powerful, terms.

MERCY AND JUSTICE

Yet this is not the whole meaning of the powerless Christ, comprehended by faith even while it is rejected by the derision and mockery of priests and soldiers. The Christian faith makes a distinction on
the one hand between the Father and the Son, between the God above
history and the God in history; and on the other hand declares that
the two are one. To declare that the two are one is to insist that the
distinction between the historical and the trans-historical, between
the facet of the divine which appears in history and the plenitude of
the divine which bears all history and creation, must not be made too
unqualifiedly.

It must not be made absolutely because the weakness of Christ is
not merely the weakness which God's revelation in history makes
necessary. It is in part the weakness of God, as He is in His nature. It is
the weakness of His love.

The weakness of God's love is not the weakness of goodness striving against the recalcitrance of some "given" stuff of creation. It is
the self-imposed weakness of His love. If God has created free spirits
who have the capacity to defy Him in their freedom, He has created
forms of life so independent that even the power of God, acting merely as power, cannot reach the final source of their defiance. The
divine power, the very structure of the world, the requirements for
mutual living which are made part of the very character of human
existence, all these are able to set an ultimate limit to man's defiance
of the order of creation. The justice and the "wrath" of God can
prevent any human rebellion from developing its defiance to the
point of ultimate triumph. The devil, according to Christian myth, is
able to defy God but not absolutely. The divine order is supported by
the divine power.

But such power does not reach the heart of the rebel. We can, as instruments of the divine justice, set a limit to the defiance of tyranny against the justice of our civilized institutions. The nations which engaged in such defiance have been brought low, and their cities lie in dust and ashes. The imagination of faith is right in discerning this doom as part of the divine justice, however much human instruments of this justice may have obscured and brought confusion into the terrible drama. But this punishment does not reach the heart of Germany or Japan. No punishment can. Justice and wrath have a negatively redemptive effect. They prove to men and nations that there are limits beyond which their rebellion cannot go. But punishment may prompt men and nations to despair as well as to repentance. There can indeed be no repentance if love does not shine through the justice. It shines through whenever it becomes apparent that the executor of judgment suffers willingly, as guiltless sufferer, with the guilty victim of punishment. Thus the love of parents shines through the punishment which they may have to mete out to childish recalcitrance. If it does not shine through, childish recalcitrance may harden into adolescent rebellion and mature despair. Because such love seldom shines through the punishment which "righteous" victors exact of the "unrighteous" vanquished, the repentance of vanquished nations is extremely difficult.

The Christian story is that, whatever the inadequacies of forgiveness and love may be in the operations of human justice, men ultimately face divine forgiveness as well as divine wrath. The Christ upon the cross is the point of illumination where the ultimate mercy is apprehended. It is not a mercy which cancels out the divine justice; nor does it prove the divine justice to be merely love. There is a hard and terrible facet to justice which stands in contradiction to love. It is not for that reason evil. Justice is good and punishment is necessary. Yet justice alone does not move men to repentance. The inner core of their rebellion is not touched until they behold the executor of judgment suffering with and for the victim of punishment.

This is the meaning of "atonement" as apprehended by faith. It is the final meaning and the final mystery of the relation of God to man. Since it is meaning and not pure mystery, faith must explicate what it means even as we seek to do so in these words. Since it is mystery it cannot be fully explicated; which is why all theories of the atonement are less illuminating (and sometimes positively confusing) than the apprehension of the mystery and the meaning by faith. Faith rises above all philosophies and theologies in sensing that the weakness of God is His final power. It is the weakness of love which touches the heart of the offender. The mystery lies in the fact that this mercy is partly the fulfillment and partly the contradiction to the justice which punishes. The fact that justice and mercy are one is symbolically expressed in the idea of the unity of Father and Son. The fact that justice and mercy stand in contradiction is symbolically expressed in the distinction between Father and Son and in the idea that the Son bears the wrath of the Father. In less metaphysical and more historic-symbolic terms the unity of mercy and justice are expressed in the biblical idea that "God so loved the world that he gave his only begotten son" (John 3:16). The distinction between justice and mercy is expressed by the idea that the Son bears the sufferings which the wrath of the Father exacts.

OBSCURING THE PARADOX

The moralists of every age and faith, including the Christian faith, regard these insights as meaningless subleties of theologians or as incredible biblical myths which can impress only the ignorant and credulous. They make these disparaging judgments because they have never plumbed the problem of justice and mercy through to its final depth. Even now they divide into two schools, the hard and the soft school. The hard school would seek to persuade a fallen foe to repentance by the rigor of the punishment of the victors. And the soft school would remit punishment and substitute mercy for judgment. The power which maintains the order of the world is good and not evil; but its virtue does not reach into the secret of the human heart. The justice which checks and punishes evil is also good and not evil; but its force is negative and the persuasive power of repentance and redemption is not in it. Thus the final majesty of God is the majesty of His mercy. It is both the completion and the contradiction of His power. This is the truth apprehended in the cross, which resolves the mystery of the relation of justice to mercy, and gives it meaning.

Naturally the final paradoxes of faith are always in peril of disintegration, inside the Christian community as well as outside. Thus there have been Christian heresies (particularly in the extreme form of Marcionism) which make an absolute distinction between the God of power who is not good and the God of mercy who is good but not powerful. Some very persuasive forms of the Christian faith drift to the very edge of this heresy. In the first world war the most famous of English chaplains, Studdert-Kennedy, allowed his tragic sense of life to be elaborated into a homiletical theology which resolved the Christian paradox and denied every form of the divine majesty and power except the power of love.

One of his best known poems stated his theology as follows:

> God, the God I love and worship, reigns in sorrow on the Tree,
> Broken, bleeding, but unconquered, very God of God to me.
> All that showy pomp of splendour, all that sheen of angel wings,
> Was not borrowed from the baubles that surround our earthly
>   kings. . . .
> . . . For Thy glory is the glory of Love's loss,
> And Thou hast no other splendour but the splendour of the Cross.
> For in Christ I see the martyrs and the beauty of their pain,
> And in Him I hear the promise that my dead shall rise again.
> High and lifted up, I see Him on the eternal Calvary,
> And two piercèd hands are stretching east and west o'er land and sea.
> On my knees I fall and worship that great Cross that shines above,
> For the very God of Heaven is not Power, but Power of Love.[2]

A non-Christian interpretation of the problem of suffering, also presented during the first world war, in H. G. Wells' *God, the Invisible King*, arrived at somewhat the same picture of a kind but not very powerful divine ruler who suffered with man in fighting against the recalcitrance of something in the universe more powerful than himself. Recently some Christian philosophers have sought to present the same doctrine in Christian form.

But all these efforts, however small or great their ingredients of Scriptural content, manage to obscure the sublimity of the paradox which the revelation of God in Christ contains. They are provisionally plausible because they are philosophically more consistent than the Christian doctrine. But they are not true to all of the facts of existence and they fail to illumine the final mystery of justice and mercy, of power and goodness, which is revealed from the cross.

Faith, by a wisdom which touches sublimities beyond the ken of philosophies, will thus continue to cherish the scandal of the cross and accept the mockery and derision of the various crowd at Calvary

---

2. G. A. Studdert-Kennedy, "High and Lifted Up," in *The Sorrows of God, and Other Poems.*

as a kind of tribute to the truth which transcends and fulfills the highest insights of reason. The words of derision: "He saved others, himself he cannot save," gives us a clue to the innermost character of a man in history who perished upon the cross. It also gives us a clue to the mystery of the very character of God.

3

TWO SERMONS

1. THE PROVIDENCE OF GOD

You have heard that it was said, "You shall love your neighbor and hate your enemy." But I say to you, Love your enemies and pray for those who persecute you, so that you may be sons of your Father who is in heaven; for he makes his sun rise on the evil and on the good, and sends rain on the just and on the unjust. For if you love those who love you, what reward have you? Do not even the tax collectors do the same? And if you salute only your brethren, what more are you doing than others? Do not even the Gentiles do the same? You, therefore, must be perfect, as your heavenly Father is perfect.

Matt. 5:43–48, RSV

My text is taken from the New Testament lesson: "But I say to you, Love your enemies and pray for those who persecute you, so that you may be sons of your Father who is in heaven; for he makes his sun rise on the evil and on the good, and sends rain on the just and on the unjust."

This text has been preached upon many times in the memory of all of us. Usually, however, the emphasis has been upon the moral admonition that we should love our enemies, and not much attention has been paid to the justification of the love of the enemy that Jesus gives by reference to the impartial character of God's love. It is on the second theme that I want to speak this morning.

There are many things to say about the first theme, for Jesus is suggesting in his Sermon on the Mount that you cannot be moral if you are too strictly moral. The highest morality of forgiveness is, as Berdyaev says, "the morality beyond morality." Nobody who is strictly moral can forgive, because forgiveness is at once the fulfillment of every concept of justice, and its annulment. Jesus justifies this "morality beyond all morality" by saying God is like that. The love of God is an impartial goodness beyond good and evil. The providence of God is an impartial concern for all men without any special privileges in it.

Thus, the structure of meaning for the Christian faith is completed against all the contradictions in history, where there are no simple correlations of reward for good and punishment for evil. God is like nature, says Jesus, like the impartial nature which you could accuse of not being moral at all, because the sun shines upon both the evil and the good, and the rain descends upon the just and the unjust. A nonmoral nature is made into the symbol of the transmoral mercy. Here is a very radical concept, and one of those words of Scripture that we never quite take in. It is a word of Scripture that has particular significance because it is set squarely against most of our religion, inside the Christian Church as well as anywhere else.

When we say that we believe in God, we are inclined to mean that we have found a way to the ultimate source and end of life, and this gives us, against all the chances and changes of life, some special security and some special favor. And if we do not mean that—which is religion on a fairly adolescent and immature level—at least we mean that we have discovered amidst the vast confusions of life what is usually called the moral order, according to which evil is punished and good rewarded, and we could hardly feel that life had any meaning if we were not certain of that.

The Bible is full of this debate between what might be called the instinct of religion and the gospel of Christ. The natural instincts of religion demand that my life be given meaning by a special security against all of the insecurities of life. If it should seem as if goodness and evil—punishment for evil and reward for good—were not being properly correlated in life, then God will guarantee finally that they will be properly correlated.

Thus, in the Scriptures the words of the Psalms, "A thousand may fall at your side, ten thousand at your right hand, but it will not come near you" (Ps. 91:7). Or the many intercessory prayers, the intent of which is "A thousand at your side, ten thousand at your right hand," let it not come to my loved one. What a natural prayer that is and finally how impossible! "For in the time of trouble He shall hide me, and he shall set me upon a rock" (cf. Ps. 27:5). In a word, plead my cause, O Lord, against them that strive with me, fight against them that fight against me.

Examples can be multiplied and it must also be realized how very natural are these kinds of prayers. Has there ever been a conflict in the human community where we have not felt we could not fight the battle were not the Lord on our side? Perhaps, as Abraham Lincoln said, we did not as frequently ask the question of whether we were on the Lord's side. These are natural religious instincts, the natural efforts to close prematurely the great structure of life's meaning. Much more justified is the other aspect of this sense of special providence—not that God would give me special privileges, special securities against the other man—but that in a very hazardous world where it is not certain that good will be rewarded and evil punished, at least God should set that right.

"Blessed is he who considers the poor!" to use another word of the Psalm, "The Lord delivers him in the day of trouble" (Ps. 41:1). Many years ago, tithing was popular in some of the churches. A member of my congregation had started tithing as a twelve-year-old boy and had become a millionaire. He was quite convinced that the millions were the reward of his tithing.

"Blessed is he who considers the poor! The Lord delivers him in the day of trouble." I was never much convinced by this millionaire businessman because of my first pastoral experience when I took the church of my deceased father for six months. The first pastoral problem I had was dealing with an old man whom I greatly respected, who really had the grace of God in him. He had considered the poor to the degree of giving striking miners so much credit at his grocery store that he lost his business. In the seventy-eighth year of his life, he had to face the problem of bankruptcy, and the fact that there was no simple correlation between his goodness and the fortunes of his life.

Both kinds of faith were wrong. First, that if we pray to God fervently enough he will establish some special security for us against the security of the other person. Or secondly, the belief that there are simple moral correlations between the vast processes either of nature or of history and human virtue. The history of our Puritan fathers in New England illustrates how wrong are both of these propositions. There were some very great virtues and graces in their lives. But the doctrine of special providence represents the real defect in our Puritan inheritance. These Puritan forefathers of ours were sure that every rain and every drought was connected with the virtue and vice of their enterprise—that God always had his hand upon them to reward them for their goodness, and to punish them for their evil.

Their belief in special providence was unfortunate, particularly so when a religious community developed in the vast possibilities of America, where inevitably the proofs of God's favor turned out to be greater than the proofs of God's wrath. It may be the reason why we Americans are so self-righteous. It may be also the reason why we still have not come to terms, in an ultimate religious sense, with our responsibilities; with the problems of the special favors that our nation enjoys compared with other nations. But first of all we have to realize that this picture of God's love is not true. The Scriptures also are full of testimony that it is not true. Certainly it is the point of the Book of Job. Job first hopes that God is a God of simple justice, but it is proved to him that this cannot be the case. Then Job protests against the fact that if he does wrong he is convicted as a sinner, but if he does right, he is no better off: "I cannot lift up my head." Ours is a confused kind of world, says Job, in which there is no guarantee that the righteous man will prosper. Is there a God in this kind of world?

These are the protests that run through the Scriptures as they run through life. "My feet had almost stumbled," says the great seventy-third Psalm. "My steps had well nigh slipped . . . when I saw the prosperity of the wicked. . . . Their eyes swell out with fatness, . . . and they say, 'How can God know?'" (Ps. 73:1–11).

"When I saw the prosperity of the wicked"—here is man in history involved in the web of relationships and meanings, but not of simple ones. There must be some moral meaning here. Is there not some punishment of wickedness in life? And I do not mean any of the arbitrary punishment which we inflict by our courts. For life is not completely at variance with itself. There *is* reward for goodness in life, and there *is* punishment for evil, but not absolutely. The same law which punishes the criminal punishes the Savior. And there are three crosses: two for criminals who cannot meet the moral mediocrities of life, and one for the Savior who rises above it. This is life.

Martin Buber, some years ago, made a remark about the special spiritual problems that we face in our world, where we cannot bring to any simple end the structure of moral meaning in which we stand. "When the Nazis ruled," he said, "even when they were at the height of their rule, I knew in my heart that they would fall, that they would be punished."

But now we face a future with greater threats of destruction than during the Nazi period. And this will continue partly because it is a problem that involves all the confusions of modern history against which our own goodness is not adequate. There is no simple moral resolution of the nuclear dilemma. These are the facts of our historic existence; life cannot be correlated easily into simple moral meanings; nor can the Christian faith be validated by proving special acts of providence in your own or somebody else's favor.

I have a certain embarrassment about this issue in the great debate between Christianity and secularism. I am convinced of the Christian faith in the God revealed in Christ and whom Christ says is partially revealed in the impartialities of nature. Yet it seems to me also true that a certain type of secularism has advantages over us on any point where, to quote William James, Christianity becomes "an effort to lobby in the courts of the Almighty for special favors."

Against this lobbying for special favors, one must admit that there is an element of nobility either in modern or ancient Stoicism. Marcus Aurelius said: "If so be the gods deliberated in particular on those things that should happen to me, I must stand to their deliberation, but if so be that they have not deliberated for me in particular, certainly they have on the whole and in general deliberated on those things which happen to me. In consequence and coherence of this general deliberation, I am bound to embrace and to accept them." There is a certain nobility in Stoic courage. It has no sense of an ultimate relationship to God as a final expression of the Christian faith, but as far as it goes, is it not true?

Modern man, under the influence of natural science, sees the problem more critically than it was seen before. We see that nature, whatever may be God's ultimate sovereignty over it, moves by its own laws. Even so good a theologian as the late William Temple did not understand this. He tried to solve it by saying that the laws of nature are merely God's habitual way of doing things. If he does not want to act in the habitual way, he will choose another way. Surely this is too voluntaristic a conception of how the forces of nature work.

An analogous proposition would be that my heart beats in a habitual way, but if I choose, I could have it do something else. No, my heart has its own automatic processes as do the forces of nature. Many in our modern world have come to despair about this vast realm of seeming meaninglessness.

Though we have some sympathy from a modern scientific culture which says such special providence is not true, what concerns us more as Christians is the protest of Jesus against the underlying assumptions. It is not true that God gives special favors, and it is not true that there are simple moral meanings in the processes of history. We cannot speak simply of a moral order which if defied, would destroy us. Though Jesus is concerned about the whole dimension of the gospel, it is not so much whether these things are true or not upon their own levels, but whether they would be right. God's love would not be right if it were this kind of a love. This is the point that Christ makes in the Sermon on the Mount, that God's love would not be right. The Christian faith believes that within and beyond the tragedies and the contradictions of history we have laid hold upon a loving heart, the proof of whose love is first impartiality toward all of his children, and secondly a mercy which transcends good and evil.

How shall we appropriate this insistence of Christ in our life? All of us, including some who are not conventionally religious, have a desire for an ultimate security. Even people who are not conventionally religious often pray in the hour of crisis. In that sense, all men are religious. Yet under the discipline of the gospel, we should bring each one of these prayers under scrutiny.

This does not change radically the problem of intercessory prayer. Perhaps we have to consider life in three different dimensions. First, there is the vast dimension of nature where we cannot expect that God will put up a special umbrella for us against this or that possible disaster. In the realm of nature, we face the problem of natural evil. Jesus was asked, "Master, who sinned, this man or his parents, that he was born blind?" Jesus' answer repudiated the idea of special providence: "It was not that this man sinned or his parents have sinned but that the works of God might be made manifest in him" (John 9:3). There is no meaning to this blindness except the ultimate possible meaning of how the blindness might become a source of grace. It is a most terrible thing to correlate natural evil immediately to any moral and spiritual meaning, and yet it is a wonderful thing to correlate it ultimately. Likewise Jesus replied, when asked about those killed by the fall of the tower in Siloam, "Were they worse offenders than all the others who dwell in Jerusalem? I tell you, no!" (Luke 13:4). Do not try to relate natural catastrophes to moral meanings. Do not ask the question whether people killed in an earthquake are more guilty, more sinful, than others. "I tell you, no!" Ask the question, rather, what ultimate use, what final point for the grace of God is there in this calamity? But do not correlate it in such a way that it ceases to be a calamity, for this belongs to the realm of nature.

In the realm of history we have another problem, of course, because history is a realm of human freedom and human agency, and if it did not have any moral meaning at all, it would be intolerable. If there were not some reward for goodness, life would be absolutely askew. If there were no likelihood that forgiveness would produce the spirit of forgiveness, and mutuality the spirit of mutuality and reciprocity, it would be hard to love and trust each other. Yet in the processes of history these things are not simply correlated. The suffering of the innocent is one of the most terrible things in the collective enterprise of man. When, towards the end of the Second World War, we started to bomb the Germans into submission, we bombed Hamburg first, the city that had more anti-Nazi votes than any other German city. These anguishes are the facts of life as we find them in history.

There are no simple correlations. This does not mean that we will not pray for our loved ones in the hazards and tumults of history, when so frequently their destiny is a curious combination of the physical and the spiritual. We certainly will not stop praying for their health, particularly in view of what we know about psychosomatic characteristics in the human personality today. We will pray for the health of other people and pray for their healing.

This is the realm of history which is a vast middle ground between the realm of grace and the realm of nature. But ultimately, of course, our Christian faith lives in the realm of grace, in the realm of freedom. This is God's freedom and my freedom, beyond the structures of my body, the realm of grace where I know God and am persuaded, as St. Paul says, that he knows me.

In that realm, finally, all concern for immediate correlations and coherences and meanings falls away. The Christian faith stands in the sense of an ultimate meaning. We may be persuaded that God is on our side—not against somebody else—but on our side in this ultimate sense. We are "sure that neither death nor life, nor angels, nor principalities, nor things present, nor things to come, . . . will be able to separate us from the love of God in Christ Jesus our Lord" (Rom. 8:38–39).

It is on that level of meaning that the Christian faith makes sense. The lower levels are a threat, not only to the sense of the meaning of

life, but finally to the morals of life. We must not deny that there is a
kind of religion that enhances the ego and gives it an undue place in
the world. But from the standpoint of our faith we should take our
humble and contrite place in God's plan of the whole, and leave it to
him to complete the fragmentation of our life.

O God, who has promised that all things will work together for good to
those that love you, grant us patience amidst the tumults, pains and
afflictions of life, and faith to discern your love, within, above, and
beyond the impartial destinies of this great drama of life. Save us from
every vainglorious pretension by which we demand favors which violate
your love for all your children, and grant us grace to appropriate every
fortune, both good and evil, for the triumph of the suffering, crucified,
and risen Lord in our souls and life. In whose name we ask it.

2. THE WHEAT AND THE TARES

Lord, thou hast been our dwelling place in all
   generations.
Before the mountains were brought forth,
   or ever thou hadst formed the earth and the world,
   even from everlasting to everlasting, thou art God.

Thou turnest man to destruction;
   and sayest, Return, ye children of men.
For a thousand years in thy sight
   are but as yesterday when it is past,
   and as a watch in the night.

Thou carriest them away as with a flood; they are as a sleep:
   in the morning they are like grass which groweth up.
In the morning it flourisheth, and groweth up;
   in the evening it is cut down, and withereth.

For we are consumed by thine anger,
   and by thy wrath are we troubled.
Thou hast set our iniquities before thee,
   our secret sins in the light of thy countenance.

For all our days are passed away in thy wrath:
   we spend our years as a tale that is told.
The days of our years are threescore years and ten;
   and if by reason of strength they be fourscore years,
yet is their strength labour and sorrow;
   for it is soon cut off, and we fly away.

Ps. 90:1–10, AV

*Another parable put he forth unto them, saying, The kingdom of heaven
is likened unto a man which sowed good seed in his field: But while
men slept, his enemy came and sowed tares among the wheat, and
went his way. But when the blade was sprung up, and brought forth
fruit, then appeared the tares also. So the servants of the householder
came and said unto him, Sir, didst not thou sow good seed in thy field?
from whence then hath it tares? He said unto them, An enemy hath
done this. The servants said unto him, Wilt thou then that we go and
gather them up? But he said, Nay; lest while ye gather up the tares, ye
root up also the wheat with them. Let both grow together until the
harvest: and in the time of harvest I will say to the reapers, Gather ye
together first the tares, and bind them in bundles to burn them: but
gather the wheat into my barn.*

Matt. 13:24–30, AV

I want to begin my sermon with the well-known ninetieth Psalm,
and end it with the parable of the wheat and the tares, which is the

New Testament lesson of the morning. The ninetieth Psalm begins with the words, "Lord, Thou hast been our dwelling place in all generations. Before the mountains were brought forth, or ever thou hadst formed the earth and the world, even from everlasting to everlasting, Thou art God." Then it goes on to describe the human situation in typically biblical terms. "Thou carriest them [that is, us] away as with a flood; . . . In the morning they are like grass which groweth up. In the morning it flourisheth; . . . in the evening it is cut down and withereth." The brevity of human life! "Thou carriest them away as with a flood." We are like corks that bob up and down in the river of time. The brevity of human life may fill us with melancholy because it seems to reduce life to such insignificance. We bring our years to an end like a tale that is told, says the Psalmist.

The second point in the analysis of the human situation is implicit rather than explicit. Man is indeed like a cork that is drawn down the river of time, carried away as with a flood. But he could not be altogether that, because he knows about it; he speculates about it as the Psalmist does, and about the significance of it. Man stands outside of the river of time, so that he can anticipate his death either with hope or with melancholy. Also he can create. He is not only a creature, but he is a creator because he is not quite in the river of time; although he might forget how much of a creature he is when he begins to create. Therefore we come to the third point.

This drama of human history is indeed partly our construct, but it stands under a sovereignty much greater than ours. "A thousand years are in thy sight but as yesterday when it is past, and as a watch in the night." The drama of our individual life and the whole drama of human history stands under a mysterious and eternal sovereignty. It is a mysterious sovereignty which the prophets are always warning that we must not spell out too much. "My thoughts are not your thoughts, my ways are not your ways." But it is not complete mystery because—and this is the distinction between the biblical view and the philosophical view—in spite of the mystery, there are also glints of meaning in it. This God is the mysterious creator of the world, but he is also a just and merciful God.

The New Testament adds to this story by suggesting there is a clue to the mystery. This is the light that shineth in darkness, the drama of the life of our Lord Jesus Christ. Here we have a sense that the mystery of God's creativity and the mystery of his severe judgment and the mystery of his mercy are related, and the clue to the mystery lies in the combination of his justice and his mercy. How are they related; this is our question, and how are these all brought together and revealed? The light that shineth in darkness enables us to live our life, not merely in the sense of its brevity, but with a sense of a purpose for it, and also with the sense of a purpose, and judgment and ultimate fulfillment beyond any judgments or fulfillments that we can envisage.

There are various alternatives—modern and ancient—to what the biblical faith tells us about our human story. One of the great alternatives Aldous Huxley has defined as the "perennial philosophy," which many modern intellectuals, when they become religious, think is a plausible alternative to biblical faith.

According to this alternative view of life, attention is fastened on the second part of the human situation; man is in the river of time but is transcendent over it. This transcendence of his is indeterminate. He can rise higher and higher, and he can look at the whole thing and ask whether it has any meaning. Let him, therefore, rise higher and higher until he, in a sense, meets God. This is the strategy of detachment, according to which we all have our private airplanes, spiritually speaking, and these spiritual airplanes have indeterminate altitude records. There is no limit to how high you can go. You start, and raise yourself up from the human scene to the point where at first it seems creative, because you see, and are apologetic for, all your vanities and pretensions. You rise a little higher, and then you become apologetic for anything that you have done responsibly and creatively. And then you also begin to look at your fellowmen, and you see mothers caring for their children, scholars engaged in their enterprises, businessmen in the marketplace, politicians fighting for their causes, and you say, "What is the good of this? This is all in the river of time. This is all so brief, and also it may be corrupt."

Playing God to the universe, in other words, can be very exhilarating but very irresponsible. It is a strategy of weakness rather than of strength; if you happen to be very weak, you can look at the world from the highest altitude you can think of. If you get high enough in an airplane, you know that the farm of the good farmer and of the bad farmer look equally like garden plots. All distinctions disappear. All moral responsibilities disappear. Indeterminate extension of our freedom over time is certainly no answer to the problem of life.

Probably not many Christians are tempted to this alternative, yet it is a perennial temptation through the ages; if you would have a religious census of the world you would find that more people than the Christians or the Jews have some vision of this alternative to biblical religion.

Which brings us now again to the strategy of life as we have it in the faith of the Bible. We look at the brevity of our life. We admit that we are creatures. We know that we are unique creatures, that God has made us in his image, that we have a freedom to do something that nature does not know, that we can project goals beyond the limitations, ambitions, desires, and lusts of nature. We are the creatures who, gloriously, tragically, and pathetically, make history. As we make it, we have to make distinctions between good and evil. We know that selfishness is dangerous. We must be unselfish. The more we rise above our immediate situation and see the situation of the other person, the more creative we are. Therefore, our life story is concerned with making rigorous distinctions between right and wrong, between good and evil. Part of the Christian faith corresponds to this interpretation. Certainly a part of the Old Testament is not quite sure whether man is in relationship to God, or whether the primary job for the righteous is to war against the unrighteous. We have to admit that it makes a very big difference when we defend freedom against tyranny, and truth against the lies of the world. How else could we build history except by these rigorous distinctions between good and evil, right and wrong?

But now we come to the New Testament lesson, the puzzling lesson of the parable of the wheat and the tares. The man sowed a field of wheat and the enemy sowed tares among the wheat. And the servants, following the impulse of each one of us, asked if they should root out the tares so that the wheat could grow. This is a parable taken from agriculture to illustrate a point of morals, and it violates every principle of agriculture or of morals. After all, every farmer and every gardener makes ceaseless war against the tares. How else could the flowers and the wheat grow? And we have to make ceaseless war against evil within ourselves and in our fellowmen, or how could there be any kind of decency in the world? Against all moral impulse, we have this eschatological parable.

"Nay," said the householder. "Lest while ye gather up the tares, you root up also the wheat." The suggestion is that a great deal of evil may come from the selfishness of men, but perhaps more evil may come from the premature judgments of men about themselves and each other. "Let both grow together until the harvest." These wonderful words of Scripture suggest that while we have to judge, there is a judgment beyond our judgment, and there are fulfillments beyond our fulfillments.

Consider how much more evil and good, creativity and selfishness, are mixed up in actual life than our moralists, whether they be Christian or secular, realize. How little we achieve charity because we do not recognize this fact.

Let us consider the matter of creativity and the desire for approval. What could be more evil than the avaricious desire for the approval of our fellowmen? But how closely related it is to the impulse of creativity. The diary of Virginia Woolf notes that when she put out a new novel, she had an almost morbid interest in the reviews. She was an established artist. Was her anxiety justified? Could not she just take for granted that people would praise her or would accept her work? Yet she had a morbid concern, as anyone who has written a book understands. You may think that you are creative, but you suspect you may have slipped. You have to be approved in order to establish your creativity; the wheat and the tares are very mixed up. "Let both grow together until the harvest." When we think of ourselves, we ought to remember that there is an ultimate judgment against excessive self-concern. But when we deal with our fellowman, we must do so in charity.

How curiously are love and self-love mixed up in life, much more complexly than any scheme of morals recognizes. The simple words of the parable are more profound than the wisdom of all our moralists. There is a self-love which is the engine of creativity. It may not be justified ultimately for that reason, but when we look at history, we have to say that it is an engine of creativity.

There is a debate whether Cervantes wrote the great classic, *Don Quixote*, in order to pay his debts, or in order to get even with his critics. But now it does not make any difference what the motive was. *Don Quixote* is no less a great work of art.

In the field of politics we see very clearly the curious mixture of egotism and desire for public welfare. Winston Churchill, for example, was a very ambitious young man. His ambition gave him the chance to accomplish much. What he achieved was not only great statesmanship but had a quality of magnanimity that reminds us of the wisdom of the wheat and the tares. Churchill knew the mixture of good and evil in the dramas of history. We doubt whether he ever read or really heeded the parable of the wheat and the tares, yet in his magnanimity there was some of its wisdom. He showed the combination of creativity and self-love which we find particularly in politics, but is it not everywhere? There is a puzzling aspect to judgments about self-love or ambition. At what particular point do we think egotism so excessive that it becomes obviously corrupting? It is always rather corrupting, but when does it become *obviously* corrupting? We know certain people to be monstrous egotists, but can we put our finger on the spot where this mixture of love and self-love, which we all have, turns into monstrous egotism? We do have to make our judgments, but we cannot be exact in our moral measurement.

There are forms of self-love which are quite dangerous, but are enclosed in a great sea of vitality which robs them of some of their power. Let us compare America with Spain. In Spain, the somewhat medieval social and political order is according to the tradition of natural law and of the Catholic church. To us, it is stale and static. In this country, and in spite of all our weaknesses, our pride and pretensions, certainly there is life. Our national life is based upon the vitality of various interests balanced by various other interests. This is the heart of the free enterprise doctrine. These self-interests are not nearly as harmless as our conservative friends imagine them to be. Here we do have to violate the parable, and provisionally make judgments and say, "This form of self-interest must be checked." Or, "This form of self-interest must be balanced by other interest." Otherwise we will not have justice if the powerful man simply goes after his interest at the expense of the weak.

We make such provisional judgments, but all these provisional judgments stand ultimately under the truth of the parable of the wheat and the tares. "Let both grow together until the harvest." If we had more modesty about this, perhaps there would not have been such a debate between pure individualism and pure collectivism. On the one hand, this policy may be necessary. On the other hand, it may be dangerous. We had better try to find out how necessary and how dangerous it is, but not absolutely, or we will make the kind of judgment that will pull up the wheat with the tares.

What is Communism but a vast example of pulling up the tares, and not knowing the wheat that is among these tares of so called self-interest or capitalistic injustice. Is it not surprising that we should have two great evils in our time, Nazism and Communism? Nazism represented such an obvious expression of collective egotism that we do not have to wait for the ultimate judgment. We all know that Nazism was evil! But Communism is a form of evil that comes from human beings forgetting that they are creatures, imagining themselves omniscient and righteous—absolutely righteous—and trying to rebuild the whole world in terms of their ideals, not knowing that their own sins are involved in it. The Communist knows nothing about the parable of the wheat and the tares, or about the ultimate judgment that stands over human existence, and above all nothing about the ambiguity of all human motives.

There is also that kind of selfishness which we might regard as an inadvertent and rather harmless corruption of the love impulse. Is it really inadvertent? Is it actually harmless? We do not know exactly. The sinfulness of parents in their love for their children gives us an example.

The love of parents for their children is one of the symbols of the kingdom of God. But we parents are not quite perfect. There are two crises which children face: one is in their youth when they find out that their parents are not as powerful as they thought; and the second is in their adolescence when they find out that the parents are not as good as they thought they were. No doubt every parent is better than an adolescent rebel imagines in the period of rebellion. The parent who claims to be absolutely loving and then insinuates into that love the old lust for power, which every human being has, obviously is vexatious. But it also must be recognized that there is some good in this evil.

Thus human history is a mixture of wheat and tares. We must make provisional distinctions, but we must know that there are no final distinctions. "Let both grow together until the harvest." Man is a creature and a creator. He would not be a creator if he could not overlook the human scene and be able to establish goals beyond those of nature and to discriminate between good and evil. He must do these things. But he must also remember that no matter how high his creativity may rise, he is himself involved in the flow of time, and he becomes evil at the precise point where he pretends not to be, when he pretends that his wisdom is not finite but infinite, and his virtue is not ambiguous but unambiguous.

From the standpoint of the biblical faith we do not have to despair because life is so brief, but we must not pretend to more because we are so great. Because we are both small and great, we have discerned a mystery and a meaning beyond our smallness and our greatness, and a justice and a love which completes our incompletions, which corrects our judgments, and which brings the whole story to a fulfillment beyond our power to fulfill any story.

> We thank you, our God, for your judgments which are sterner than the judgments of man. Help us to remember them when moral men speak well of us. We thank you for your mercy which is kinder than the goodness of men. Help us to discern this when we are overcome by the confusion of life, and despair about our own sin. Grant us, O Lord, always to worship you in all our doings in the greatness of your creativity and the wonder of your judgment and your mercy.

4

HUMOUR AND FAITH

He that sitteth in the heavens shall laugh: the Lord shall have them in derision.

Ps. 2:4.

This word of the Second Psalm is the only instance in the Bible in which laughter is attributed to God. God is not frequently thought of as possessing a sense of humour, though that quality would have to be attributed to perfect personality. There are critics of religion who regard it as deficient in the sense of humour, and they can point to the fact that there is little laughter in the Bible. Why is it that Scriptural literature, though filled with rejoicings and songs of praise, is not particularly distinguished for the expression of laughter? There are many sayings of Jesus which betray a touch of ironic humour; but on the whole one must agree with the critics who do not find much humour or laughter in the Bible.

This supposed defect will, however, appear less remarkable if the relation of humour to faith is understood. Humour is, in fact, a prelude to faith; and laughter is the beginning of prayer. Laughter must be heard in the outer courts of religion; and the echoes of it should resound in the sanctuary; but there is no laughter in the holy of holies. There laughter is swallowed up in prayer and humour is fulfilled by faith.

HUMOUR, FAITH, AND INCONGRUITY

The intimate relation between humour and faith is derived from the fact that both deal with the incongruities of our existence. Humour is concerned with the immediate incongruities of life and faith with the ultimate ones. Both humour and faith are expressions of the freedom of the human spirit, of its capacity to stand outside of life, and itself, and view the whole scene. But any view of the whole immediately creates the problem of how the incongruities of life are to be dealt with; for the effort to understand the life, and our place in it, confronts us with inconsistencies and incongruities which do not fit into any neat picture of the whole. Laughter is our reaction to immediate incongruities and those which do not affect us essentially. Faith is the only possible response to the ultimate incongruities of existence which threaten the very meaning of our life.

We laugh at what? At the sight of a fool upon the throne of the king; or the proud man suffering from some indignity; or the child introducing its irrelevancies into the conversation of the mature. We laugh at the juxtaposition of things which do not fit together. A boy slipping on the ice is not funny. Slipping on the ice is funny only if it happens to one whose dignity is upset. A favorite device of dramatists, who have no other resources of humour, is to introduce some irrelevant interest into the central theme of the drama by way of the conversation of maid or butler. If this irrelevance is to be really funny, however, it must have some more profound relation to the theme than the conversor intended. This is to say that humour manages to resolve incongruities by the discovery of another level of congruity. We laugh at the proud man slipping on the ice, not merely because the contrast between his dignity and his undignified plight strikes us as funny; but because we feel that his discomfiture is a poetically just rebuke of his dignity. Thus we deal with immediate incongruities, in which we are not too seriously involved and which open no gap in the coherence of life in such a way as to threaten us essentially.

But there are profound incongruities which contain such a threat. Man's very position in the universe is incongruous. That is the problem of faith, and not of humour. Man is so great and yet so small, so significant and yet so insignificant. "On the one hand," says Edward Bellamy, "is the personal life of man, an atom, a grain of sand on a boundless shore, a bubble of a foam flecked ocean, a life bearing a proportion to the mass of past, present and future, so infinitesimal as to defy the imagination. On the other hand is a certain other life, as it were a spark of the universal life, insatiable in aspiration, greedy of infinity, asserting solidarity with all things and all existence, even while subject to the limitations of space and time."[1] That is the contrast.

1. In *The Religion of Solidarity.*

When man surveys the world he seems to be the very center of it; and his mind appears to be the unifying power which makes sense out of the whole. But this same man, reduced to the limits of his animal existence, is a little animalcule, preserving a precarious moment of existence within the vastness of space and time. There is a profound incongruity between the "inner" and the "outer" world, or between the world as viewed from man's perspective, and the man in the world as viewed from a more ultimate perspective. The incongruity becomes even more profound when it is considered that it is the same man who assumes the ultimate perspective from which he finds himself so insignificant.

Philosophers seek to overcome this basic incongruity by reducing one world to the dimension of the other; or raising one perspective to the height of the other. But neither a purely naturalistic nor a consistently idealistic system of philosophy is ever completely plausible. There are ultimate incongruities of life which can be resolved by faith but not by reason. Reason can look at them only from one standpoint or another, thereby denying the incongruities which it seeks to solve. They are also too profound to be resolved or dealt with by laughter. If laughter seeks to deal with the ultimate issues of life it turns into a bitter humour. This means that it has been overwhelmed by the incongruity. Laughter is thus not merely a vestibule to faith but also a "no-man's land" between faith and despair. We laugh cheerfully at the incongruities on the surface of life; but if we have no other resource but humour to deal with those which reach below the surface, our laughter becomes an expression of our sense of the meaninglessness of life.

LAUGHTER AND HUMAN JUDGMENT

Laughter is a sane and healthful response to the innocent foibles of men; and even to some which are not innocent. All men betray moods and affectations, conceits and idiosyncrasies, which could become the source of great annoyance to us if we took them too seriously. It is better to laugh at them. A sense of humour is indispensable to men of affairs who have the duty of organizing their fellowmen in common endeavors. It reduces the frictions of life and makes the foibles of men tolerable. There is, in the laughter with which we observe and greet the foibles of others, a nice mixture of mercy and judgment, of censure and forbearance. We would not laugh if we regarded these foibles as altogether fitting and proper. There is judgment, therefore, in our laughter. But we also prove by the laughter that we do not take the annoyance too seriously. However, if our fellows commit a serious offense against the common good, laughter no longer avails. If we continue to indulge in it, the element of forbearance is completely eliminated from it. Laughter against real evil is bitter. Such bitter laughter of derision has its uses as an instrument of condemnation. But there is no power in it to deter the evil against which it is directed.

There were those who thought that we could laugh Mussolini and Hitler out of court. Laughter has sometimes contributed to the loss of prestige of dying oligarchies and social systems. Thus Cervantes' *Don Quixote* contributed to the decline of feudalism, and Boccaccio's *Decameron* helped to signal the decay of medieval asceticism. But laughter alone never destroys a great seat of power and authority in history. Its efficacy is limited to preserving the self-respect of the slave against the master. It does not extend to the destruction of slavery. Thus all the victims of tyranny availed themselves of the weapon of wit to preserve their sense of personal self-respect. Laughter provided them with a little private world in which they could transvalue the values of the tyrant, and reduce his pompous power to the level of the ridiculous. Yet there is evidence that the most insufferable forms of tyranny (as in the concentration camps, for instance) could not be ameliorated by laughter.

Laughter may turn to bitterness when it faces serious evil, partly because it senses its impotence. But, in any case, serious evil must be seriously dealt with. The bitterness of derision is serious enough; but where is the resource of forgiveness to come from? It was present in the original forbearance of laughter; but it cannot be brought back into the bitterness of derision. The contradiction between judgment and mercy cannot be resolved by humour but only by vicarious pain.

Thus we laugh at our children when they betray the jealous conceits of childhood. These are the first buds of sin which grow in the soil of the original sin of our common humanity. But when sin has conceived and brought forth its full fruit, our laughter is too ambiguous to deal with the child's offense; or if it is not ambiguous it becomes too bitter. If we retain the original forbearance of laughter in our judgment it turns into harmful indulgence. Parental judgment is always confronted with the necessity of relating rigorous judgment creatively to the goodness of mercy. That relation can be achieved only as the parent himself suffers under the judgments which are exacted. Not humour but the cross is the meeting point of justice and mercy, once both judgment and mercy have become explicit. Laughter can express both together, when neither is fully defined. But, when it becomes necessary to define each explicitly, laughter can no longer contain them both. Mercy is expelled and only bitterness remains.

LAUGHTER AND DIVINE JUDGMENT

What is true of our judgments of each other is true of the judgment of God. In the word of our text, God is pictured laughing at man and having him in derision because of the vanity of man's imagination and pretensions. There is no suggestion of a provisional geniality in this divine laughter. Derisiveness is pure judgment. It is not possible to resolve the contradiction between mercy and judgment, on the level of the divine, through humour; because the divine judgment is ultimate judgment. That contradiction, which remains an unsolved mystery in the Old Testament, is resolved only as God is revealed in Christ. There is no humour but suffering in that revelation. There is, as we have observed, a good deal of ironic humour in the sayings of Christ. But there is no humour in the scene of Christ upon the Cross. The only humour on Calvary is the derisive laughter of those who cried, "He saved others; himself he can not save. . . . If he be the son of God let him come down from the cross" (Matt. 27:42); and the ironic inscription on the cross, ordered by Pilate: "The King of the Jews." These ironic and derisive observations were the natural reactions of common sense to dimensions of revelation which transcend common sense. Since they could not be comprehended by faith, they prompted ironic laughter.

There is no humour in the cross because the justice and the mercy of God are fully revealed in it. In that revelation, God's justice is made the more terrible because the sin of man is disclosed in its full dimension. It is a rebellion against God from which God himself suffers. God cannot remit the consequences of sin; yet He does show mercy by taking the consequences upon and into Himself. This is the main burden of the disclosure of God in Christ. This is the final clue to the mystery of the divine character.

Mercy and justice are provisionally contained in laughter; and the contradiction between them is tentatively resolved in the sense of humour. But the final resolution of justice, fully developed, and of mercy, fully matured, is possible only when the sharp edge of justice is turned upon the executor of judgment without being blunted. This painful experience of vicarious suffering is far removed from laughter. Only an echo of the sense of humour remains in it. The echo is the recognition in the sense of humour that judgment and mercy belong together, even though they seem to be contradictory. But there is no knowledge in the sense of humour of how the two are related to each other and how the contradiction between them is to be resolved.

LAUGHTER AT THE SELF

The sense of humour is even more important provisionally in dealing with our own sins than in dealing with the sins of others. Humour is a proof of the capacity of the self to gain a vantage point from which it is able to look at itself. The sense of humour is thus a by-product of self-transcendence. People with a sense of humour do not take themselves too seriously. They are able to "stand off" from themselves, see themselves in perspective, and recognize the ludicrous and absurd aspects of their pretensions. All of us ought to be ready to laugh at ourselves because all of us are a little funny in our foibles, conceits and pretensions. What is funny about us is precisely that we take ourselves too seriously. We are rather insignificant little bundles of energy and vitality in a vast organization of life. But we pretend that we are the very center of this organization. This pretension is ludicrous; and its absurdity increases with our lack of awareness of it. The less we are able to laugh at ourselves the more it becomes necessary and inevitable that others laugh at us.

It is significant that little children are really very sober, though they freely indulge in a laughter which expresses a pure animal joy of existence. But they do not develop the capacity of real humour until the fifth or sixth year, at which time they may be able to laugh at themselves and at others. At about this age their intense preoccupation with self and with an immediate task at hand is partly mitigated. The sense of humour grows, in other words, with the capacity of self-transcendence. If we can gain some perspective upon our own self we are bound to find the self's pretensions a little funny.

This means that the ability to laugh at oneself is the prelude to the sense of contrition. Laughter is a vestibule to the temple of confession. But laughter is not able to deal with the problem of the sins of the self in any ultimate way. If we become fully conscious of the tragedy of sin we recognize that our preoccupation with self, our exorbitant demands upon life, our insistence that we receive more attention than our needs deserve, effect our neighbors harmfully and defraud them of their rightful due. If we recognize the real evil of sin, laughter cannot deal with the problem. If we continue to laugh after having recognized the depth of evil, our laughter becomes the instrument of irresponsibility. Laughter is thus not only the vestibule of the temple of confession but the no-man's land between cynicism and contrition. Laughter may express a mood which takes neither the self nor life seriously. If we take life seriously but ourselves not too seriously, we cease to laugh. The contradiction in man between "the good that he would and does not do, and the evil that he would not do, and does" (see Rom. 7:15–20) is no laughing matter.

There is furthermore another dimension in genuine contrition which laughter does not contain. It is the awareness of being judged from beyond ourselves. There is something more than self-judgment in genuine contrition. "For me it is a small thing to be judged of men," declares St. Paul, "neither judge I myself; for I know nothing against myself; he who judges me is the Lord" (Rom. 4:3–4). In an ultimate sense the self never knows anything against itself. The self of today may judge the self's action of yesterday as evil. But that means that the self of today is the good self. We are within depths of mystery which are never completely fathomed. Man is a spirit; and among the qualities of his spirit are the capacity to regard himself and the world; and to speculate on the meaning of the whole. This man is, when he is the observer, the very center of the universe. Yet the same man "brings his years to an end like a tale that is told" (Ps. 90:9). This man groweth up like grass in the morning which in the evening is cut down and withereth. The brevity of human existence is the most vivid expression and climax of human weakness.

The incongruity of man's greatness and weakness, of his mortality and immortality, is the source of his temptation to evil. Some men seek to escape from their greatness to their weakness; they try to deny the freedom of their spirit in order to achieve the serenity of nature. Some men seek to escape from their weakness to their greatness. But these simple methods of escape are unavailing. The effort to escape into the weakness of nature leads not to the desired serenity but to sensuality. The effort to escape from weakness to greatness leads not to the security but to the evils of greed and lust for power, or to the opposite evils of a spirituality which denies the creaturely limitations of human existence.

The philosophies of the ages have sought to bridge the chasm between the inner and the outer world, between the world of thought in which man is so great and the world of physical extension in which man is so small and impotent. But philosophy cannot bridge the chasm. It can only pretend to do so by reducing one world to the dimensions of the other. Thus naturalists, materialists, mechanists, and all philosophers, who view the world as primarily a system of physical relationships, construct a universe of meaning from which man is the full dimension of spirit can find no home. The idealistic philosophers, on the other hand, construct a world of rational coherence in which mind is the very stuff of order, the very foundation of existence. But their systems do not do justice to the large areas of chaos in the world; and they fail to give an adequate account of man himself, who is something less, as well as something more, than mind.

HUMOUR AND INCONGRUITY

The sense of humour is, in many respects, a more adequate resource for the incongruities of life than the spirit of philosophy. If we are able to laugh at the curious quirks of fortune, in which the system of order and meaning which each life constructs within and around itself is invaded, we at least do not make the mistake of prematurely reducing the irrational to a nice system. Things "happen" to us. We make our plans for a career, and sickness frustrates us. We plan our life, and war reduces all plans to chaos. The storms and furies of the world of nature, which can so easily reduce our private schemes to confusion, do of course have their own laws. They "happen" according to a discernible system of causality. There is no question about the fact that there are systems of order in the world. But it is not so easy to discern a total system of order and meaning which will comprehend the various levels of existence in an orderly whole.

To meet the disappointments and frustrations of life, the irrationalities and contingencies with laughter, is a high form of wisdom. Such laughter does not obscure or defy the dark irrationality. It merely yields to it without too much emotion and friction. A humorous acceptance of fate is really the expression of a high form of self-detachment. If men do not take themselves too seriously, if they have some sense of the precarious nature of the human enterprise, they prove that they are looking at the whole drama of life not merely from the circumscribed point of their own interests but from some further and higher vantage point. One thinks for instance of the profound wisdom which underlies the capacity of laughter in the Negro people. Confronted with the cruelties of slavery, and socially too impotent to throw off the yoke, they learned to make their unpalatable situation more sufferable by laughter. There was of course a deep pathos mixed with the humour, a proof of the fact that laughter had reached its very limit.

LAUGHTER IN THE FACE OF EVIL AND DEATH

There is indeed a limit to laughter in dealing with life's frustrations. We can laugh at all of life's surface irrationalities. We preserve our sanity the more surely if we do not try to reduce the whole crazy-quilt of events in which we move to a premature and illusory order. But the ultimate incongruities of human existence cannot be "laughed off." We can not laugh at death. We do try of course.

A war era is particularly fruitful of *Galgenhumor* (gallows humour). Soldiers are known on occasion to engage in hysterical laughter when nerves are tense before the battle. They speak facetiously of the possible dire fate which might befall this or that man of the company. "Sergeant," a soldier is reported to have said before a recent battle, "don't let this little fellow go into battle before me. He isn't big enough to stop the bullet meant for me." The joke was received with uproarious good humour by the assembled comrades. But when the "little fellow" died in battle the next day, everyone felt a little ashamed of the joke. At any rate it was quite inadequate to deal with the depth and breadth of the problem of death.

If we persist in laughter when dealing with the final problem of human existence, when we turn life into a comedy we also reduce it to meaninglessness. That is why laughter, when pressed to solve the ultimate issue, turns into a vehicle of bitterness rather than joy. To laugh at life in the ultimate sense means to scorn it. There is a note of derision in that laughter and an element of despair in that derision.

Just as laughter is the "no-man's land" between cynicism and contrition when we deal with the incongruous element of evil in our own soul, so is it also the area between despair and faith when dealing with evil and incongruity in the world about us. Our provisional amusement with the irrational and unpredictable fortunes which invade the order and purpose of our life must move either toward bitterness or faith, when we consider not this or that frustration and this or that contingent event, but when we are forced to face the issue of the basic incongruity of death.

Either we have a faith from the standpoint of which we are able to say, "I am persuaded, that neither death, nor life . . . shall be able to separate us from the love of God, which is in Christ Jesus our Lord" (Rom. 8:38–39), or we are overwhelmed by the incongruity of death and are forced to say with Ecclesiastes: "I said in mine heart concerning the estate of the sons of men . . . that they might see that they themselves are beasts. For that which befalleth the sons of men befalleth beasts; . . . as the one dieth, so dieth the other; yea they all have one breath; so that a man hath no preeminence above a beast; for all is vanity" (Eccles. 3:18–19).

The final problem of human existence is derived from the fact that in one context and from one perspective man has no preeminence above the beast; and yet from another perspective his preeminence is very great. No beast comes to the melancholy conclusion that "all is vanity"; for the purposes of its life do not outrun its power, and death does not therefore invade its life as an irrelevance. Furthermore it has no prevision of its own end and is therefore not tempted to melancholy. Man's melancholy over the prospect of death is the proof of his partial transcendence over the natural process which ends in death. But this is only a partial transcendence and man's power is not great enough to secure his own immortality.

This problem of man, so perfectly and finally symbolized in the fact of death, can be solved neither by proving that he has no preeminence above the beast, nor yet proving that his preeminence is a guarantee that death has no final dominion over him. Man is both great and small, both strong and weak, both involved in and free of the limits of nature; and he is a unity of strength and weakness of spirit and creatureliness. There is therefore no possibility of man extricating himself by his own power from the predicament of his amphibious state.

FAITH AND THE LIMITATIONS OF LAUGHTER

The Christian faith declares that the ultimate order and meaning of the world lies in the power and wisdom of God who is both Lord of the whole world of creation and the father of human spirits. It believes that the incongruities of human existence are finally overcome by the power and the love of God, and that the love which Christ revealed is finally sufficient to overcome the contradiction of death.

This faith is not some vestigial remnant of a credulous and pre-scientific age with which "scientific" generations may dispense. There is no power in any science or philosophy, whether in a pre- or post-scientific age, to leap the chasm of incongruity by pure thought. Thought which begins on one side of the chasm can do no more than deny the reality on the other side. It seeks either to prove that death is no reality because spirit is eternal, or that spirit is not eternal because death is a reality. But the real situation is that man, as a part of the natural world, brings his years to an end like a tale that is told; and that man as a free spirit finds the brevity of his years incongruous and death an irrationality; and that man as a unity of body and spirit can neither by taking thought reduce the dimension of his life to the limit of nature, nor yet raise it to the dimension of pure spirit. Either his incomplete and frustrated life is completed by a power greater than his own, or it is not completed.

Faith is therefore the final triumph over incongruity, the final assertion of the meaningfulness of existence. There is no other triumph and will be none, no matter how much human knowledge is enlarged. Faith is the final assertion of the freedom of the human spirit, but also the final acceptance of the weakness of man and the final solution for the problem of life through the disavowal of any final solutions in the power of man.

Insofar as the sense of humour is a recognition of incongruity, it is more profound than any philosophy which seeks to devour incongruity in reason. But the sense of humour remains healthy only when it deals with immediate issues and faces the obvious and surface irrationalities. It must move toward faith or sink into despair when the ultimate issues are raised.

That is why there is laughter in the vestibule of the temple, the echo of laughter in the temple itself, but only faith and prayer, and no laughter, in the holy of holies.

5

≋

THE ASSURANCE OF GRACE

Whenever the tension between spirit and nature is adequately maintained and the imperatives of spirit are pressed rigorously against the
immediate impulses of nature, the result is not only a morality of
purer disinterestedness but a religion of grace which seeks to console
the human spirit to its inevitable defeat in the world of nature and
history. It is significant that in the Christian religion, Jesus, who in
his own life incarnated the spirit of pure love to a unique and remarkable degree, became for Paul the symbol and revelation of a divine
forgiveness which knew how to accept human intentions for achievements. The relation of the religion of Jesus to that of Paul is a perfect
illustration of the relation of a religious morality of pure disinterestedness to a supra-moral religion of grace. The force of the same
religious urge is revealed in both of them.

A high religion creates both disinterestedness and the realization
that pure love and disinterestedness are impossible of achievement.
It declares on the one hand, "Be ye therefore perfect even as your
Father in heaven is perfect" (Matt. 5:48), and on the other it confesses, "Why callest thou me good; no one is good save God" (Luke
18:19). The same rigor which discovers the inertia of natural impulse
sufficiently to make a high morality possible also reveals the resistance of nature to spirit so clearly that the demands of pure spirit
are seen to be frustrated in nature and history. Pure religion is thus at
the same time the inspiration of a high morality and a consolation for
the frustrations which moral purpose faces in history.

The consolations of the assurance of grace in religious faith have no
meaning to the modern man and the modern spirit because the modern spirit is still under the illusion that the logic of the spirit needs
only to be recognized to be fulfilled. For it, life is a simple process in
which spirit gains ever more impressive victories over natural im-

pulse. Its optimistic monism is too thoroughgoing, and there are not enough dualistic elements in its thought, for an adequate ethic or religion. The naturalistic monism of modern culture is possible both because the ethical character of the forces of nature is overestimated and because the rigor of the ethical demand is softened by prudential qualifications. This superficial monism is destroyed whenever ethical passion rises to a pitch where prudence is discarded or when philosophical and religious penetration discloses life in both its heights and depths. It may be claimed, therefore, that religion and morality are related to each other in terms of mutual support: a profound religion makes a pure ethical passion possible, and a pure ethical passion makes religion necessary.

GRACE IN THE RELIGION OF JESUS

In the religion of Jesus, ethical tension and relaxation from tension through the assurance of grace are curiously intermingled so that the latter does not become a peril to the former. This is less true of the religion of Paul, and the Christian orthodoxy which is derived from it. In Paul, the dualism and pessimism are more consistently and philosophically developed, and the chasm between nature and God must therefore be bridged by a more specific act of divine grace, which for Paul and Christian orthodoxy is to be found in the historic incarnation and redemption. In Jesus, the mythology which expresses his thought is much more paradoxical and unphilosophical, and he is therefore more able to do justice both to the tension required for an adequate ethic and the release from tension necessary to an adequate religion.

Essentially, the experience of grace in religion is the apprehension of the absolute from the perspective of the relative. The unachieved is in some sense felt to be achieved or realized. The sinner is "justified" even though his sin is not overcome. The world, as revealed in its processes of nature, is known to be imperfect, and yet it is recognized as a creation of God. Man is regarded as both a sinner and a child of God. In these paradoxes true religion makes present reality bearable even while it insists that God is denied, frustrated and defied in the immediate situation.

In Jesus' religio-poetic conceptions of life and the world, the impartiality of nature, which to the humanist represents nature's injustice and indicates her inability to support the moral values conceived by man, is regarded as a revelation of divine mercy which "maketh his sun to rise on the evil and the good and sendeth rain on the just and the unjust" (Matt. 5:45). The conception here is of a God who, in spite of his transcendence, does not negate the forces of nature but reveals himself in them. Here religious faith transmutes nature's unconcern for the moral distinctions between human good and evil into a revelation of the highest spiritual achievement: forgiving love. The very pinnacle of the spirit is found in the broad basis of natural process. The whole world process is endowed with spiritual meaning which reveals both the judgments and the mercy of God. In this imaginative insight, the relation of the assurance of forgiveness to the demand for perfection in high religion is revealed at its best. Nothing in conceptions of orthodox and conventional religion approaches this profundity.

In the same way, Jesus finds glimpses of God, of pure spirit, of perfect love, in human nature, in the love of parents for their children, for instance, and in the innocency of little children; yet he also knew that out of the heart of this same human nature "proceed evil thoughts, murders, adulteries, fornications, thefts, false witness, blasphemies" (Matt. 15:19). His confidence in the goodness of human nature is not as simple as that of liberal Christianity. The kingdom of God, in his view, will be established not by the goodness of loving men but by the grace of God. Yet there are glimpses of the eternal and the absolute in human nature.

The relation of ethical tension and religious relaxation is perhaps most perfectly revealed in the beatitudes of Jesus, in which bliss is promised to the unsatisfied. The knowledge and the certainty of God are a gift to, and an achievement of, those who strive after perfection without the illusion of having attained it, the "poor in spirit," and those who "hunger and thirst after righteousness" (Matt. 5:3, 6). Those who imagine themselves righteous are consistently condemned. Those who strive after pure spirit are consoled in the inevitable frustration which attends their striving, because in their very search after perfection they are initiated into the true character of spirit and realize that perfection is love and not justice. Thus they obtain mercy while they learn to be merciful.

GRACE AND MORAL PASSION

The contrite recognition of the imperfections in the self further reduces the strain of living in an imperfect world because it reduces the
presumptions and demands which the soul makes upon the world
and upon its fellowmen. When the evils from which men suffer are
recognized as having their root in sins which the self shares with all
mankind, they are borne more patiently and with less resentment
than would otherwise be the case. In the mythology of Genesis, even
the inadequacies of nature are ascribed to the sin of man, a somewhat
too simple solution for the problem of evil, but one which does credit
to man's moral imagination.

It must be immediately evident that every religious assurance of
grace and every concomitant emotion of contrition contain certain
perils to a socio-moral passion which strives to correct the imperfections of society and which must count upon impatient and, on the
whole, self-righteous men to perform the task. The knowledge of the
equal sinfulness of all human nature is not completely compatible
with a social purpose which sets the relatively good ideal against the
relative injustices of society. This incompatibility between the temper of classical religion and strenuous morality proves that the relation of religion and morality is never simple and is not exhausted in
their mutual support of each other on certain levels. In certain areas
the conflict is permanent; but its permanency does not justify the
suppression of one in favor of the other.

All men who live with any degree of serenity live by some assurance of grace. In every life there must at least be times and seasons
when the good is felt as a present possession and not as a far-off goal.
The sinner must feel himself "justified," that is, he must feel that his
imperfections are understood and sympathetically appreciated as
well as challenged. Whenever he finds himself in a circle of love
where he is "completely known and all forgiven," something of the
mercy of God is revealed to him and he catches a glimpse of the very
perfection which has eluded him. Perhaps the most sublime insight
of Jewish prophets and the Christian gospel is the knowledge that
since perfection is love, the apprehension of perfection is at once the
means of seeing one's imperfection and the consoling assurance of
grace which makes this realization bearable. This ultimate paradox

of high religion is not an invention of theologians or priests. It is constantly validated by the most searching experiences of life.

GRACE IN NATURE AND HISTORY

It is a literal fact that the processes of nature and history are revelations of grace as well as of judgment. Logically every life deserves destruction. Since it is predatory either individually or collectively, it ought to die at the hands of those it has exploited. Though it may perish in the end, the God of history and nature is truly longsuffering, "slow to anger and plenteous in mercy" (Ps. 103:8). If, for instance, the white man were to expiate his sins committed against the darker races, few white men would have the right to live. They live partly because they are strong enough to maintain themselves against their enemies and partly because their enemies have not taken vengeance upon them. They survive, in other words, both by the law of nature and by the law of grace. That is why the same facts of history lend themselves both to cynical and to religious interpretations.

The religious imagination sees truly when it regards the slow processes of history and the impartialities of nature as revelations of divine mercy. The same radiant morning sun may dispel the stupor of the man who has spent the night in a drunken orgy and call the diligent husbandman to his daily tasks. That aspect of nature is just as significant as the fact that the same wintry storm may "destroy both good and bad alike." If in the latter case nature seems to be inframoral in her judgments, it is not wrong to discover supramoral justice (mercy) in the former case. Thus vital religion catches glimpses of ultimate perfection in the very imperfections of man and history. Only a very rational religion relegates perfection completely to another world of pure transcendence. The modern Barthian emphasis on "the qualitative distinction between time and eternity" has much more in common with Greek Platonism than with the paradoxical religion of Jesus.

MISUNDERSTANDINGS OF GRACE

The experience of grace has been stereotyped by religious orthodoxy and made to depend upon the dispensations of religious institutions, the acceptance of dogmas, and upon faith in the efficacy of grace in specific facts of history (revelation and incarnation).

The fact that Christian orthodoxy relates and fastens the experience of grace, which in the religion of Jesus is organically related to the total moral and religious experience in human life, to the one fact of the incarnation need not lead to a magical and unmoral interpretation of grace. Religious faith needs specific symbols; and the Jesus of history is a perfect symbol of the absolute in history, because the perfect love to which pure spirit aspires is vividly realized in the drama of his life and cross. Thus a man becomes the symbol of God, and the religious sense that the absolute invades the relative and the historical is adequately expressed. Naturally, rational theology has difficulty in bringing the paradoxes of this mythological conception into the canons of rationality. In both orthodox and liberal theology, the profound mythological conceptions of the incarnation and atonement are rationalized, and their profundity is endangered, by canons of logic and consistency.

In orthodoxy, it is feared that some human imperfection and some relativity of history may still cling to the symbol of the absolute, because the symbol is historical, a man living in Galilee and speaking the language of a particular time and place. These relativities are rigorously effaced or obscured by the insistence that Christ was "the Only Begotten Son of God; Begotten of his Father before all the Worlds, God of God, Light of Light, Very God of Very God, Begotten not made, Being of one substance with the Father." The modern mind may find little plausibility in such a confession, but it is quite consistent with a dualistic world-view which is unable to find the absolute and perfect in the nature of the historic and the relative.

Unfortunately, the consistent dualism of orthodoxy complicates the task, necessary to the original meaning of the mythology, of relating the absolute to history. It does not adequately express the deeper feelings of the human spirit, which knows itself to be a citizen of two worlds, the world of spirit and the world of nature, which knows these two worlds to be at war with each other, but also believes that there is some ultimate resolution and reconciliation in the conflict.

The long controversy about the two natures of Christ in the history of Christian theology represents the futile effort of reason to comprehend or to define the mythological absurdities and profundities of the original myth. It is both interesting and pathetic that the dualism of Christian orthodoxy should be finally stated in its most consistent terms in our own day in reaction to Christian liberalism and that the dialectical theology (Barthianism), which draws these final pessimistic and dualistic conclusions, should find no meaning in history or nature except as the one event in history (the incarnation) illumines the scene. It is significant too that this one event in history really ceases to be an event in history and that the symbol of the absolute never really becomes incarnate.

Against this kind of consistent dualism and pessimism, Christian liberalism seems to have a more plausible rationalism. It believes that the Jesus of history was a symbol of the absolute, because he personifies "the highest human values." The goodness of human nature, and finally the ethical character of history itself, are thus the revelations of the absolute. If this seems more plausible and rational to our day than the position of Christian orthodoxy, it is only because our culture has been an optimistic one and has not realized what frustrations and defeats the spirit meets in the impulses of nature and history.

In consistent orthodoxy, the absolute and the relative, the divine and human, the spiritual and the natural are so completely separated that the ultimate faith of religion in the meaningfulness of life rests upon one event in history which is not truly historical. Religion is thus reduced to magic. In liberal theology, on the other hand, the tension between spirit and nature is not fully recognized, and all history and nature (including human nature) are consequently invested prematurely with the aura of the absolute and the perfect. In both cases, rationalism has destroyed the original mythological profundity of the Christian religion, which sought to express the idea that the conflict between spirit and nature is a real conflict, that no complete victory of spirit in history is possible, but that defeat is turned into victory when the unachieved perfection is discovered to be a forgiving love which justifies (understands) man's imperfection.

GRACE AS "MYTHICAL"

Every effort to state the idea of the grace and forgiveness of God in purely rational terms suffers from the same difficulties encountered in stating the conception of the relation of God to the world. The idea of grace can be stated adequately only in mythical terms. In the mythos of Jesus, the holy God reveals his holiness in terms of mercy and this mercy redeems the sinner. This redemption means that the sinner knows himself to be in the embrace of divine love in spite of his sin. The holiness of God thus creates both the consciousness of sin and the consolation which makes the consciousness of sin bearable.

When put in rational terms, this experience means that the man who is involved in the relativities of the natural and historical process finds himself nevertheless in contact with the final and the absolute life which is above the process. Thus the tension between the absolute and the relative is overcome.

But the rationalization of the mythos robs it of some of its significance. In purely rational terms, the sin of man becomes merely the imperfection and relativity inherent in the process of history, and the sense of personal responsibility for evil actions is lost. Since in every human life the egoism of natural impulse is actually transmuted into a willful conflict of life with life, the mythos of the fall and sin therefore does justice to the actual facts which a rational conception of human imperfection fails to reveal. But a rational conception not only blunts the idea of evil as sin into an idea of evil as imperfection; it also transmutes the apprehension of perfection into an experience which threatens to remove the concept of imperfection. Thus the sinner who is "justified" feels himself to have attained perfection. If, on the other hand, a rational effort is made to avoid the dangers of this confusion of perfection and imperfection, it results in a dualism of which Neo-Platonism is a typical example and in which the ethical distinctions between good and evil are lost in metaphysical distinctions between the world of pure form and of concrete reality.

Christian orthodoxy derived from Paul is very frequently close to errors of Neo-Platonic dualism. Christian liberalism, on the other hand, falls into the monistic errors of rationalism and fails to develop either a conception of sin for which grace is really required, or yet a conception of grace which maintains the idea of the sinfulness and imperfection of the world as it illumines the imperfect world with the aura of the absolute and perfect. The experience of grace, in short, can only be expressed in mythological terms if it is not to become a peril to the ethical life. For only in the concepts of religious myth can an imperfect world mirror the purposes of a divine Creator, and can the mercy of God make the fact of sin and imperfection bearable, without destroying moral responsibility for the evil of imperfection or obscuring its realities in actual history.

KEEPING ETHICAL TENSION ALIVE

Ideally, the Christian religion therefore is rooted in a mythology which does justice both to the necessity for moral tension in life and the need for the relaxation of this tension. Practically, the Christianity of the churches has subordinated ethical tension to the assurance of grace, or (as in the case of liberal Christianity) it has destroyed ethical tension by a too monistic and naturalistic mythology. If ethical tension has been maintained, it has expressed itself, in both orthodoxy and liberalism, in too purely individualistic terms, so that the moral vigor, which is most relevant to the urgent moral problems of an era which must deal with the life and death of social systems, is expressed outside the churches. It comes to its completest expression among those who have learned in bitter experience how real the conflict between spirit and nature is in history.

The radical idealists who express this moral vigor in the modern day are so completely immersed in the specific problems which face them that they can hardly be expected to do justice to the perennial problems of the human spirit, or to know that a relative victory over evil, however important, is not the final victory.

When the storms and fevers of this era are passed, and modern civilization has achieved a social system which provides some basic justice compatible with the necessities of a technical age, the perennial problems of humanity will emerge once more. Religious insights which seem for the moment to be inimical to moral progress and moral vigor will come into their own again. There will be unjust men in this new society of justice; and good men will feel that they are not as just as they ought to be. The perils of nature and the inhumanities of man will continue to take their toll in human life. Men's hopes will be shattered by untoward fortune; family circles will be invaded by death, and widows and orphans will seek not only security from society but some faith in the meaning of life which will make the chaos of the moment bearable; good will still be turned into evil, when the devotion of naïvely virtuous men is sluiced by the design of knaves and the ignorance of fools, into ignoble causes and dangerous channels. Men will continue, in short, to find the promptings of the spirit frustrated by the forces of nature within them and the hopes of the spirit shattered by the forces of nature about them. They will suffer both at the hands of nature and at the hands of man, and they will find the semi-conscious cruelties of conscious men more difficult to bear than "the trampling march of unconscious power."

When these problems of man in nature and man in society are seen again as perennial problems of the human spirit, and not merely as injustices of an era, men will have to learn once more that though evil must be resisted, there are limits to the possibility of resistance and some evil must be borne. The weak will cry out against the injustices of the strong, and they will confront the eternal problem of how to prevent bitterness from corroding their spirit and spoiling the purity of their testimonies. Men will learn that nature can never be completely tamed to do man's will. Her blind caprices, her storms and tempests, will continue on occasion to brush aside man's handiwork as a housewife destroys a cobweb; and her inexorable processes will run counter to men's hopes and designs. Then men will see again the importance of accommodating the vision of perfection to an imperfect world, without losing the urge to perfect the world. In order to do that, they must find suggestions of meaning in chaos and glimpses of ultimate perfection within imperfection.

The inevitable imperfections of life and history will be borne with greater serenity if the ego recognizes that the blind forces of nature which frustrate the spirit are in the self as well as outside it. In classical Christianity it is suggested again and again that repentance is the beginning of redemption, even that it is synonymous with redemption. This is a profound insight; for the evils and frustrations of life and history would be, in fact, unbearable if contrition did not reduce the presumptions and pretensions of the self and reveal the fact that some of the confusions from which the spirit suffers have their direct source in the chaos of the self, and that others may be regarded as punishment for the sins of the self even if they have not been obviously caused by them. The consciousness of sin in classical religion is closely related to the cynic's interpretation of human nature; but it is never purely pessimistic. Classical religious faith is always saved from despair because it knows that sin is discovered by the very faith through which men catch a glimpse of the reality of spirit. Both the heights and depths of the world of spirit are known.

The knowledge of the depths within the self saves the self from pride, prevents a bitter criticism of the sins of others, and makes a sullen rebellion against the imperfections of nature and history impossible. The knowledge of the heights keeps profound self-knowledge from degenerating into bitter disillusionment.

These religious insights guarantee the ethically striving soul a measure of serenity and provide the spiritual relaxation without which all moral striving generates a stinking sweat of self-righteousness, and an alternation of fanatic illusions and fretful disillusionments. Naturally it is not easy to preserve a decent balance between the ethical urge to realize perfection in history and the religious need of reconciliation with imperfection. In particular periods of history the one will devour the other. Sometimes the ethical urge will degenerate into an illusion-crammed ethical utopianism; at other times religious insights will betray the soul into a premature peace with and transcendence over the world's imperfections. But the human spirit will always discover in time that sanity and wholesomeness are possible only when two partially incompatible and partially supplementary attitudes toward life are both embraced and espoused. Then it will find its way back to the profound mythologies which do justice to both; and it will disavow not only the moribund religion which solves the problem of the spirit in nature by magic, but also the superficial rational moralism which dreams of gaining a quick and easy victory of the spirit over nature.

6

PRAYERS

O Lord, hear our prayers not according to the poverty of our asking, but according to the richness of your grace, so that our lives may conform to those desires which accord with your will.

When our desires are amiss, may they be overruled by a power greater than ours, and by a mercy more powerful than our sin.

———+ +———

Grant us, our Father, your grace, that, seeing ourselves in the light of your holiness, we may be cleansed of the pride and vainglory which obscure your truth; and knowing that from you no secrets are hid, we may perceive and confront those deceits and disguises by which we deceive ourselves and our fellowmen. So may we worship you in spirit and in truth and in your light, see light.

———+ +———

Many, O Lord, are the wonderful works which you have wrought. They cannot be reckoned up in order. If we should declare and speak of them, they are more than we can number. We give praise for the creation of the world, for the majesty of the mountains and for the mighty deeps, for the myriad number of all your creatures, each sustaining its life according to the plan you have ordained. We give praise for the life of man, whom you have created in your image and called into fellowship with you, whom you have endowed with memory and foresight, so that all our yesterdays are gathered together in our present moment and all our tomorrows are the objects of our hopes and apprehension.

O Lord, you have made us very great. Help us to remember how weak we are, so that we may not deny our kinship with the creatures of the field and our common dependence with them upon summer and winter, day and night. O Lord, you have made us very small, and we bring our years to an end like a tale that is told; help us to remember that beyond our brief day is the eternity of your love.

———————+ +———————

We give you thanks, O Lord, for life and love and the joy of existence, for the echo in human hearts to all pure and lovely things, for the promise of life and youth and the dawn of the unknown, and for the hope and assurance of fulfillment. We rejoice in the glory of manhood and womanhood, in the innocence of children and the serene wisdom of age. We rejoice in the sweetness of companionship and in the joy of understanding hearts, in the faith of strong souls and the wholesomeness of simple people whom pride has not touched. We give you thanks for the pleasures of art and literature, for the enrichment of personality through every ministry of truth and beauty and goodness.

We confess that we are not worthy of the riches of life for which the generation of men have labored that we might enter into this heritage. We confess the sorry confusion of our common life, the greed which disfigures our collective life and sets man against his fellowmen. We confess the indifference and callousness with which we treat the sufferings and the insecurity of the poor, and the pettiness which mars the relations between us. May we with contrite hearts seek once more to purify our spirits, and to clarify our reason so that a fairer temple for the human spirit may be built in human society.

———————+ +———————

Our Father, we thank you for all the provisions made for the needs of men, for the ordered course of nature and for the miracle of the abundance by which our life is sustained. Grant us grace to distribute this abundance, not according to the caprice of what nature has given to one and withheld from another, but according to your love for all your children. Most especially do we pray for your spirit upon this nation, that it may not perish in surfeit while much of the world perishes in need. Grant that we may have ears to hear and eyes to see the need of the anxious and troubled peoples of the world.

———————+ +———————

Almighty God, our heavenly Father, guide, we beseech you, the nations of the world into the ways of justice and truth and establish among them the peace which is the fruit of righteousness. Temper the pride of victors by the knowledge that your judgment is meant for victors and vanquished. Transfigure the despair of the vanquished into hope, and let not the pride of the victors obscure the mercy of the judge before whom they will be judged. Bind us together, victors and vanquished, uneasy partners and former enemies, into a new community and thus make the wrath of man to praise you.

———+ +———

We pray to you this day mindful of the sorry confusion of our world. Look with mercy upon this generation of your children so steeped in misery of their own contriving, so far strayed from your ways and so blinded by passions. We pray for the victims of tyranny, that they may resist oppression with courage and may preserve their integrity by a hope which defies the terror of the moment. We pray for wicked and cruel men, whose arrogance reveals to us what the sin of our own hearts is like when it has conceived and brought forth its final fruit. O God, who resists the proud and gives grace to the humble, bring down the mighty from their seats.

We pray for ourselves who live in peace and quietness, that we may not regard our good fortune as proof of our virtue, or rest content to have our ease at the price of other men's sorrow and tribulation.

We pray for all who have some vision of your will, despite the confusions and betrayals of human sin, that they may humbly and resolutely plan for and fashion the foundations of a just peace between men, even while they seek to preserve what is fair and just among us against the threat of malignant power. Grant us grace to see what we can do, but also to know what are the limits of our powers, so that courage may feed on trust in you, who are able to rule and overrule the angry passions of men and make the wrath of men to praise you.

———+ +———

O God, the sovereign of nations and the judge of men, look with compassion upon this sad world so full of misery and sorrow. Enlighten our eyes that we may see the justice of your judgments. Increase our faith that we may discern the greatness of your mercy. Save us from the sorrow of the world which works death and despair.

Fill us with the godly sorrow which works repentance, and the desire to do your will. Teach us how we may build a common life in which the nations of the world may find peace and justice. Show us what we ought to do. Show us also what are the limits of our powers and what we cannot do. So may our purpose to do your will be supported by our faith, for you are able to overrule our will and the make the wrath of man to praise you. Recall us to our dignity as co-workers together with you. Remind us of our weakness that we may look to you who works in us both to will and to do your good pleasure and supplies what is needed beyond our powers.

———————————+   +———————————

O Lord, whose kingdom is not of this world but yet whose truth is the judgment seat before which we must all be made manifest, reveal yourself to us above and beyond the confusion of counsel in which we stand. Reveal yourself as our judge so that we may not be at ease if the world thinks well of us, nor be dismayed if it judges us severely. Your judgments are more severe and your mercy is greater than the justice and goodness of the world. Grant us grace to submit ourselves to your will, that dying to our own desires, we may arise to newness of life.

———————————+   +———————————

Look with mercy upon this company of your people, the church. You have called us out of many lands and places to serve you in the ministry of your word. Teach us rightly to divide the word of truth. Grant that our love may grow in all knowledge and discernment. Help us each to walk worthily in the vocation wherewith we are called, forbearing one another in love and endeavoring to keep the unity of the spirit in the bond of peace. Teach us to look not each at his own things, but at the things of the other, so that we may impart and receive from one another whatever gift of the spirit you have given to each. O Lord, bind us together in the body of Christ that we may grow unto a perfect man, unto the measure of the stature of the fullness of Christ.

We pray, O Lord, for your church, that it may be healed of its divisions by your grace; that it may teach your word with courage to a sinful world, and may mediate with true charity your love and mercy to all men. Strengthen every ministry of reconciliation therein with your spirit. Grant that it may be a true community of grace in which the pride of race or nation is humbled, where the strong and mighty are brought to judgment, and the meek and lowly are lifted up. Make it more faithful to its Lord, and more instant to meet the needs of men.

III
THE CHURCH AND
THE MODERN WORLD

7

THE CHRISTIAN CHURCH IN A SECULAR AGE

For the past two hundred years the Christian church has been pro-
claiming its gospel in a world which no longer accepted the essentials
of the Christian faith. The Western world, particularly the more
advanced industrial nations, has come increasingly under the sway of
what has been called a secular culture. Secularism is most succinctly
defined as the explicit disavowal of the sacred. The holy in every
religion is that reality upon which all things depend, in terms of
which they are explained and by which they are judged. It is the
ultimate mystery, but also the ultimate source of all meaning. For the
Christian faith, holiness is ascribed only to the God who is the
creator, judge and redeemer of the world. The world is made and
sustained by Him. Its historical realities are thus the fruits of His
creative will. The world is judged by Him. Its sins stand under His
divine judgment. The world is redeemed by Him. Without His grace
mediated through Christ, human existence remains a problem to
itself, being unable to escape by any effort of its own from the contradictions of a sinful existence.

THE RELIGION OF SECULARISM

In contrast to this faith, modern secularism has been interpreted by
the Christian church too much in terms of secularism's own disavowal of religious faith. Strictly speaking, there is no such thing as
secularism. An explicit denial of the sacred always contains some
implied affirmation of a holy sphere. Every explanation of the meaning of human existence must avail itself of some principle of explanation which cannot be explained. Every estimate of values involves

some criterion of value which cannot be arrived at empirically. Consequently the avowedly secular culture of today turns out upon close examination to be either a pantheistic religion which identifies existence in its totality with holiness, or a rationalistic humanism for which human reason is essentially god, or a vitalistic humanism which worships some unique or particular vital force in the individual or the community as its god, that is, as the object of its unconditioned loyalty.

This latter faith, the product of the romantic movement in Western civilization, is the most obvious form of idolatry. It is also the most explicitly religious. Its emergence, particularly on the European continent, in these latter days of a dying bourgeois culture, proves the irrelevance of critical categories which imply a simple and unqualified contrast between the religious and the secular. There are no irreligious cultures; and if there were, it could not be assumed that a religious culture is intrinsically superior to an irreligious one. The question is not whether we worship a god. That is not the question, on the one hand, because all men do, whether implicitly or explicitly; and on the other hand, the worship of false gods is in no sense preferable to complete agnosticism, if the latter were possible.

The civilization and culture in which we are called upon to preach the Christian gospel is, in other words, not irreligious, but a devotee of a very old religion, dressed in a new form. It is the old religion of self-glorification. This is a very old religion because it involves the quintessence of human sin, as defined by St. Paul in the first chapter of Romans. Speaking of the Gentiles and their culpability in the sight of God he declares: "So that they are without excuse: because that, when they knew God, they glorified Him not as God, neither were thankful; but became vain in their imaginations, and their foolish heart was darkened. Professing themselves to be wise, they became fools [and what an accurate description that is of the vainglory of our modern era], and changed the glory of the uncorruptible God into an image made like to corruptible man, and to birds and four-footed beasts, and creeping things" (Rom. 1:20–23).

Every form of modern secularism contains an implicit or explicit self-glorification and deification in the sense described in the letter to the Romans. Humanistic rationalism, forgetting that human reason as well as human physical existence is a derived, dependent, created and finite reality, makes it into a principle of interpretation of the

meaning of life; and believes that its gradual extension is the guarantee of the ultimate destruction of evil in history. It mistakes the
image of God in man for God Himself. It does not realize that the
freedom by which man is endowed in his rational nature is the occasion for his sin as well as the ground of morality. It does not understand that by this reason nature's harmless will-to-live is transmuted
into a sinful will-to-power. It is by this reason that men make pretentious claims for their partial and relative insights, falsely identifying
them with absolute truth. Thus rationalism always involves itself in
two descending scales of self-deification. What begins as the deification of humanity in abstract terms ends as the deification of a particular type of man, who supposedly possesses ultimate insights. In Aristotelian rationalism this latter development is expressed in the
deification of the aristocrat, whom to glorify the slave exists. In modern rationalism the final result is a glorification of bourgeois perspectives.

The recent emergence of a more explicit type of self-glorification in
race, state and nation, in religions of *Blut und Boden* represents the
victory of romanticism over rationalism, to speak in purely cultural
terms. More profoundly considered, this romantic development is a
cynical reaction to the hypocritical pretensions of the rationalists.
Let those of us who live in such parts of Western civilization in which
the old rational humanism and universalism is not yet completely
disintegrated guard ourselves against premature self-righteous judgments. It may be that our type of humanism represents a more
sincere attempt to establish universal values and expresses an honest
devotion to European civilization rather than to the defiant strength
of a particular nation. But on the other hand, this bourgeois humanism tends to be oblivious to its own partial, national and bourgeois
perspectives. Having erroneously identified its truth with the eternal
truth, it naturally elicits the reaction of a curious kind of cynical
romanticism. It is not without significance that rational humanism
is still most robust in the nations which hold a dominant position,
politically and economically, in the Western world, more particularly the Anglo-Saxon nations; while what we abhor as primitivistic
romanticism flourishes in the less satisfied nations. Hypocrisy and
implicit or covert self-glorification are always the particular temptation of the victors; and cynicism and a more explicit self-glorification
the sin of the vanquished. The necessity of compensating for out-

raged self-esteem is the cause of this greater degree of explicitness in the deification of self.

The whole story of modern culture might be truly chronicled in terms of the parable of the Prodigal Son (Luke). The more rationalistic humanism is the son in the first stages of his emancipation from his father. The temper of modern culture is expressed quite precisely in the words of the son: "Father, give me the portion of goods that falleth to me." Our civilization did not want to recognize its dependence upon a divine father, who is the source of all life and the judge of all human actions. It wanted an autonomous culture. It separated the "goods that falleth to me" from the divine patrimony and forgot the dangers of anarchy in this independence. The more romantic type of modern humanism, as revealed in the religio-political movements of the Continent, represent a more advanced state of disintegration. Here the son is "wasting his substance in riotous living," a civilization allowing the vital energies of peoples and nations to express themselves in anarchic conflict with one another, and insisting that any vital or unique energy is morally self-justifying. The "mighty famine" when the son begins to be in want is still in the future, but our civilization is destined for such a catastrophe as so certain a consequence of the anarchy of its conflicting national passions and ambitions, that one may well speak of it as part of the contemporary picture.

To leave for a moment the parable of the Prodigal Son, a further reaction to bourgeois rationalism and humanism must be recorded which seeks to eliminate the errors of this dominant form of secularism. I refer to Marxism and the revolt of the proletarians in the Western world against the privileged sections of the community. In this newer form of humanism there is an explicit recognition of the finiteness of the human mind and the relation of human ideals to human interests; to the sinfulness, in short, of all human culture. Yet this very philosophy which sees the pretensions of all "the wise, the mighty and the noble" so clearly insists that it will be able to arrive at an absolute and universal position. In this creed the life of the proletariat has some mystic union with the absolute.

Here then we have a nice combination of the romantic and the rationalistic strains in modern culture, a glorification of the vitality of the burden bearers of the world as the instrument of an ultimate universalistic humanism; but no recognition that this fateful class is also composed of sinful men and that their sin will become more apparent as soon as they cease to be the oppressed and become the victors. Inasfar as Marxism seeks to establish genuinely universal values it must not be equated with the fascism which defies every common interest in the name of its own self-justifying vitality. Nor can its superiority over the pretentious rationalism of bourgeois life be denied. But unfortunately, as every culture which is not confronted with the one holy God, the creator, lord and judge of the world, it also ends in the sin of self-glorification.

THE CHRISTIAN MESSAGE

The question is, what shall the Christian church say to this modern culture, which began its adventure in autonomy with such gay self-assurance, which is already so deeply involved in "riotous living" and which faces so certain a doom of a mighty famine?

The Message of Repentance

We must, of course, preach the gospel to this, as to every generation. Our gospel is one which assures salvation in the cross of Christ to those who heartily repent of their sins. It is a gospel of the cross; and the cross is a revelation of the love of God only to those who have first stood under it as a judgment. It is in the cross that the exceeding sinfulness of human sin is revealed. It is in the cross that we become conscious how, not only what is worst, but what is best in human culture and civilization is involved in man's rebellion against God. It was Roman law, the pride of all pagan civilization, and Hebraic religion, the acme of religious devotion, which crucified the Lord. Thus does the cross reveal the problem of all human culture and the dilemma of every human civilization.

Repentance is the first key into the door of the Kingdom of God. "God resisteth the proud and giveth grace to the humble" (1 Peter 5:5). Whenever men trust their own righteousness, their own achievements, whenever they interpret the meaning of life in terms of the truth in their own culture, or find in their own capacities a sufficient steppingstone to the holy and the divine, they rest their life upon a frail reed which inevitably breaks and leaves their life meaningless.

Perhaps that is why the truest interpretations of the Christian faith have come in moments of history when civilizations were crumbling and the processes of history and the judgments of God had humbled human arrogance. The faith of the Hebrew prophets was thus formulated when the culture religion of Israel was threatened and finally overcome by the mighty civilizations of Assyria and Babylon. Augustine wrote the *City of God* when Roman civilization, once mighty enough to seem identical with civilization itself, had become the helpless victim of barbarians; and the renewal of the Christian gospel in the Protestant Reformation was, historically speaking, the consequence as well as the cause of the crumbling of a once proud medieval civilization. Proud men and successful civilizations find it difficult to know God, because they are particularly tempted to make themselves God. That is why "not many mighty, not many noble, not many wise after the flesh are called" (1 Cor. 1:26). Without the godly sorrow that worketh repentance there can be no salvation.

The Message of Hope

Just as the Christian gospel calls the proud to repent, it assures those who despair of a new hope. It is interesting how every religion which imparts a superficial meaning to life, and grounds that meaning in a dubious sanctity, finally issues in despair. Those who make the family their god must despair when the family is proved to be only a little less mortal than the individual. Those who make a god of their nation must despair when the might of their nation crumbles, as every creaturely and sinful might must: "For we are consumed by thine anger and by thy wrath are we troubled" (Ps. 90:7). That is the despair which awaits many a young nationalistic pagan of Europe today. They might even, if they could see truly, despair in the triumph of their nation, for the nation in triumph is less worthy of reverence than the nation in defeat. Pride accentuates its sins, and there are no sufferings to prompt pity as a handmaiden of love in the heart of the patriot.

Every humanistic creed is a cosmos of meaning sustained by a thin ice on the abysmal deeps of meaninglessness and chaos. Only the faith in God, who has been "our dwelling place in all generations," and who was God "before the mountains were brought forth or ever the earth and the world were made" (Ps. 90:1–2), can survive the vicissitudes of history, can rescue human existence from the despair in which it is periodically involved by its sinful pretensions, and the tragic disappointment of its facile hopes.

The fulfillment of life, according to our Christian faith, is possible only through the mercy of God. All superficial questions about the meaning of life, all simple religions which imagine that faith in any god is better than no faith at all, fail to recognize that the ultimate question is not whether life has a meaning (which it must have or no one could live), but whether or not the meaning is tragic. The only serious competitor to Christianity as a spiritual religion is Buddhism, and in Buddhism life is conceived in terms of pure tragedy. Christianity is a faith which takes us through tragedy to beyond tragedy, by way of the cross to a victory in the cross. The God whom we worship takes the contradictions of human existence into Himself. This knowledge is a stumbling block to the Jews, and to the Gentiles foolishness, but to them that are called it is the power and the wisdom of God. This is a wisdom beyond human knowledge, but not contrary to human experience. Once known, the truth of the gospel explains our experiences which remain inexplicable on any other level. Through it we are able to understand life in all of its beauty and its terror, without being beguiled by its beauty or driven to despair by its terror.

NOT OF THE WORLD, BUT IN THE WORLD

While the gospel which we preach reveals a world which in its ground and its fulfillment transcends human history, it does not abstract us from this present history with all of its conflicts and tragic disappointments of arrogant hopes. We are in the world, and God's will, His judgment and His mercy impinge upon our daily actions and historic problems. We must bring forth fruits meet for repentance. What can those fruits be but the fruits of "love, joy, peace?" (Gal. 5:22). When the church proclaims the love commandment to the world as the law of God, it must guard against the superficial moralism of telling the world that it can save itself if men will only stop being selfish and learn to be loving. We dare not forget that in us, as well as in those who do not acknowledge the Christian gospel, there is a law in our members that wars against the law that is in our mind. The law of love is not kept simply by being preached. Yet it is the law of life and must be both preached and practised. It is a terrible heresy to suggest that, because the world is sinful, we have a right to construct a Machiavellian politics or a Darwinian sociology as normative for Christians.

What is significant about the Christian ethic is precisely this: that it does not regard the historic as normative. Man may be, as Thomas Hobbes observed, a wolf to his fellowman. But this is not his essential nature. Let Christianity beware, particularly radical Protestantism, that it does not accept the habits of a sinful world as the norms of a Christian collective life. For the Christian only the law of love is normative. He would do well to remember that he is a sinner who has never perfectly kept the law of God. But neither must he forget that he is a child of God who stands under that law.

Much of what passes for theological profundity today is no more than a subtle re-enactment of the part of the son in the Lord's parable, who promised to do the father's will and did not, leaving his will to be done by the son who had refused to promise it. How accurately that little parable of Christ pictures the superior passion for human justice of many outside the Church as against those who are in it. Frequently, believing Christians are tempted by their recognition of the sinfulness of human existence to disavow their own responsibility for a tolerable justice in the world's affairs. Justice is not love. Justice presupposes the conflict of life with life and seeks to mitigate it. Every relative justice therefore stands under the judgment of the law of love, but it is also an approximation of it.

A Christian pessimism which becomes a temptation to irresponsibility toward all those social tasks which constantly confront the life of men and nations, tasks of ordering the productive labor of men, of adjudicating their conflicts, of arbitrating their divergent desires, of raising the level of their social imagination and increasing the range of their social sympathies—such a pessimism cannot speak redemptively to a world constantly threatened by anarchy and suffering from injustice. The Christian gospel which transcends all particular and contemporary social situations can be preached with power only by a church which bears its share of the burdens of immediate situations in which men are involved, burdens of establishing peace, of achieving justice, and of perfecting justice in the spirit of love. Thus is the Kingdom of God which is not of this world made relevant to every problem of the world.

THE DANGER OF PROFANIZATION

If the problem of presenting the Christian ethic to a non-Christian world without the spirit of self-righteousness is difficult, an even more far-reaching problem is the presentation of the gospel to a secular age. The truths of the Christian gospel are simple and clear. But it is not easy for any human institution to mediate them without pride or hypocrisy; and the church is a human institution, though it is that institution where it is known that all human life stands under a divine judgment and within a divine mercy. The real difficulty of preaching the gospel of God's mercy to the prodigal son, our modern culture, lies in the temptation to play the part of the elder brother in the Lord's parable. One might indeed elaborate this parable without disloyalty to its meaning, with the suggestion that the younger son might well have been prompted to leave his father's house because of the insufferable self-righteousness of the elder brother. At any rate, it is quite obvious that no Christian church has a right to preach to a so-called secular age without a contrite recognition of the shortcomings of historic Christianity which tempted the modern age to disavow its Christian faith.

Secularism is, on the one hand, the expression of man's sinful self-sufficiency. It may be, on the other hand, a reaction to profanity. Some men are atheists because of a higher implicit theism than that professed by believers. They reject God because His name has been taken in vain, and they are unable to distinguish between His holiness and its profanization. It is popular today in Christian circles to speak somewhat contemptuously of the errors and illusions of the secular culture which challenged Christianity so optimistically in the last two centuries and finds itself in such confusion today. It would be well to remember, however, that the primary conscious motive of this secularism (whatever may have been its unconscious and more sinful motives) was to break the chains which a profane Christianity had placed upon man.

A profane Christianity, like the elder brother, ostensibly maintains its sense of dependence upon the Father, but it uses this relationship to satisfy a sinful egotism. It falsely identifies its relative and partial human insights with God's wisdom, and its partial and relative human achievements with God's justice. A profane Christianity falsely identifies the church with the Kingdom of God. Since the historic church is always touched with human finiteness, is subject to sociological forces and pressures, and victim of the prejudices and illusions of particular ages, any tendency to obscure or deny this fact becomes the final and most terrible expression of human sinfulness. Of that sin no church has been free.

Protestants may believe, and not without a measure of truth, that this sin of profaning the holiness of God, of using His name in vain, is a particular danger in Catholicism, for Catholicism has a doctrine of the church in which what is human and what is divine in the Church is constantly subject to a confused identification of the one with the other. Yet no historic Christian institution is free of this sin. Every vehicle of God's grace, the preacher of the word, the prince of the church, the teacher of theology, the historic institution, the written word, the sacred canon—all these are in danger of being revered as if they were themselves divine. The aura of the divine word, which is transmitted through them, falsely covers their human frailties. The Christian church has never followed St. Paul rigorously enough in his disavowal of divinity: "And when the people saw what Paul had done they lifted up their voices saying, in the speech of Lyconia: The gods have come down to us in the likeness of men . . . which when the Apostles Paul and Barnabas heard of they rent their clothes and ran in among the people crying out and saying, Sirs, why do ye these things? We also are men of like passions with you and preach unto you, that ye should turn from these vanities unto the living God, which made heaven and earth and the sea and all things that are therein" (Acts 14:11–15).

SECULARISM AS A REACTION AGAINST A PROFANE CHRISTIANITY

Modern secularism was forced to resist a profanization of the holiness of God both in the realm of the truth and in the realm of the good, in both culture and ethics. In the realm of culture the Christian religion was tempted to complete the incompleteness of all human culture by authoritative dicta, supposedly drawn from Scripture. It forgot that theology is a human discipline subject to the same relativities as any other human discipline. If modern culture was wrong in regarding the Anselmic axiom *"Credo ut intelligam"* as absurd because it failed to understand that reason cannot function without the presuppositions of faith, Christian culture was wrong in insinuating the specific insights and prejudices of a particular age into the *"credo."* While modern science was wrong in assuming that its descriptions of detailed historical sequences in nature and history offered an adequate insight into the meaning of life, Christian culture was wrong in regarding its knowledge of the transhistorical sources of the meaning of life as adequate explanations of detailed sequences and efficient causation.

Thus we have been subjected for centuries to a conflict between a theology which had become a bad science, and a science which implied an unconscious theology, a theology of unconscious presuppositions about the ultimate meaning of life. These presuppositions were doubly wrong. They were wrong in content and erroneous in being implicit rather than explicit. But surely the responsibility for this confusing conflict rests as much with a theology which had become a bad science as with a science which is a bad theology. In one sense all orthodox Christian theology has been guilty of the sin of profanity. It has insisted on the literal and historic truth of its myths, forgetting that it is the function and character of religious myth to speak of the eternal in relation to time, and that it cannot therefore be a statement of temporal sequences.

No Christian theology, worthy of its name, can therefore be without gratitude to the forces of modern secularism inasfar as their passion for truth was a passion for God. They failed indeed to recognize that every search for truth begins with a presupposition of faith. They did not know for this reason how vulnerable they were to the sneer of Pilate: "What is truth?"; and they could not consequently appreciate the affirmation of Christ: "I am the truth" (cf. John 14:6). But this secularization of truth is no more culpable than the religious profanization of truth which blandly appropriates the truth in Christ for every human vagary and prejudice, for every relative insight and temporal perspective.

The profanity of historic Christianity in regard to the problem of righteousness has been even more grievous than in regard to the problem of truth. Every human civilization is a compromise between the necessities and contingencies of nature and the Kingdom of God with its absolute love commandment. This is as true of a Christian as of an unchristian civilization. In a Christian, as well as in an unchristian civilization, the strong are tempted to exploit the weak, the community is tempted to regard itself as an end in itself, and the rulers are tempted to use their power for their own advantage. When the welter of relative justice and injustice, which emerges out of this conflict and confluence of forces, is falsely covered with the aura of the divine, and when the preservation of such a civilization is falsely enjoined as a holy duty, and when its rebels and enemies are falsely regarded as enemies of God, it is only natural that those who are most conscious of the injustices of a given social order, because they suffer from them, should adopt an attitude of cynical secularism toward the pretensions of sanctity made in behalf of a civilization. A profanization of the holiness of God leads inevitably to an effort to eliminate the sacred from human life. Invariably this effort is partially informed by a covert and implicit sense of the sacred, morally higher than the historic sanctity against which it protests. One need only study the perverted religious intensity of the nineteenth-century Russian nihilists to understand how a warfare against God may be prompted by a prophetic passion for God and scorn for the dubious political divinities which seek to borrow His holiness.

It is impossible to understand the secularism of either the commercial classes or the radical proletarians of the past hundred and fifty years, if it is not appreciated to what degree this secularism represents a reaction to the too intimate and organic relation of Christianity with a feudal society. The priest of religion and the landlord of an agrarian society were too closely related to each other and the former was too frequently the apologist and auxiliary gendarme of the latter.

It may seem that this charge falls more heavily upon Catholicism than upon Protestantism, not only because of the historic relation of the former with a medieval culture and feudal civilization, but also because the latter is less prone to identify itself with the detailed economic and political arrangements of any society. But with its higher degree of detachment, Protestantism has sometimes also revealed a higher degree of social irresponsibility. It has allowed its pessimism to betray it into a negative sanctification of a given social order, on the assumption that any given order is preferable to anarchy and that the disturbance of the status quo might lead to anarchy.

Thus Catholicism and Protestantism, between them, have exhausted the possibilities of error in Christianity's relation to society. In either case peace and order through power were estimated too highly and the inevitable injustice of every stabilization of power was judged too leniently. Frequently Christianity was content to regard deeds of personal generosity and charity as adequate expressions of the Christian love commandment within a civilization in which every basic relationship was a complete denial of that commandment.

The secularism both of our modern bourgeois civilization and of the more proletarian civilizations which threaten to replace it, is therefore something more than the religion of self-glorification. It combines this sin with a passion for justice which frequently puts the historic church to shame. If the Christian church is to preach its gospel effectively to men of such a culture, it must understand the baffling mixture of a new profanity and resistance to an old profanity which is comprehended in this culture.

JUDGMENT MUST BEGIN AT THE HOUSE OF GOD

Such a recognition is the clue to the problem of an effective proclamation of the Christian gospel in our day. If we preach repentance, it must be repentance for those who accept the Lord as well as for those who pretend to deny Him. If we preach the judgment of God upon a sinful world, it must be judgment upon us as well as upon those who do not acknowledge His judgments. If we preach the mercy of God, it must be with a humble recognition that we are in need of it as much as those who do not know God's mercy in Christ. If we preach the obligation of the love commandment, the preacher must know that he violates that commandment as well as those who do not consciously accept its obligation. Nothing is cheaper and more futile than the preaching of a simple moralism which is based upon the assumption that the world need only to be told that selfishness is sin and that love is the law of life to beguile it from the anarchy of sin in which it is at present engulfed. Such a moralism, to which the modern church is particularly prone, is blind to the real tragedy and persistence of sin in the world.

To preach to others and become ourselves castaways is a peril in which all holy business is done. It is a peril to which the church must succumb if it does not constantly hear the challenge of God to Jeremiah to "separate the precious from the vile" (Jer. 15:19), to distinguish between what is genuinely the Lord's will and our will,

His holiness and our sin, in the work of the Christian church. The Kingdom of God was ushered in by the preaching of John the Baptist. The most profound element in John's message of repentance was expressed in the words, "And think not to say within yourselves, We have Abraham to our Father; for I say unto you that God is able of these stones to raise up children unto Abraham" (Matt. 3:9). Not only the racial inheritors of a divine promise are tempted to rest complacently in the assurance "We have Abraham to our Father." That is a temptation which assails all inheritors of a divine promise, including the Christian Church, the "Israel of God." It is wholesome therefore for the Church to stand under the stinging rebuke "God is able of these stones to raise up children unto Abraham," a rebuke in the form of a statement of fact which history has validated again and again.

If the conscience of the church feels the relevance to its own life of that rebuke, it can preach the gospel of a holy God, holy in righteousness and in mercy, without making sinful claims for itself in the name of that holiness, and it will be able to speak to the conscience of this generation, rebuking its sins without assuming a role of self-righteousness and overcoming its despair without finding satisfaction in the sad disillusionment into which the high hopes of modernity have issued.

8

≡

THE CHRISTIAN WITNESS
IN THE SOCIAL AND
NATIONAL ORDER

The natural inclination of the convinced Christian, when viewing the tragic realities of our contemporary world, is to bear witness to the truth in Christ against the secular substitutes for the Christian faith which failed to anticipate, and which may have helped to create, the tragic world in which we now live. Did they not destroy the sense of a divine sovereignty to which we are all subject? And did they not invent schemes of redemption from evil which made repentance unnecessary?

This inclination may also define our responsibility. But I doubt whether it is our primary responsibility. It is also our opportunity to bring the truth of the Word of God to bear upon the secular roots of our present predicament because our current history is actually a remarkable illustration of the way Nemesis overtakes the pride of man and how divine judgment is visited upon men and nations who exalt themselves above measure.

TWO SECULAR ILLUSIONS: LIBERALISM AND MARXISM

The liberal part of our culture thought that the Christian idea of the sinfulness of all men was outmoded. In its place it put the idea of a harmless egotism, rendered innocuous either by a prudent self-interest or by a balance of all social forces which would transmute the selfishness of all into a higher social harmony. The vanity of that idea was proved by the ever more dynamic disproportions of power in our society and the ever greater destruction of community in a technical society.

Sometimes the liberal part of our culture conceived the idea of redemption through growth and development. Men suffered (so it was argued) not from sin but from impotence. But fortunately the whole historical process was itself redemptive. It translated man from impotence to power, from ignorance to intelligence, from being the victim to becoming the master of historical destiny. This illusion proved as tragic as the first one. Since the sin of man lies in the corruption of his will and not in his weakness, the possibilities of evil grow with the development of the very freedom and power which were supposed to emancipate man.

The obvious illusions of the liberal world prompted a Marxist rebellion against the whole liberal culture. In place of confidence in a simple harmony of all social forces, it proclaimed confidence in a new harmony of society through a revolutionary destruction of property, thus making a social institution the root of evil in man and promising redemption through its destruction. In place of the idea of redemption through endless growth and development, it promised redemption through the death of an old order and the rise of a new one. But this was not redemption through the perpetual dying to self of the Christian gospel. It was the promise of a new life for us through the death of our foes.

The tragedy of our age has been deepened by the fact that (1) this alternative to secular liberalism proved in many respects even more illusory and erroneous, (2) the two forms of error have involved the world in a bitter civil war which rends society asunder from the national to the international community.

It proved even more erroneous because the prophets of this new religion turned into tyrannical priest-kings who, having lost all sense of the contingent character of all human interests and ideas, filled the world with the cruelty of their self-righteousness. It proved more erroneous because the doctrine of the socialization of property, when raised to a doctrine of religious redemption, rather than followed pragmatically, merely combines economic and political power in the hands of one oligarchy and produces tyranny. The obvious evils and cruelties of this alternative have given the proponents of the old order good pretexts not to repent of their own sins, but to be content with calling attention to the perils of the alternative.

Perhaps it is because there is a little truth and so much error in both secular alternatives to the Christian faith that they have involved the world in such a hopeless civil war, in which each side had enough truth to preserve its sense of high mission and enough error to frighten the other side with the possible consequences of its victory.

THE CHURCH'S NEED FOR REPENTANCE

We must undoubtedly bear witness against both types of secular illusion from the standpoint of the truth which we have, not of ourselves, but from the gospel. In such a witness, the contemporary situation offers the gospel truth a powerful support. We must preach the gospel in the day in which the modern man, who was so confident that he could control his own destiny, is hopelessly caught in an historic fate in which the human will seems to have become completely impotent and frustrated. The vaunted virtues of each side are vices from the standpoint of the other side, and sins in the sight of God. The word of the Psalmist fits our situation exactly: "The heathen have raged and the people have imagined vain things. But he who sitteth in the heavens shall laugh" (cf. Psalm 2:2,4).

But let us not presume to laugh with God. God's derisive laughter is the justified divine judgment upon this new and yet very old pride of modern man. We must not laugh, lest we forget that His judgment is upon us, as well as upon them. We are too deeply implicated in the disaster of our day to permit ourselves more than provisional testimony against a so-called secular society. That society in both its liberal and Marxist variety came into being, partly because of the deep involvement of Christianity in the social sins of our day and in the stubbornness of the social injustices.

A brief catalog of the sins of the Church proves the depth of our involvement.

(1) There is no social evil, no form of injustice whether of the feudal or the capitalist order, which has not been sanctified in some way or other by religious sentiment and thereby rendered more impervious to change. In a sense, the word of Marx is true: "The beginning of all criticism is the criticism of religion." For it is on this ultimate level that the pretensions of men reach their most absurd form. The final sin is always committed in the name of religion.

(2) A part of the Church, fearing involvement in the ambiguities of politics, has declared the problems of politics to be irrelevant to the Christian life. It has abandoned modern men in the perplexities of the

modern community and has seen brotherhood destroyed in a technical society without a qualm. Usually this neutrality has not even been honestly neutral. The neutral Church is usually an ally of the established social forces.

(3) A part of the Church, facing the complexities of the political order, has been content with an insufferable sentimentality. These problems would not arise, it has declared, if only men would love one another. It has insisted that the law of love is a simple possibility, when every experience proves that the real problem of our existence lies in the fact that we ought to love one another, but do not. And how do we establish tolerable community in view of the fact that all men, including Christians, are inclined to take advantage of each other? Even now, many Christians fatuously hope that this Christian conference [the Amsterdam Assembly] will speak some simple moral word which will resolve by love the tragic conflict in the world community. The most opportunistic statesman, who recognizes the complexities which this sentimentality obscures, is a publican who may enter the Kingdom of God before the Phariseeism which imagines that we can lift ourselves above the tragic moral ambiguities of our existence by a simple act of the will.

(4) A part of the Church, conscious of these perplexities, has been ready to elaborate detailed schemes of justice and of law for the regulation of the political and social life of mankind, below the level of love and of grace. But it has involved itself in a graceless and inflexible legalism. It does not know that all law can easily be the instrument of sin; that inflexible propositions of justice, particularly in the rapidly shifting circumstances of modern technical development, may hinder rather than help the achievement of true justice. One contribution which Christianity certainly ought to make to the problem of political justice is to set all propositions of justice under the law of love, resolving the fruitless debate between pragmatists and legalists and creating the freedom and maneuverability necessary to achieve a tolerable accord between men and nations in ever more complex human relations. We need a pragmatic attitude toward every institution of property and of government, recognizing that none of them are as sacrosanct as some supposedly Christian or secular system of law has made them, that all of them are subject to corruption, and that their abolition is also subject to corruption. This freedom need not degenerate into lawlessness, if it is held in the

knowledge that "all things are yours, and ye are Christ's and Christ is God's" (1 Cor. 3:21).

BEYOND REPENTANCE TO REDEMPTION

We have spoken negatively. The Christian Church must bear witness against every form of pride and vainglory, whether in the secular or in the Christian culture, and be particularly intent upon our own sins lest we make Christ the judge of the other but not of ourselves. But the experience of repentance does not stand alone. It is a part of a total experience of redemption. Positively our task is to present the Gospel of redemption in Christ to nations as well as to individuals. According to our faith, we are always involved in sin and in death because we try too desperately to live, to preserve our pride, to maintain our prestige. Yet it is possible to live truly if we die to self, if the vainglory of man is broken by divine judgment that life may be truly reformed by divine grace. This promise of new life is for individuals. Yet who can deny its relevance for nations and empires, for civilizations and cultures also, even though these collective forms of life do not have the exact integrity of the individual soul nor do they have as direct an access to divine judgment and grace?

The situation in the collective life of mankind today is that we have made shipwreck of our common life through the new powers and freedom which a technical civilization has placed at our disposal. The shipwreck, manifested in the misery and insecurity of the whole world, is an objective historical judgment. It is the death which has followed upon a vainglorious life of the nations. Without faith, it is nothing but death. Without faith, it generates the sorrow of the world, which is despair. Without faith, this confusion is the mark of meaninglessness which follows the destruction of the simple systems of life's meaning which have had ourselves, our nation, and our culture at its center. It is by faith in the God revealed in One who died and rose again that death can become the basis of new life, that meaninglessness turns into meaning, that judgment is experienced as grace. Our business is so to mediate the divine judgment and grace that nations, classes, states and cultures, as well as individuals, may discern the divine author of their wounds, that they may also know the possibility of a new and whole life. In a day of complacency and security, the Christian church must anticipate the judgment which is to come, and declare that the day of the Lord will be darkness and not light. In the day of judgment and catastrophe, the Christian gospel has a message of hope for those who truly repent.

THE CHURCH'S MESSAGE OF JUDGMENT AND MERCY

It is true that the human situation is such that repentance is always required, even as evil always flourishes. But it is wrong to preach this Gospel *sub specie aeternitatis*, as if there were no history with its time and seasons, and with its particular occasions. Nor is our preaching of any avail if we only persuade men and nations to acknowledge the original sin which infects us all, but not the particular sins of which we are guilty. Not the least of our tasks is to expound a judgment and a mercy which tempers the wind to the shorn sheep.

Must we not warn victorious nations that they are wrong in regarding their victory as a proof of their virtue, lest they engulf the world in a new chain of evil by their vindictiveness, which is nothing else than the fury of their self-righteousness? And is our word to the defeated nations not of a different order, reminding them that their warfare is accomplished seeing that they have received at the Lord's hand double for all their sins, and that the punishment is really at the Lord's hand even though it is not nicely proportioned to the evil committed?

Must we not warn powerful and secure nations and classes that they have an idolatrous idea of their own importance and that as surely as they say, "I sit as a queen and shall never know sorrow," so surely shall "in one moment her sorrow come?" (Rev. 18:7). And must we not remind those who are weak and defrauded and despised that God will avenge the cruelties from which they suffer but will also not bear the cruel resentment which corrupts their hearts?

Must we not say to the rich and secure classes of society that their vaunted devotion to the laws and structures of society which guarantee their privileges is tainted with self-interest? And must we not say to the poor that their dream of a propertyless society of perfect justice turns into a nightmare of new injustice because it is based only upon the recognition of the sin which the other commits and knows nothing of the sin which the poor man commits when he is no longer poor but has become a commissar?

Everywhere life is delivered unto death because it is ensnared in self-delusion and practices every evasion rather than meet the true

God. And everywhere the church is caught in this dance of death because it allows the accents of national pride and of racial prejudice, the notes of self-esteem and complacency, to color its message, so that the whole business of religion in our day could seem to the cynical observer (even as it must appear to the righteous God) as a vast effort to lobby in the courts of the Almighty to gain a special advantage for our cause in the divine adjudication. If the slogan "Let the church be the church" is to have a meaning other than its withdrawal from the world, must it not mean that by prayer and fasting it has at least extricated itself in some degree from its embarrassing alliances with this or that class, race and nation, so that it may speak the word of God more purely and more forthrightly to each man and nation, but also to each generation, according to the peculiar needs of the person and the hour?

A new life is possible for those who die to the old self, whether nations or individuals, at any time and in any situation. But on the positive side, there are also special words to be spoken to an age beside timeless words. The new life which we require collectively in our age is a community wide enough to make the world-wide interdependence of nations in a technical age sufferable; and a justice carefully enough balanced to make the dynamic forces of a technical society yield a tolerable justice rather than an alternation of intolerable anarchy and intolerable tyranny. To accomplish this purpose some of our own preconceptions must go, and the same law of love which is no simple possibility for man or society must be enthroned as yet the final standard of every institution, structure and system of justice.

To those who exalt freedom, we must declare that freedom without community is not love, but leads to man making himself his own end. To those who exalt community, we must declare that no historic community deserves the final devotion of man, since his stature and structure is such that only God can be the end of his life.

Against those who make the state sacrosanct, we must insist that the state is always tempted to set its majesty in rebellious opposition to the divine majesty. To those who fear the extension of the state for the regulation of modern economic life, we must point out that their fears are frequently prompted not by a concern for justice but by a jealous desire to maintain their own power.

A tolerable community under modern conditions cannot be easily established; it can be established at all only if much of what has been regarded as absolute is recognized to be relative; and if everywhere men seek to separate the precious from the vile, and sharply distinguish between their interests and the demands which God and the neighbor make upon them.

"WORKING WHILE IT IS STILL DAY"

Perhaps our generation will fail. Perhaps we lack the humility and charity for the task. There are ominous signs of our possible and even probable failure. There is the promise of a new life for men and nations in the gospel, but there is no guarantee of historic success. There is no way of transmuting the Christian gospel into a system of historical optimism. The final victory over man's disorder is God's and not ours; but we do have responsibility for proximate victories. Christian life without a high sense of responsibility for the health of our communities, our nations, and our cultures degenerates into an intolerable other-worldliness. We can neither renounce this earthly home of ours nor yet claim that its victories and defeats give the final meaning to our existence.

Jesus wept over Jerusalem and regretted that it did not know the things that belonged to its peace (Luke 19:41). In the Old Testament, we have the touching story of Abraham bargaining with God about the size of the saving remnant which would be needed to redeem the city (Gen. 19:22–23). Would fifty or forty or thirty be required? He and the Lord finally settled for twenty. Only a small leaven is needed; only a little center of health can become the means of convalescence for a whole community. That fact measures the awful responsibility of the people of God in the world's cities of destruction.

But there is a climax in this story which is frequently disregarded. It is a terrible climax which has relevance for our own day. However small the saving remnant which God requires for the reconstruction of our communities, it was not forthcoming in Sodom and Gomorrah. Perhaps it is valid to express the surmise that the leavening minority in Sodom may have been quantitatively adequate but that its righteousness was irrelevant for saving Sodom and Gomorrah. One has the uneasy feeling that we are in that position. There is so little health in the whole of our modern civilization that one cannot find the island of order from which to proceed against disorder. Our choices have become terribly circumscribed. Must we finally choose between atomic annihilation or subjection to universal tyranny?

If such a day should come, we will remember that the mystery of God's sovereignty and mercy transcends the fate of empires and civilizations. He will be exalted though they perish. However, He does not desire their perdition but rather that they turn from their evil ways and live. From us He demands that we work while it is day, since the night cometh when no man can work.

9

Why the Christian Church Is Not Pacifist

Whenever the actual historical situation sharpens the issue, the debate whether the Christian Church is, or ought to be, pacifist is carried on with fresh vigor both inside and outside the Christian community. Those who are not pacifists seek to prove that pacifism is a heresy; while the pacifists contend, or at least imply, that the church's failure to espouse pacifism unanimously can only be interpreted as apostasy, and must be attributed to its lack of courage or to its want of faith.

There may be an advantage in stating the thesis, with which we enter this debate, immediately. The thesis is, that the failure of the church to espouse pacifism is not apostasy, but is derived from an understanding of the Christian gospel which refuses simply to equate the Gospel with the "law of love." Christianity is not simply a new law, namely, the law of love. The finality of Christianity cannot be proved by analyses which seek to reveal that the law of love is stated more unambiguously and perfectly in the life and teachings of Christ than anywhere else. Christianity is a religion which measures the total dimension of human existence not only in terms of the final norm of human conduct, which is expressed in the law of love, but also in terms of the fact of sin. It recognizes that the same man who can become his true self only by striving infinitely for self-realization beyond himself is also inevitably involved in the sin of infinitely making his partial and narrow self the true end of existence. It believes, in other words, that though Christ is the true norm (the "second Adam") for every man, every man is also in some sense a crucifier of Christ.

The good news of the gospel is not the law that we ought to love one another. The good news of the gospel is that there is a resource of divine mercy which is able to overcome a contradiction within our souls, which we cannot ourselves overcome. This contradiction is that, though we know we ought to love our neighbor as ourself, there is a "law in our members which wars against the law that is in our mind" (Rom. 7:23), so that, in fact, we love ourselves more than our neighbor.

The grace of God which is revealed in Christ is regarded by Christian faith as, on the one hand, an actual "power of righteousness" which heals the contradiction within our hearts. In that sense Christ defines the actual possibilities of human existence. On the other hand, this grace is conceived as "justification," as pardon rather than power, as the forgiveness of God, which is vouchsafed to man despite the fact that he never achieves the full measure of Christ. In that sense Christ is the "impossible possibility." Loyalty to him means realization in intention, but does not actually mean the full realization of the measure of Christ. In this doctrine of forgiveness and justification, Christianity measures the full seriousness of sin as a permanent factor in human history. Naturally, the doctrine has no meaning for modern secular civilization, nor for the secularized and moralistic versions of Christianity. They cannot understand the doctrine precisely because they believe there is some fairly simple way out of the sinfulness of human history.

It is rather remarkable that so many modern Christians should believe that Christianity is primarily a "challenge" to man to obey the law of Christ; whereas it is, as a matter of fact, a religion which deals realistically with the problem presented by the violation of this law. Far from believing that the ills of the world could be set right "if only" men obeyed the law of Christ, it has always regarded the problem of achieving justice in a sinful world as a very difficult task. In the profounder versions of the Christian faith the very utopian illusions, which are currently equated with Christianity, have been rigorously disavowed.

THE TRUTH AND HERESY OF PACIFISM

Nevertheless, it is not possible to regard pacifism simply as a heresy. In one of its aspects modern Christian pacifism is simply a version of Christian perfectionism. It expresses a genuine impulse in the heart of Christianity, the impulse to take the law of Christ seriously and not to allow the political strategies, which the sinful character of man makes necessary, to become final norms. In its profounder forms, this Christian perfectionism did not proceed from a simple faith that the "law of love" could be regarded as an alternative to the political strategies by which the world achieves a precarious justice. These strategies invariably involve the balancing of power with power; and they never completely escape the peril of tyranny on the one hand, and the peril of anarchy and warfare on the other.

In medieval ascetic perfectionism and in Protestant sectarian perfectionism (of the type of Meno Simons, for instance) the effort to achieve a standard of perfect love in individual life was not presented as a political alternative. On the contrary, the political problem and task were specifically disavowed. This perfectionism did not give itself to the illusion that it had discovered a method for eliminating the element of conflict from political strategies. On the contrary, it regarded the mystery of evil as beyond its power of solution. It was content to set up the most perfect and unselfish individual life as a symbol of the Kingdom of God. It knew that this could only be done by disavowing the political task and by freeing the individual of all responsibility for social justice.

It is this kind of pacifism which is not a heresy. It is rather a valuable asset for the Christian faith. It is a reminder to the Christian community that the relative norms of social justice, which justify both coercion and resistance to coercion, are not final norms, and that Christians are in constant peril of forgetting their relative and tentative character and of making them too completely normative.

There is thus a Christian pacifism which is not a heresy. Yet most modern forms of Christian pacifism are heretical. Presumably inspired by the Christian gospel, they have really absorbed the Renaissance faith in the goodness of man, have rejected the Christian doctrine of original sin as an outmoded bit of pessimism, have reinterpreted the cross so that it is made to stand for the absurd idea that perfect love is guaranteed a simple victory over the world, and have rejected all other profound elements of the Christian gospel as "Pauline" accretions which must be stripped from the "simple gospel of Jesus." This form of pacifism is not only heretical when judged by the standards of the total gospel. It is equally heretical when judged by the facts of human existence. There are no historical realities which remotely conform to it. It is important to recognize this lack of conformity to the facts of experience as a criterion of heresy.

All forms of religious faith are principles of interpretation which we use to organize our experience. Some religions may be adequate principles of interpretation at certain levels of experience, but they break down at deeper levels. No religious faith can maintain itself in defiance of the experience which it supposedly interprets. A religious faith which substitutes faith in man for faith in God cannot finally validate itself in experience. If we believe that the only reason men do not love each other perfectly is because the law of love has not been preached persuasively enough, we believe something to which experience does not conform. If we believe that if Britain had only been fortunate enough to have produced 30 percent instead of 2 percent of conscientious objectors to military service, Hitler's heart would have been softened and he would not have dared to attack Poland, we hold a faith which no historic reality justifies.

Such a belief has no more justification in the facts of experience than the communist belief that the sole cause of man's sin is the class organization of society and the corollary faith that a "classless" society will be essentially free of human sinfulness. All of these beliefs are pathetic alternatives to the Christian faith. They all come finally to the same thing. They do not believe that man remains a tragic creature who needs the divine mercy as much at the end as at the beginning of his moral endeavors. They believe rather that there is some fairly easy way out of the human situation of "self-alienation." In this connection it is significant that Christian pacifists, rationalists like Bertrand Russell, and mystics like Aldous Huxley, believe essentially the same thing. The Christians make Christ into the symbol of their faith in man. But their faith is really identical with that of Russell or Huxley.

The common element in these various expressions of faith in man is the belief that man is essentially good at some level of his being. They believe that if you can abstract the rational-universal man from what is finite and contingent in human nature, or if you can only cultivate some mystic-universal element in the deeper levels of man's consciousness, you will be able to eliminate human selfishness and the consequent conflict of life with life. These rational or mystical views of man conform neither to the New Testament's view of human nature nor yet to the complex facts of human experience.

THE ABSOLUTE ETHIC OF JESUS

In order to elaborate the thesis more fully, that the refusal of the Christian Church to espouse pacifism is not apostasy and that most modern forms of pacifism are heretical, it is necessary first of all to consider the character of the absolute and unqualified demands which Christ makes and to understand the relation of these demands to the gospel.

It is very foolish to deny that the ethic of Jesus is an absolute and uncompromising ethic. It is, in the phrase of Ernst Troeltsch, an ethic of "love universalism and love perfectionism." The injunctions "resist not evil," "love your enemies," "if ye love them that love you what thanks have you?" "be not anxious for your life," and "be ye therefore perfect even as your father in heaven is perfect," are all of one piece, and they are all uncompromising and absolute. Nothing is more futile and pathetic than the effort of some Christian theologians who find it necessary to become involved in the relativities of politics, in resistance to tyranny or in social conflict, to justify themselves by seeking to prove that Christ was also involved in some of these relativities, that he used whips to drive the money-changers out of the Temple, or that he came "not to bring peace but a sword," or that he asked the disciples to sell a cloak and buy a sword. What could be more futile than to build a whole ethical structure upon the exegetical issue whether Jesus accepted the sword with the words: "It is enough," or whether he really meant: "Enough of this" (Luke 22:36)?

Those of us who regard the ethic of Jesus as finally and ultimately normative, but as not immediately applicable to the task of securing justice in a sinful world, are very foolish if we try to reduce the ethic so that it will cover and justify our prudential and relative standards and strategies. To do this is to reduce the ethic to a new legalism. The significance of the law of love is precisely that it is not just another law, but a law which transcends all law. Every law and every standard which falls short of the law of love embodies contingent factors and makes concessions to the fact that sinful man must achieve tentative harmonies of life with life which are less than the best. It is dangerous and confusing to give these tentative and relative standards final and absolute religious sanction.

Curiously enough the pacifists are just as guilty as their less absolutist brethren of diluting the ethic of Jesus for the purpose of justifying their position. They are forced to recognize that an ethic of pure non-resistance can have no immediate relevance to any political situation; for in every political situation it is necessary to achieve justice by resisting pride and power. They therefore declare that the ethic of Jesus is not an ethic of non-resistance, but one of non-violent resistance; that it allows one to resist evil provided the resistance does not involve the destruction of life or property.

There is not the slightest support in Scripture for this doctrine of non-violence. Nothing could be plainer than that the ethic uncompromisingly enjoins non-resistance and not non-violent resistance. Furthermore, it is obvious that the distinction between violent and non-violent resistance is not an absolute distinction. If it is made absolute, we arrive at the morally absurd position of giving moral preference to the non-violent power which Doctor Goebbels wields, over the type of power wielded by a general. This absurdity is really derived from the modern (and yet probably very ancient and very Platonic) heresy of regarding the "physical" as evil and the "spiritual" as good. The reductio ad absurdum of this position is achieved in a book which has become something of a textbook for modern pacifists, Richard Gregg's *The Power of Non-Violence.* In this book, non-violent resistance is commended as the best method of defeating your foe, particularly as the best method of breaking his morale. It is suggested that Christ ended his life on the cross because he had not completely mastered the technique of non-violence, and must for this reason be regarded as a guide who is inferior to Gandhi, but whose significance lies in initiating a movement which culminates in Gandhi.

One may well concede that a wise and decent statesmanship will seek not only to avoid conflict, but to avoid violence in conflict. Parliamentary political controversy is one method of sublimating political struggles in such a way as to avoid violent collisions of interest. But this pragmatic distinction has nothing to do with the more basic distinction between the ethic of the "Kingdom of God," in which no concession is made to human sin, and all relative political strategies which, assuming human sinfulness, seek to secure the highest measure of peace and justice among selfish and sinful men.

THE TENSION BETWEEN "BE NOT ANXIOUS"
AND "LOVE THY NEIGHBOR"

If pacifists were less anxious to dilute the ethic of Christ to make it conform to their particular type of non-violent politics, and if they were less obsessed with the obvious contradiction between the ethic of Christ and the fact of war, they might have noticed that the injunction "resist not evil" is only part and parcel of a total ethic which we violate not only in war-time, but every day of our life, and that overt conflict is but a final and vivid revelation of the character of human existence. This total ethic can be summarized most succinctly in the two injunctions "Be not anxious for your life" and "Love thy neighbor as thyself" (cf. Matt. 6:31, 19:19).

In the first of these, attention is called to the fact that the root and source of all undue self-assertion lies in the anxiety which all men have in regard to their existence. The ideal possibility is that perfect trust in God's providence ("for your heavenly father knoweth what things ye have need of") and perfect unconcern for the physical life ("fear not them which are able to kill the body") would create a state of serenity in which one life would not seek to take advantage of another life. But the fact is that anxiety is an inevitable concomitant of human freedom, and is the root of the inevitable sin which expresses itself in every human activity and creativity. Not even the most idealistic preacher who admonishes his congregation to obey the law of Christ is free of the sin which arises from anxiety. He may or may not be anxious for his job, but he is certainly anxious about his prestige. Perhaps he is anxious for his reputation as a righteous man. He may be tempted to preach a perfect ethic the more vehemently in order to hide an unconscious apprehension of the fact that his own life does not conform to it. There is no life which does not violate the injunction "Be not anxious." That is the tragedy of human sin. It is the tragedy of man who is dependent upon God, but seeks to make himself independent and self-sufficing.

In the same way there is no life which is not involved in a violation of the injunction, "Thou shalt love thy neighbor as thyself." No one is so blind as the idealist who tells us that war would be unnecessary "if only" nations obeyed the law of Christ, but who remains unconscious of the fact that even the most saintly life is involved in some measure of contradiction to this law. Have we not all known loving fathers and mothers who, despite a very genuine love for their children, had to be resisted if justice and freedom were to be gained for the children? Do we not know that the sinful will-to-power may be compounded with the most ideal motives and may use the latter as its instruments and vehicles? The collective life of man undoubtedly stands on a lower moral plane than the life of individuals, yet nothing revealed in the life of races and nations is unknown in individual life. The sins of pride and of lust for power and the consequent tyranny and injustice are all present, at least in an inchoate form, in individual life. Even as I write, my little five-year-old boy comes to me with the tale of an attack made upon him by his year-old sister. This tale is concocted to escape paternal judgment for being too rough in playing with his sister. One is reminded of Germany's claim that Poland was the aggressor and the similar Russian charge against Finland.

THE TENSION BETWEEN TYRANNY AND ANARCHY

The pacifists do not know human nature well enough to be concerned about the contradictions between the law of love and the sin of man, until sin has conceived and brought forth death. They do not see that sin introduces an element of conflict into the world and that even the most loving relations are not free of it. They are, consequently, unable to appreciate the complexity of the problem of justice. They merely assert that if only men loved one another, all the complex, and sometimes horrible, realities of the political order could be dispensed with. They do not see that their "if" begs the most basic problem of human history. It is because men are sinners that justice can be achieved only by a certain degree of coercion on the one hand, and by resistance to coercion and tyranny on the other hand. The political life of man must constantly steer between the Scylla of anarchy and the Charybdis of tyranny.

Human egotism makes large-scale co-operation upon a purely voluntary basis impossible. Governments must coerce. Yet there is an element of evil in this coercion. It is always in danger of serving the purposes of the coercing power rather than the general weal. We cannot fully trust the motives of any ruling class or power. That is why it is important to maintain democratic checks upon the centers of power. It may also be necessary to resist a ruling class, nation or race, if it violates the standards of relative justice which have been set up for it. Such resistance means war. It need not mean overt conflict or violence. But if those who resist tyranny publish their scruples against violence too publicly, the tyrannical power need only threaten the use of violence against non-violent pressure to persuade the resisters to quiescence. The relation of pacifism to the abortive effort to apply non-violent sanctions against Italy in the Ethiopian dispute is instructive at this point.

The refusal to recognize that sin introduces an element of conflict into the world invariably means that a morally perverse preference is given to tyranny over anarchy (war). If we are told that tyranny would destroy itself, if only we would not challenge it, the obvious answer is that tyranny continues to grow if it is not resisted. If it is to be resisted, the risk of overt conflict must be taken. The thesis that German tyranny must not be challenged by other nations because Germany will throw off this yoke in due time, merely means that an unjustified moral preference is given to civil war over international war, for internal resistance runs the risk of conflict as much as external resistance. Furthermore, no consideration is given to the fact that a tyrannical state may grow too powerful to be successfully resisted by purely internal pressure, and that the injustices which it does to other than its own nationals may rightfully lay the problem of the tyranny upon other nations.

It is not unfair to assert that most pacifists who seek to present their religious absolutism as a political alternative to the claims and counter-claims, the pressures and counter-pressures of the political order, invariably betray themselves into this preference for tyranny. Tyranny is not war. It is peace, but it is a peace which has nothing to do with the peace of the Kingdom of God. It is a peace which results from one will establishing a complete dominion over other wills and reducing them to acquiescence.

One of the most terrible consequences of a confused religious absolutism is that it is forced to condone such tyranny as that of Germany in the nations which it has conquered and now cruelly oppresses. It usually does this by insisting that the tyranny is no worse than that which is practised in the so-called democratic nations. Whatever may be the moral ambiguities of the so-called democratic nations, and however serious may be their failure to conform perfectly to their democratic ideals, it is sheer moral perversity to equate the inconsistencies of a democratic civilization with the brutalities which modern tyrannical states practise. If we cannot make a distinction here, there are no historical distinctions which have any value. All the distinctions upon which the fate of civilization has turned in the history of mankind have been just such relative distinctions.

One is persuaded to thank God in such times as these that the common people maintain a degree of "common sense," that they preserve an uncorrupted ability to react against injustice and the cruelty of racial bigotry. This ability has been lost among some Christian idealists who preach the law of love but forget that they, as well as all other men, are involved in the violation of that law; and who must (in order to obscure this glaring defect in their theory) eliminate all relative distinctions in history and praise the peace of tyranny as if it were nearer to the peace of the Kingdom of God than war. The overt conflicts of human history are periods of judgment when what has been hidden becomes revealed. It is the business of Christian prophecy to anticipate these judgments to some degree at least, to call attention to the fact that when men say "peace and quiet" "destruction will come upon them unaware" (cf. Ps. 35:8, Ez. 7:25), and reveal to what degree this overt destruction is a vivid portrayal of the constant factor of sin in human life. A theology which fails to come to grips with this tragic factor of sin is heretical, both from the standpoint of the gospel and in terms of its blindness to obvious facts of human experience in every realm and on every level of moral goodness.

THE TENSION BETWEEN RIGHTEOUSNESS AND MERCY

The gospel is something more than the law of love. The gospel deals with the fact that men violate the law of love. The gospel presents Christ as the pledge and revelation of God's mercy which finds man in his rebellion and overcomes his sin.

The question is whether the grace of Christ is primarily a power of righteousness which so heals the sinful heart that henceforth it is able to fulfil the law of love; or whether it is primarily the assurance of divine mercy for a persistent sinfulness which man never overcomes completely. When St. Paul declared: "I am crucified with Christ; nevertheless I live, yet it is no more I that live but Christ that dwelleth in me" (Gal. 2:20), did he mean that the new life in Christ was not his own by reason of the fact that grace, rather than his own power, enabled him to live on the new level of righteousness? Or did he mean that the new life was his only in intention and by reason of God's willingness to accept intention for achievement? Was the emphasis upon sanctification or justification?

This is the issue upon which the Protestant Reformation separated itself from classical Catholicism, believing that Thomistic interpretations of grace lent themselves to new forms of self-righteousness in place of the Judaistic-legalistic self-righteousness which St. Paul condemned. If one studies the whole thought of St. Paul, one is almost forced to the conclusion that he was not himself quite certain whether the peace which he had found in Christ was a moral peace, the peace of having become what man truly is; or whether it was primarily a religious peace, the peace of being "completely known and all forgiven," of being accepted by God despite the continued sinfulness of the heart. Perhaps St. Paul could not be quite sure about where the emphasis was to be placed, for the simple reason that no one can be quite certain about the character of this ultimate peace. There must be, and there is, moral content in it, a fact which Reformation theology tends to deny and which Catholic and sectarian theology emphasizes. But there is never such perfect moral content in it that any man could find perfect peace through his moral achievements, not even the achievements which he attributes to grace rather than the power of his own will. This is the truth which the Reformation emphasized and which modern Protestant Christianity has almost completely forgotten.

We are, therefore, living in a state of sorry moral and religious confusion. In the very moment of world history in which every contemporary historical event justifies the Reformation emphasis upon the persistence of sin on every level of moral achievement, we not only identify Protestant faith with a moralistic sentimentality which neglects and obscures truths in the Christian gospel (which it was the mission of the Reformation to rescue from obscurity), but we even neglect those reservations and qualifications upon the theory of sanctification upon which classical Catholicism wisely insisted.

We have, in other words, reinterpreted the Christian gospel in terms of the Renaissance faith in man. Modern pacifism is merely a final fruit of this Renaissance spirit, which has pervaded the whole of modern Protestantism. We have interpreted world history as a gradual ascent to the Kingdom of God which waits for final triumph only upon the willingness of Christians to "take Christ seriously." There is nothing in Christ's own teachings, except dubious interpretations of the parable of the leaven and the mustard seed, to justify this interpretation of world history. In the whole of the New Testament, gospels and epistles alike, there is only one interpretation of world history. That pictures history as moving toward a climax in which both Christ and anti-Christ are revealed.

The New Testament does not, in other words, envisage a simple triumph of good over evil in history. It sees human history involved in the contradictions of sin to the end. That is why it sees no simple resolution of the problem of history. It believes that the Kingdom of God will finally resolve the contradictions of history; but for it the Kingdom of God is no simple historical possibility. The grace of God for man and the Kingdom of God for history are both divine realities and not human possibilities.

The Christian faith believes that the atonement reveals God's mercy as an ultimate resource by which God alone overcomes the judgment which sin deserves. If this final truth of the Christian religion has no meaning to modern men, including modern Christians, that is because even the tragic character of contemporary history has not yet persuaded them to take the fact of human sinfulness seriously.

LOVE AS A PRINCIPLE OF INDISCRIMINATE CRITICISM

The contradiction between the law of love and the sinfulness of man raises not only the ultimate religious problem how men are to have peace if they do not overcome the contradiction, and how history will culminate if the contradiction remains on every level of historic achievement; it also raises the immediate problem how men are to achieve a tolerable harmony of life with life, if human pride and selfishness prevent the realization of the law of love.

The pacifists are quite right in one emphasis. They are right in asserting that love is really the law of life. It is not some ultimate possibility which has nothing to do with human history. The freedom of man, his transcendence over the limitations of nature and over all historic and traditional social situations, makes any form of human community which falls short of the law of love less than the best. Only by a voluntary giving of life to life and a free interpenetration of personalities could man do justice both to the freedom of other personalities and the necessity of community between personalities. The law of love therefore remains a principle of criticism over all forms of community in which elements of coercion and conflict destroy the highest type of fellowship.

To look at human communities from the perspective of the Kingdom of God is to know that there is a sinful element in all the expedients which the political order uses to establish justice. That is why even the seemingly most stable justice degenerates periodically into either tyranny or anarchy. But it must also be recognized that it is not possible to eliminate the sinful element in the political expedients. They are, in the words of St. Augustine, both the consequence of, and the remedy for, sin. If they are the remedy for sin, the ideal of love is not merely a principle of indiscriminate criticism upon all approximations of justice. It is also a principle of discriminate criticism between forms of justice.

As a principle of indiscriminate criticism upon all forms of justice, the law of love reminds us that the injustice and tyranny against which we contend in the foe is partially the consequence of our own injustice, that the pathology of modern Germans is partially a consequence of the vindictiveness of the peace of Versailles, and that the ambition of a tyrannical imperialism is different only in degree and not in kind from the imperial impulse which characterizes all of human life.

The Christian faith ought to persuade us that political controversies are always conflicts between sinners and not between righteous men and sinners. It ought to mitigate the self-righteousness which is an inevitable concomitant of all human conflict. The spirit of contrition is an important ingredient in the sense of justice. If it is powerful enough it may be able to restrain the impulse of vengeance sufficiently to allow a decent justice to emerge. This is an important issue facing Europe in anticipation of the conclusion of the present war. It cannot be denied that the Christian conscience failed terribly in restraining vengeance after the last war. It is also quite obvious that the natural inclination to self-righteousness was the primary force of this vengeance (expressed particularly in the war guilt clause of the peace treaty). The pacifists draw the conclusion from the fact that justice is never free from vindictiveness, that we ought not for this reason ever to contend against a foe. This argument leaves out of account that capitulation to the foe might well subject us to a worse vindictiveness. It is as foolish to imagine that the foe is free of the sin which we deplore in ourselves as it is to regard ourselves as free of the sin which we deplore in the foe.

The fact that our own sin is always partly the cause of the sins against which we must contend is regarded by simple moral purists as proof that we have no right to contend against the foe. They regard the injunction "Let him who is without sin cast the first stone" (John 8:7) as a simple alternative to the schemes of justice which society has devised, and whereby it prevents the worst forms of anti-social conduct. This injunction of Christ ought to remind every judge and every juridical tribunal that the crime of the criminal is partly the consequence of the sins of society. But if pacifists are to be consistent they ought to advocate the abolition of the whole judicial process in society. It is perfectly true that national societies have more impartial instruments of justice than international society possesses to date. Nevertheless, no impartial court is as impartial as it pretends to be, and there is no judicial process which is completely free of vindictiveness. Yet we cannot dispense with it; and we will have to continue to put criminals into jail. There is a point where the final cause of the criminal's anti-social conduct becomes a fairly irrelevant issue in comparison with the task of preventing his conduct from injuring innocent fellows.

The ultimate principles of the Kingdom of God are never irrelevant to any problem of justice, and they hover over every social situation as an ideal possibility; but that does not mean that they can be made into simple alternatives for the present schemes of relative justice. The thesis that the so-called democratic nations have no right to resist overt forms of tyranny, because their own history betrays imperialistic motives, would have meaning only if it were possible to achieve a perfect form of justice in any nation and to free national life completely of the imperialistic motive. This is impossible; for imperialism is the collective expression of the sinful will-to-power which characterizes all human existence. The pacifist argument on this issue betrays how completely pacifism gives itself to illusions about the stuff with which it is dealing in human nature. These illusions deserve particular censure, because no one who knows his own heart very well ought to be given to such illusions.

LOVE AS A PRINCIPLE OF DISCRIMINATE CRITICISM

The recognition of the law of love as an indiscriminate principle of criticism over all attempts at social and international justice is actually a resource of justice, for it prevents the pride, self-righteousness and vindictiveness of men from corrupting their efforts at justice. But it must be recognized that love is also a principle of discriminate criticism between various forms of community and various attempts at justice. The closest approximation to a love in which life supports life in voluntary community is a justice in which life is prevented from destroying life and the interests of the one are guarded against unjust claims by the other. Such justice is achieved when impartial tribunals of society prevent men "from being judges in their own cases," in the words of John Locke. But the tribunals of justice merely codify certain equilibria of power. Justice is basically dependent upon a balance of power. Whenever an individual or a group or a nation possesses undue power, and whenever this power is not checked by the possibility of criticizing and resisting it, it grows inordinate. The equilibrium of power upon which every structure of justice rests would degenerate into anarchy but for the organizing center which controls it. One reason why the balances of power, which prevent injustice in international relations, periodically degenerate into overt anarchy is because no way has yet been found to establish an adequate organizing center, a stable international judicatory, for this balance of power.

A balance of power is something different from, and inferior to, the harmony of love. It is a basic condition of justice, given the sinfulness of man. Such a balance of power does not exclude love. In fact, without love the frictions and tensions of a balance of power would become intolerable. But without the balance of power even the most loving relations may degenerate into unjust relations, and love may become the screen which hides the injustice. Family relations are instructive at this point. Women did not gain justice from men, despite the intimacy of family relations, until they secured sufficient economic power to challenge male autocracy. There are Christian "idealists" today who speak sentimentally of love as the only way to justice, whose family life might benefit from a more delicate "balance of power."

Naturally the tensions of such a balance may become overt; and overt tensions may degenerate into conflict. The center of power, which has the function of preventing this anarchy of conflict, may also degenerate into tyranny. There is no perfectly adequate method of preventing either anarchy or tyranny. But obviously the justice established in the so-called democratic nations represents a high degree of achievement; and the achievement becomes the more impressive when it is compared with the tyranny into which alternative forms of society have fallen. The obvious evils of tyranny, however, will not inevitably persuade the victims of economic anarchy in democratic society to eschew tyranny. When men suffer from anarchy they may foolishly regard the evils of tyranny as the lesser evils. Yet the evils of tyranny in fascist and communist nations are so patent, that we may dare to hope that what is still left of democratic civilizations will not lightly sacrifice the virtues of democracy for the sake of escaping its defects.

We have a very vivid and conclusive evidence about the probable consequences of a tyrannical unification of Europe. The nature of the German rule in the conquered nations of Europe gives us the evidence. There are too many contingent factors in various national and international schemes of justice to justify any unqualified endorsement of even the most democratic structure of justice as "Christian." Yet it must be obvious that any social structure in which power has been made responsible, and in which anarchy has been overcome by methods of mutual accommodation, is preferable to either anarchy or tyranny. If it is not possible to express a moral preference for the justice achieved in democratic societies, in comparison with tyrannical societies, no historical preference has any meaning. This kind of justice approximates the harmony of love more than either anarchy or tyranny.

If we do not make discriminate judgments between social systems we weaken the resolution to defend and extend civilization. Pacifism either tempts us to make no judgments at all, or to give an undue preference to tyranny in comparison with the momentary anarchy which is necessary to overcome tyranny. It must be admitted that the anarchy of war which results from resistance to tyranny is not always creative; that, at given periods of history, civilization may lack the resource to fashion a new and higher form of unity out of momentary anarchy. The defeat of Germany, and the frustration of the Nazi effort to unify Europe in tyrannical terms, is a negative task. It does not guarantee the emergence of a new Europe with a higher level of international cohesion and new organs of international justice. But it is a negative task which cannot be avoided. All schemes for avoiding this negative task rest upon illusions about human nature. Specifically, these illusions express themselves in the failure to understand the stubbornness and persistence of the tyrannical will, once it is fully conceived. It would not require great argumentative skill to prove that Nazi tyranny never could have reached such proportions as to be able to place the whole of Europe under its ban, if sentimental illusions about the character of the evil which Europe was facing had not been combined with less noble motives for tolerating Nazi aggression.

A simple Christian moralism is senseless and confusing. It is senseless when, as in the World War, it seeks uncritically to identify the cause of Christ with the cause of democracy without a religious reservation. It is just as senseless when it seeks to purge itself of this error by an uncritical refusal to make any distinctions between relative values in history. The fact is that we might as well dispense with the Christian faith entirely if it is our conviction that we can act in history only if we are guiltless. This means that we must either prove our guiltlessness in order to be able to act; or refuse to act because we cannot achieve guiltlessness. Self-righteousness or inaction are the alternatives of secular moralism. If they are also the only alternatives of Christian moralism, one rightly suspects that Christian faith has become diluted with secular perspectives.

In its profoundest insights, the Christian faith sees the whole of human history as involved in guilt, and finds no release from guilt except in the grace of God. The Christian is freed by that grace to act in history, to give his devotion to the highest values he knows, to defend those citadels of civilization of which necessity and historic destiny have made him the defender; and he is persuaded by that grace to remember the ambiguity of even his best actions. If the providence of God does not enter the affairs of men to bring good out of evil, the evil in our good may easily destroy our most ambitious efforts and frustrate our highest hopes.

THE CONTRIBUTION OF A TRUE PACIFISM

Despite our conviction that most modern pacifism is too filled with secular and moralistic illusions to be of the highest value to the Christian community, we may be grateful for the fact that the Christian church has learned, since the last war, to protect its pacifists and to appreciate their testimony. Even when this testimony is marred by self-righteousness, because it does not proceed from a sufficiently profound understanding of the tragedy of human history, it has its value.

It is a terrible thing to take human life. The conflict between man and man and nation and nation is tragic. If there are men who declare that, no matter what the consequences, they cannot bring themselves to participate in this slaughter, the church ought to be able to say to the general community: We quite understand this scruple and we respect it. It proceeds from the conviction that the true end of man is brotherhood, and that love is the law of life. We who allow ourselves to become engaged in war need this testimony of the absolutist against us, lest we accept the warfare of the world as normative, lest we become callous to the horror of war, and lest we forget the ambiguity of our own actions and motives and the risk we run of achieving no permanent good from this momentary anarchy in which we are involved.

But we have a right to remind the absolutists that their testimony against us would be more effective if it were not corrupted by self-righteousness and were not accompanied by the implicit or explicit accusation of apostasy. A pacifism which really springs from the Christian faith, without secular accretions and corruptions, could not be as certain as modern pacifism is that it possesses an alternative for the conflicts and tensions from which and through which the world must rescue a precarious justice.

A truly Christian pacifism would set each heart under the judgment of God to such a degree that even the pacifist idealist would know that knowledge of the will of God is no guarantee of his ability or willingness to obey it. The idealist would recognize to what degree he is himself involved in rebellion against God, and would know that this rebellion is too serious to be overcome by just one more sermon on love, and one more challenge to man to obey the law of Christ.

IV
THEOLOGICAL ETHICS:
RESOURCES FOR ENGAGEMENT

10

AUGUSTINE'S POLITICAL REALISM

The terms "idealism" and "realism" are not analogous in political and in metaphysical theory; and they are certainly not as precise in political, as in metaphysical, theory.

In political and moral theory "realism" denotes the disposition to take all factors in a social and political situation, which offer resistance to established norms, into account, particularly the factors of self-interest and power. In the words of a notorious "realist," Machiavelli, the purpose of the realist is "to follow the truth of the matter rather than the imagination of it; for many have pictures of republics and principalities which have never been seen." This definition of realism implies that idealists are subject to illusions about social realities, which indeed they are.

"Idealism" is, in the esteem of its proponents, characterized by loyalty to moral norms and ideals, rather than to self-interest, whether individual or collective. It is, in the opinion of its critics, characterized by a disposition to ignore or be indifferent to the forces in human life which offer resistance to universally valid ideals and norms. This disposition, to which Machiavelli refers, is general whenever men are inclined to take the moral pretensions of themselves or their fellowmen at face value; for the disposition to hide self-interest behind the facade of pretended devotion to values, transcending self-interest, is well-nigh universal. It is, moreover, an interesting human characteristic, proving that the concept of "total depravity," as it is advanced by some Christian realists, is erroneous. Man is a curious creature with so strong a sense of obligation to his fellows that he cannot pursue his own interests without pretending to serve his fellowmen.

The definitions of "realists" and "idealists" emphasize disposition, rather than doctrines; and they are therefore bound to be inexact. It must remain a matter of opinion whether or not a man takes adequate account of all the various factors and forces in a social situation. Was Plato a realist, for instance, because he tried to guard against the self-interest of the "guardians" of his ideal state by divesting them of property and reducing their family responsibilities to a minimum? Does this bit of "realism" cancel out the essential unrealism, inherent in ascribing to the "lusts of the body" the force of recalcitrance against the moral norm; or in attributing pure virtue to pure mind?

THE DISTINCTIVE NATURE OF AUGUSTINE'S REALISM

Augustine was, by general consent, the first great "realist" in Western history. He deserves this distinction because his picture of social reality in his *Civitas Dei* gives an adequate account of the social factions, tensions, and competitions which we know to be well-nigh universal on every level of community; while the classical age conceived the order and justice of its polis to be a comparatively simple achievement, which would be accomplished when reason had brought all subrational forces under its dominion.

This difference in the viewpoints of Augustine and the classical philosophers lies in Augustine's biblical, rather than rationalistic, conception of human selfhood, with the ancillary conception of the seat of evil being in the self. Augustine broke with classical rationalism in his conception of the human self, according to which the self is composed of mind and body; the mind being the seat of virtue because it has the capacity to bring all impulses into order; and the body, from which come the "lusts and ambitions," being the cause of evil. According to Augustine, the self is an integral unity of mind and body. It is something more than mind and is able to use mind for its purposes. The self has, in fact, a mysterious identity and integrity transcending its functions of mind, memory, and will. "These three things, memory, understanding, and love are mine and not their own," he declares, "for they do what they do not for themselves but for me; or rather I do it by them. For it is I who remember by memory and understand by understanding and love by love."[1] It must be

1. *De Trin.*, 15.22.

observed that the transcendent freedom of this self, including its capacity to defy any rational or natural system into which someone may seek to coordinate it (its capacity for evil), makes it difficult for any philosophy, whether ancient or modern, to comprehend its true dimension. That is why the classical wise men obscured it by fitting its mind into a system of universal mind and the body into the system of nature; and that is also why the modern wise men, for all their rhetoric about the "dignity" of the individual, try to cut down the dimension of human selfhood so that it will seem to fit into a system of nature.

This conception of selfhood is drawn from the Bible, rather than from philosophy, because the transcendent self which is present in, though it transcends, all of the functions and effects of the self, is comprehensible only in the dramatic-historical mode of apprehension which characterizes biblical faith. Augustine draws on the insights of neo-Platonism to illustrate the self's power of self-transcendence; but he rejects Plotinus' mystic doctrine, in which the particular self, both human and divine, is lost in a vast realm of undifferentiated being.

Augustine's conception of the evil which threatens the human community on every level is a corollary of his doctrine of selfhood. "Self-love" is the source of evil rather than some residual natural impulse which mind has not yet completely mastered. This excessive love of self, sometimes also defined as pride or *superbia*, is explained as the consequence of the self's abandonment of God as its true end and of making itself "a kind of end." It is this powerful self-love or, in a modern term, "egocentricity," this tendency of the self to make itself its own end or even to make itself the false center of whatever community it inhabits, which sows confusion into every human community. The power of self-love is more spiritual than the "lusts of the body," of which Plato speaks; and it corrupts the processes of the mind more than Plato or Aristotle knew. That is why Augustine could refute the classical theory with the affirmation that "it is not the bad body which causes the good soul to sin but the bad soul which causes the good body to sin." At other times Augustine defines the evil in man as the "evil will," but with the understanding that it is the self which is evil in the manifestation of its will. "For he who extols the whole nature of the soul as the chief good and condemns the nature of the flesh as if it were evil, assuredly is fleshly both in the love of the soul and in the hatred of the flesh."[2] This concise statement of the Christian position surely refutes the absurd charge of moderns that the Christian faith is "dualistic" and generates contempt for the body. It also establishes the only real basis for a realistic estimate of the forces of recalcitrance which we must face on all levels of the human community, particularly for a realistic estimate of the spiritual dimension of these forces and of the comparative impotence of "pure reason" against them.

Compared with a Christian realism, which is based on Augustine's interpretation of biblical faith, a great many modern social and psychological theories, which fancy themselves anti-Platonic or even anti-Aristotelian and which make much of their pretended "realism," are in fact no more realistic than the classical philosophers. Thus modern social and psychological scientists are forever seeking to isolate some natural impulse such as "aggressiveness" and to manage it; with equal vanity they are trying to find a surrogate for Plato's and Aristotle's disinterested "reason" in a so-called "scientific method." Their inability to discover the corruption of self-interest in reason or in man's rational pursuits; and to measure the spiritual dimension of man's inhumanity and cruelty, gives an air of sentimentality to the learning of our whole liberal culture. Thus we have no guidance amid the intricacies of modern power politics, except as the older disciplines, less enamored of the "methods of natural science," and the common sense of the man in the street, supply the necessary insights.

THE "CITY OF THIS WORLD"

Augustine's description of the social effects of human egocentricity or self-love is contained in his definition of the life of the "city of this world," the *civitas terrena*, which he sees as commingled with the *civitas dei*. The "city of this world" is dominated by self-love to the point of contempt of God; and is distinguished from the *civitas dei* which is actuated by the "love of God" to the point of contempt of self. This "city" is not some little city-state, as it is conceived in

2. *De Civ. Dei*, 15.5.

classical thought. It is the whole human community on its three levels of the family, the commonwealth, and the world.

A potential world community is therefore envisaged in Augustine's thought. But, unlike the Stoic and modern "idealists," he does not believe that a common humanity or a common reason gives promise of an easy actualization of community on the global level. The world community, declares Augustine, "is fuller of dangers as the greater sea is more dangerous."[3] Augustine is a consistent realist in calling attention to the fact that the potential world community may have a common human reason, but it speaks in different languages and "Two men, each ignorant of each other's language" will find that "dumb animals, though of a different species, could more easily hold intercourse than they, human beings though they be."[4] This realistic reminder that common linguistic and ethnic cultural forces, which bind the community together on one level, are divisive on the ultimate level, is a lesson which our modern proponents of world government have not yet learned.

Augustine's description of the *civitas terrena* includes an emphasis on the tensions, frictions, competitions of interest, and overt conflicts to which every human community is exposed. Even in the family, one cannot rely on friendship "seeing that secret treachery has often broken it up."[5] This bit of realism will seem excessive until we remember that our own generation has as much difficulty in preserving the peace and integrity in the smallest and most primordial community, the family, as in integrating community on the highest global level.

The *civitas terrena* is described as constantly subject to an uneasy armistice between contending forces, with the danger that factional disputes may result in "bloody insurrection" at any time. Augustine's realism prompts him to challenge Cicero's conception of a commonwealth as rooted in a "compact of justice." Not so, declares Augustine. Commonwealths are bound together by a common love, or collective interest, rather than by a sense of justice; and they could not maintain themselves without the imposition of power.

3. Ibid., 19.7.
4. Ibid.
5. Ibid., 19.5.

"Without injustice the republic would neither increase nor subsist. The imperial city to which the republic belongs could not rule over provinces without recourse to injustice. For it is unjust for some men to rule over others."[6]

This realism has the merit of describing the power realities which underlie all large scale social integrations whether in Egypt or Babylon or Rome, where a dominant city-state furnished the organizing power for the Empire. It also describes the power realities of national states, even democratic ones, in which a group, holding the dominant form of social power, achieves oligarchic rule, no matter how much modern democracy may bring such power under social control. This realism in regard to the facts which underlie the organizing or governing power refutes the charge of modern liberals that a realistic analysis of social forces makes for state absolutism; so that a mild illusion in regard to human virtue is necessary to validate democracy. Realistic pessimism did indeed prompt both Hobbes and Luther to an unqualified endorsement of state power; but that is only because they were not realistic enough. They saw the dangers of anarchy in the egotism of the citizens but failed to perceive the dangers of tyranny in the selfishness of the ruler. Therefore they obscured the consequent necessity of placing checks upon the ruler's self-will.

Augustine's realism was indeed excessive. On the basis of his principles he could not distinguish between government and slavery, both of which were supposedly the rule over man by man and were a consequence of, and remedy for, sin; nor could he distinguish between a commonwealth and a robber band, for both were bound together by collective interest; "For even thieves must hold together or they cannot effect what they intend." The realism fails to do justice to the sense of justice in the constitution of the Roman Empire; or, for that matter, to the sense of justice in a robber band. For even thieves will fall out if they cannot trust each other to divide the loot, which is their common aim, equitably. But the excessive emphasis upon the factors of power and interest, a wholesome corrective to Cicero's and modern Ciceronian moralistic illusions, is not fatal to the establishment of justice so long as the dangers of tyranny are weighed as realistically as the dangers of anarchy.

6. Ibid., 19.21.

Augustine's realistic attitude toward government rests partly upon the shrewd observation that social peace and order are established by a dominant group within some level of community; and that this group is not exempt from the corruption of self-interest merely because the peace of society has been entrusted to it. (One thinks, incidentally, how accurately the Augustinian analysis fits both the creative and the ambiguous character of the American hegemony in the social cohesion of the free world.)

The realism is partly determined by his conception of a "natural order" which he inherited from the early Christian fathers, who in turn took it from that part of the Stoic theory which emphasized the primordial or primitive as the natural. This Stoic and Christian primitivism has the merit of escaping the errors of those natural law theories which claim to find a normative moral order amid the wide variety of historic forms or even among the most universal of these forms. The freedom of man makes these Stoic conceptions of the "natural" impossible. But it has the weakness which characterizes all primitivism, whether Stoic, Christian, or Romantic, for it makes primitive social forms normative. A primitive norm, whether of communal property relations or unorganized social cohesion, may serve provisionally as an occasion for the criticism of the institutions of an advancing civilization, more particularly the institutions of property and government; but it has the disadvantage of prompting indiscriminate criticism. This lack of discrimination is obvious in primitivistic Stoicism, in early Christianity, in seventeenth-century Cromwellian sectarianism, in Romanticism, and in Marxism and anarchism.

Augustine expressed this idea of a primitive social norm as follows:

> This is the prescribed order of nature. It is thus that God created man. For 'let them,' He says, 'have dominion over the fish of the sea and the fowl of the air and over every creeping thing, which creepeth on the earth.' He did not intend that His rational creature, made in His image, should have dominion over anything but irrational creation—not man over man but man over beasts. And hence the righteous men of primitive times were made shepherds of cattle rather than kings of men.[7]

This primitivism avoids the later error of the absolute sanctification of government. But its indiscriminate character is apparent by his failure to recognize the difference between legitimate and illegiti-

7. Ibid., 19.15.

mate, between ordinate and inordinate subordination of man to man. Without some form of such subordination the institutions of civilization could not exist.

THE COMMINGLING OF THE TWO CITIES

If Augustine's realism is contained in his analysis of the *civitas terrena*, his refutation of the idea that realism must lead to cynicism or relativism is contained in his definition of the *civitas dei*, which he declares to be "commingled" with the "city of this world" and which has the "love of God" rather than the "love of self" as its guiding principle. The tension between the two cities is occasioned by the fact that, while egotism is "natural" in the sense that it is universal, it is not natural in the sense that it does not conform to man's nature as one who transcends himself indeterminately and can only have God rather than self for his end. A realism becomes morally cynical or nihilistic when it assumes that the universal characteristic in human behavior must also be regarded as normative. The biblical account of human behavior, upon which Augustine bases his thought, can escape both illusion and cynicism because it recognizes that the corruption of human freedom may make a behavior pattern universal without making it normative. Good and evil are not determined by some fixed structure of human existence. Man, according to the biblical view, may use his freedom to make himself falsely the center of existence; but this does not change the fact that love rather than self-love is the law of his existence, in the sense that man can only be healthy, and his communities at peace, if man is drawn out of himself and saved from the self-defeating consequences of self-love.

There are several grave errors in Augustine's account of love and of the relation of love to self-love; but before considering them we might well first pay tribute to his approach to political problems. The virtue of making love, rather than justice, into the norm for the community may seem, at first blush, to be dubious. The idea of justice seems much more relevant than the idea of love, particularly for the collective relationships of men. The medieval tradition, which makes the justice of a rational "natural law" normative even for Christians when they consider the necessities of a sinful world, seems much more realistic than modern forms of sentimental Protestantism which regards love as a simple alternative to self-love which could be achieved if only we could preach the idea persuasively enough to beguile men from the one to the other.

Augustine's doctrine of love as the final norm must be distinguished from modern sentimental versions of Christianity which regard love as a simple possibility, and which think it significant to assert the obvious proposition that all conflicts in the community would be avoided if only people and nations would love one another. Augustine's approach differs from modern forms of sentimental perfectionism in the fact that he takes account of the power and persistence of egotism, both individual and collective, and seeks to establish the most tolerable form of peace and justice under conditions set by human sin. He inherited the tradition of monastic perfection; and he allows it as a vent for the Christian impulse toward individual perfection, without however changing the emphasis upon the duty of the Christian to perfect the peace of the city of this world. Furthermore, he raises questions about monastic perfection which, when driven home by the Reformation, were to undermine the whole system.

> I venture to say [he writes] that it is good for those who observe continence and are proud of it, to fall that they may be humbled. For what benefit is it to anyone in whom is the virtue of continence, if pride holds sway? He is but despising that by which man is born in striving after that which led to satan's fall . . . holy virginity is better than conjugal chastity . . . but if we add two other things, pride and humility . . . which is better, pride or humility? . . . I have no doubt that a humble married woman is to be preferred to a proud virgin. . . . A mother will hold a lesser place in the Kingdom of Heaven, because she has been married, than the daughter, seeing that she is a virgin. . . . But if thy mother has been humble and thou proud, she will have some sort of place, but thou none.[8]

While Augustine's doctrine of love is thus not to be confused with modern sentimentalities which do not take the power of self-love seriously, one may well wonder whether an approach to politics which does not avail itself of the calculations of justice, may be deemed realistic. We have already noted that Augustine avails himself of the theory of the "natural law," only in the primordial version of the theory. If primordial conditions of a "natural order" are not to be defined as normative, the only alternative is to assume a

8. Sermon cccliv, ix, 9.

"rational order" to which the whole of historical life conforms. Aquinas, in fact, constructed his theory of the natural law upon classical, and primarily Aristotelian, foundations. It was the weakness of both classical and medieval theories that they assumed an order in history, conforming to the uniformities of nature. Aristotle was aware of deviations in history, greater than those in nature; but he believed that there was nevertheless one form "which was marked by nature as the best." There is, in other words, no place in this theory of natural law for the endlessly unique social configurations which human beings, in their freedom over natural necessity, construct. The proponents of "natural law" therefore invariably introduce some historically contingent norm or social structure into what they regard as God's inflexible norm. That was the weakness of both classical and medieval social theory; and for that matter of the natural law theories of the bourgeois parties of the eighteenth century, who had found what they regarded as a more empirically perceived "natural law." But the modern empirical intelligence was no more able than the deductive rational processes of classical and medieval times, to construct a social norm not colored by the interests of the constructor, thus introducing the taint of ideology into the supposed sanctities of the law.

We must conclude, therefore, that Augustine was wise in avoiding the alleged solution of a natural law theory, which was the basis of so much lack of realism in both the classical and the medieval period, and which can persist today, long after the Aristotelian idea of fixed form for historical events has been overcome, as the dogma of a religious system which makes its supposed sanctities into an article of faith. Augustine's conception of the radical freedom of man, derived from the biblical view, made it impossible to accept the idea of fixed forms of human behavior and of social organization, analogous to those of nature, even as he opposed the classical theory of historical cycles. Furthermore, his conception of human selfhood, and of the transcendence of the self over its mind, made it impossible to assume the identity of the individual reason with a universal reason, which lies at the foundation of the classical and medieval natural law theories. It is in fact something of a mystery how the Christian insights into human nature and history, expressed by Augustine, could have been subordinated to classical thought with so little sense of the conflict between them in the formulations of Thomas Aquinas; and how they should have become so authoritative in Roman Catholicism without more debate between Augustinian and Thomistic emphases.

Augustine's formula for leavening the city of this world with the love of the city of God is more adequate than classical and medieval thought, both in doing justice to the endless varieties of historical occasions and configurations and in drawing upon the resources of love rather than law in modifying human behavior.

Every "earthly peace," declares Augustine, is good as far as it goes. "But they will not have it long for they used it not well while they had it." That is, unless some larger love or loyalty qualifies the self-interest of the various groups, this collective self-interest will expose the community to either an overt conflict of competing groups or to the injustice of a dominant group which "when it is victorious . . . will become vice's slave."

Let us use some examples from current national and international problems to illustrate the Augustinian thesis.

There is, or was, a marked social tension between the middle classes of industrial owners and the industrial workers in all modern industrial nations. In some of them, for instance in Germany and France, this tension led to overt forms of the class conflict. In others such as Britain, the smaller European nations and America, this tension was progressively resolved by various accommodations of interest. Wherein lay the difference? It did not lie in the possession of more adequate formulae of justice in some nations than in others. The difference lay in the fact that in some nations the various interest groups had, in addition to their collective interest, a "sense of justice," a disposition to "give each man his due" and a loyalty to the national community which qualified the interest struggle. Now, that spirit of justice is identical with the spirit of love, except at the highest level of the spirit of love, where it becomes purely sacrificial and engages in no calculation of what the due of each man may be. Two forms of love, the love of the other and the love of the community, were potent, in short, in modifying the acerbities and injustices of the class struggle. The two forms of love availed themselves of various calculations of justice in arriving at and defining their ad hoc agreements. But the factors in each nation and in each particular issue were too variable to allow for the application of any general rules or formulas of justice. Agreements were easier, in fact, if too much was not claimed for these formulas. Certain "principles" of justice, as distinguished from formulas or prescriptions, were indeed operative, such as liberty, equality, and loyalty to covenants; but these principles will be recognized as no more than the law of love in its various facets.

In the same manner, the international community is exposed to exactly the tensions and competitions of interest which Augustine describes. There are no formulas of justice or laws which will prevent these tensions from reaching overt conflict, if the collective interest of each nation is not modified by its loyalty to a higher value, such as the common civilization of the free nations. Where this common loyalty is lacking, as in our relation with Russia, no formula can save us from the uneasy peace in which we live. The character of this peace is just as tentative as Augustine described it. Whenever common loves or loyalties, or even common fears, lay the foundation for community, it must of course be our business to perfect it by calculations of justice which define our mutual responsibilities as exactly as possible.

It must be noted that the Augustinian formula for the leavening influence of a higher upon a lower loyalty or love, is effective in preventing the lower loyalty from involving itself in self-defeat. It corrects the "realism" of those who are myopically realistic by seeing only their own interests and failing thereby to do justice to their interests where they are involved with the interests of others. There are modern realists, for instance, who, in their reaction to abstract and vague forms of international idealism, counsel the nation to consult only its own interests. In a sense, collective self-interest is so consistent that it is superfluous to advise it. But a consistent self-interest on the part of a nation will work against its interests, because it will fail to do justice to the broader and longer interests, which are involved with the interests of other nations. A narrow national loyalty on our part, for instance, will obscure our long range interests where they are involved with those of a whole alliance of free nations. Thus the loyalty of a leavening portion of a nation's citizens to a value transcending national interest will save a "realistic" nation from defining its interests in such narrow and short range terms as to defeat the real interests of the nation.

CRITIQUE OF AUGUSTINE'S REALISM

We have acknowledged some weaknesses in the Augustinian approach to the political order which we must now define and examine more carefully.

(1) Non-Catholics commonly criticize Augustine's alleged identification of the *civitas dei* with the visible Church. But we must absolve him of this charge or insist on a qualification of the criticism. He does indeed accept the Catholic doctrine, which had grown up before his day; and he defines the visible Church as the only perfect society. There are passages in which he seems to assume that it is possible to claim for the members of the Church that they are solely actuated by the *amor dei*. But he introduces so many reservations to this assertion that he may well be defined in this, as in other instances, as the father of both Catholicism and the Reformation. Of the Church, Augustine declared, "by faith she is a virgin. In the flesh she has few holy virgins."[9] Or again: "God will judge the wicked and the good. The evil cannot now be separated from the good but must be suffered for a season. The wicked may be with us on the threshing floor . . . in the barn they cannot be."[10] The reservations which he made upon the identification of the Church and the kingdom laid the foundations for the later Reformation position.

(2) But these reservations about the sinners who might be present in the visible Church cannot obscure a graver error in his thought. This error is probably related to his conception of grace which does not allow for the phenomenon, emphasized by the Reformation, that men may be redeemed in the sense that they consciously turn from self to Christ as their end, and yet they are not redeemed from the corruption of egotism which expresses itself, even in the lives of the saints. This insight is most succinctly expressed in Luther's phrase *"simul justus et peccator"* (both justified and a sinner). When Augustine distinguished between the "two loves" which characterize the "two cities," the love of God and the love of self, and when he pictured the world as a commingling of the two cities, he does not recognize that the commingling is due not to the fact that two types of people dwell together, but because the conflict between love and self-love is in every soul. It is particularly important to recognize this

9. Sermon ccxiii, vii, 7.
10. *Comm. on Ps.* cxi, 9.

fact in political analyses; for nothing is more obvious than that personal dedication is no guarantee against the involvement of the dedicated individual in some form of collective egotism.

(3) We have frequently referred to Augustine's definition of the "two loves" which inform the "two cities" of which "the one is selfish and the other social," the one loving self to the point of contempt of God and the other loving God to the point of contempt of self. The question is whether Anders Nygren is right in *Agape and Eros* in defining the Augustinian conception of *amor dei* as rooted in a classical rather than a biblical concept.

In defense of Augustine it must be said that he is not insensible to the two facets of the love commandment and therefore does not define the *amor dei* in purely mystical terms as a flight from this world. He insists on the contrary that the *amor dei* is "social" and he offers the concord among brethren as a proof of the love of God. But nevertheless Nygren is right in suggesting that the thought of Plotinus has colored Augustine's conceptions sufficiently so that the *agape* of the New Testament is misinterpreted by Augustine's conception of *caritas* and *amor dei*. The *agape* form of love in the New Testament fails to be appreciated particularly in two of its facets:

First, the equality of the "two loves," the love of God and the love of the neighbor (enforced in the Scripture by the words "the second is like unto [the first]") is violated by Augustine under the influence of Plotinus, even as a later medieval Catholic mystic, St. John of the Cross, violated it when he regarded the love of the creature as a ladder which might lead us to the love of God, but must be subordinated to the latter. Augustine wants us to love the neighbor for the sake of God, which may be a correct formulation; but he wants us to prove the genuineness of our love of God in the love of the neighbor, or by leading him to God. Thus the meeting of the neighbor's need without regard to any ultimate religious intention is emptied of meaning. The love of the neighbor is for him not part of a double love commandment, but merely the instrument of a single love commandment which bids us flee all mortality, including the neighbor, in favor of the immutable good.

The second facet of the *agape* concept of the New Testament which tends to be obscured by Augustine is the notion of sacrificial love, the absurd principle of the cross, the insistence that the self must sacrifice itself for the other. It is not fair to Augustine to say that he neglects this facet of meaning, for he seems to emphasize it so constantly. He comes closest to its meaning when he deals with the relation of humility to love. Yet it seems fair to say that he was sufficiently imbued by classical mystical thought forms so that the emphasis lies always upon the worthiness or unworthiness of the object of our love; the insistence is that only God and not some mutable "good" or person is worthy of our love. This is a safeguard against all forms of idolatry. But it does not answer another important question: when I love a person or a community do I love myself in them or do I truly love them? Is my love a form of alteregoism? The Augustinian *amor dei* assumes that the self in its smallness cannot contain itself within itself, and therefore it is challenged to go out from itself to the most ultimate end. But it hardly reveals the full paradox of self-realization through self-giving, which is a scandal in the field of rational ethics as the cross is a scandal in the field of rational religion. Yet it is the source of ultimate wisdom. For the kind of self-giving which has self-realization as its result must not have self-realization as its conscious end; otherwise the self by calculating its enlargement will not escape from itself completely enough to be enlarged.

The weakness of Augustine in obscuring these facets of the *agape* principle may be illustrated, without unfairness I hope, by referring to his treatment of family love. He questions the love of mate or children as the final form of love, but not for New Testament reasons. He does not say: "When you love your wife and children are you maybe really loving yourself in them and using them as the instruments of your self-aggrandisements?" He declares instead, in effect: "You must not love your family too unreservedly because your wife and children are mortal. They also belong to the rivers of Babylon, and, if you give them absolute devotion, the hour of bereavement will leave you desolate." Of course, Augustine is too much the Christian to engage in a consistent mystic depreciation of the responsibilities and joys of this earthly life. After all, his whole strategy for the "commingling" of the two cities revolves around the acceptance of the ordinary responsibilities of home and state, but in performing these tasks for the ultimate, rather than the immediate end. He asks:

> What then? Shall all perish who marry and are given in marriage, who till the fields and build houses? No, but those who put their trust in these things, who prefer them to God, who for the sake of these things

are quick to offend God, these will perish. But those who either do not use these things or who use them as though they used them not, trusting more in Him who gave them than in the things given, understanding in them His consolation and mercy, and who are not absorbed in these gifts lest they fall away from the giver, these are they whom the day will not overtake as a thief unprepared.[11]

MODERN ILLUSIONS AND "THE RIVER OF BABYLON"

We must not, in criticizing Augustine for neo-Platonic elements in his thought, obscure the Christian elements which will be equally an offense to modern men who regard the world as self-sufficing and self-explanatory, who reject as absurd the Christian faith that there is not only a mystery behind and above the world of observed phenomena and intelligible meanings, but that it is a mystery whose meaning has been disclosed as a love which elicits our answering love. This modern generation, with its confidence in a world without mystery, and without meaning beyond simple intelligibility, will not be beguiled from its unbelief by a reminder that its emancipation from God has betrayed it into precisely those idolatries—the worship of false gods, the dedication to finite values as if they were ultimate—of which Augustine spoke. But it must be recorded nevertheless as a significant fact of modern history. While it is an offence to regard communism as the inevitable end-product of secularism, as some Christians would have us believe, it is only fair to point out that the vast evils of modern communism come ironically to a generation which thought it would be easy to invest all the spiritual capital of men, who mysteriously transcend the historical process, in some value or end within that process; and communism is merely the most pathetic and cruel of the idolatrous illusions of this generation.

We must be clear about the fact that all the illusions about man's character and history, which made it so difficult for either the classical or the modern age to come to terms with the vexing problems of our togetherness, seem to stem from efforts to understand man in both his grandeur and his misery by "integrating" him into some natural or rational system of coherence. Thereby they denied the mystery of his transcendence over every process which points to

11. *Comm. on Ps.* cxx, 3.

another mystery beyond himself, without which man is not only a mystery to himself but a misunderstood being.

We cannot deny that from a Christian standpoint the world is like a "river of Babylon" to use Augustine's symbol; and that Augustine is right in suggesting that ultimately we cannot find peace if we are merely tossed down the river of time. We must find security in that which is not carried down the river. "Observe however," declares Augustine (in a simile which will seem strange to generations which have made the "rivers of Babylon," the stream of temporal events, into forces of redemption, but which will not seem so strange as the modern experience proves history as such to be less redemptive than we had believed):

> The rivers of Babylon are all things which are here loved, and pass away.
>
> For example, one man loves to practice husbandry, to grow rich by it, to employ his mind on it, to get his pleasure from it. Let him observe the issue and see that what he has loved is not a foundation of Jerusalem, but a river of Babylon.
>
> Another says, it is a grand thing to be a soldier; all farmers fear those who are soldiers, are subservient to them, tremble at them. If I am a farmer, I shall fear soldiers; if a soldier, farmers will fear me. Madman! thou hast cast thyself headlong into another river of Babylon, and that still more turbulent and sweeping. Thou wishest to be feared by thy inferior; fear Him Who is greater than thou. He who fears thee may on a sudden become greater than thou, but He Whom thou oughtest to fear will never become less.
>
> To be an advocate, says another, is a grand thing; eloquence is most powerful; always to have clients hanging on the lips of their eloquent advocate, and from his words looking for loss or gain, death or life, ruin or security. Thou knowest not whither thou hast cast thyself. This too is another river of Babylon, and its roaring sound is the din of the waters dashing against the rocks. Mark that it flows, that it glides on; beware, for it carries things away with it.
>
> To sail the seas, says another, and to trade is a grand thing—to know many lands, to make gains from every quarter, never to be answerable to any powerful man in thy country, to be always travelling, and to feed thy mind with the diversity of the nations and the business met with, and to return enriched by the increase of thy gains. This too is a river of Babylon. When will the gains stop? When wilt thou have confidence and be secure in the gains thou makest? The richer thou art, the more fearful wilt thou be. Once shipwrecked, thou wilt come forth stripped of all, and rightly wilt bewail thy fate *in* the rivers of Babylon, because thou wouldest not sit down and weep *upon* the rivers of Babylon.

But there are other citizens of the holy Jerusalem, understanding their captivity, who mark how human wishes and the diverse lusts of men, hurry and drag them hither and thither, and drive them into the sea. They see this, and do not throw themselves into the rivers of Babylon, but sit down upon the rivers of Babylon and upon the rivers of Babylon weep, either for those who are being carried away by them, or for themselves whose deserts have placed them in Babylon.[12]

Whatever the defects of the Augustine approach may be, we must acknowledge his immense superiority both over those who preceded him and who came after him. A part of that superiority was due to his reliance upon biblical rather than idealistic or naturalistic conceptions of selfhood. But that could not have been the only cause, else Christian systems before and after him would not have been so inferior. Or were they inferior either because they subordinated the biblical-dramatic conception of human selfhood too much to the rationalistic scheme, as was the case with medieval Christianity culminating in the thought of Thomas Aquinas, or because they did not understand that the corruption of human freedom could not destroy the original dignity of man, as was the case with the Reformation with its doctrines of sin, bordering on total depravity and resulting in Luther's too pessimistic approach to political problems?

As for secular thought, it has difficulty in approaching Augustine's realism without falling into cynicism, or in avoiding nihilism without falling into sentimentality. Hobbes' realism was based on an insight which he shared with Augustine, namely, that in all historical encounters, the mind is the servant and not the master of the self. But he failed to recognize that the self which thus made the mind its instrument was a corrupted and not a "normal" self. Modern "realists" know the power of collective self-interest as Augustine did; but they do not understand its blindness. Modern pragmatists understand the irrelevance of fixed and detailed norms; but they do not understand that love must take the place as the final norm for these inadequate norms. Modern liberal Christians know that love is the final norm for man; but they fall into sentimentality because they fail to measure the power and persistence of self-love.

Thus Augustine, whatever may be the defects of his approach to political reality, and whatever may be the dangers of a too slavish devotion to his insights, nevertheless proves himself a more reliable

12. *Comm. on Ps.* cxxxvi, 3, 4.

guide than any known thinker. A generation which finds its communities imperiled and in decay from the smallest and most primordial community, the family, to the largest and most recent, the potential world community, might well take counsel of Augustine in solving its perplexities.

11

LOVE AND LAW IN PROTESTANTISM AND CATHOLICISM

The whole question about the relation of love to law in Christian thought is really contained in the question how love is the fulfillment of the law. The analysis of this issue may well begin with a definition of the nature of law. Subjectively considered, law is distinguished by some form of restraint or coercion, or, as Aquinas puts it, it is the direction to "perform virtuous acts by reason of some outward cause." The compulsion may be the force and prestige of the mores and customs of a community, persuading or compelling an individual to act contrary to his inclinations. But there is also an inner compulsion of law. It is the compulsion of conscience, the force of the sense of obligation, operating against other impulses in the personality. If there is no friction or tension between duty and inclination law is, at least in one sense, dissolved into love.

Materially, law usually represents detailed prescriptions of duties and obligations which the self owes to itself, to God, and to its neighbors. There may of course be general principles of law which gather together the logic of detailed prescriptions; as for instance the proposition defined in Catholic thought as the "preamble" of the natural law, "that we ought to do good and avoid evil"; or Jesus' own summary of the law and the prophets. But that summary is, significantly, the "law of love" and therefore no longer purely law, but a law transcending law. Some degree of detail is characteristic of pure law. The "positive law" of historic communities gains its force primarily from its specificity. Many a law has been annulled by our Supreme Court on the ground that "vagueness" invalidated it. Even if we do not accept the Catholic theory of a highly specific "natural law," we all

do accept principles of justice which transcend the positive enact-
ments of historic states and which are less specific and not so sharply
defined as positive law, and yet more specific than the law of love.
These are generated in the customs and mores of communities; and
they may rise to universal norms which seem to have their source not
in particular communities but in the common experience of mankind.

The question of how love is related to law must be considered in
terms of both the subjective and the material dimensions of both love
and law. Subjectively, the question is how the experience of love, in
which the "ought" is transcended, nevertheless contains a "thou
shalt." Materially, the question is how the indeterminate possibilities of love are related to the determinate and specified obligations defined by law. The dialectical relation of love to law as both its
fulfillment and its end (*pleroma* and *telos*), as fulfilling all possibilities of law and yet as standing in contradiction to it—"The law
was given by Moses, but grace and truth came by Jesus Christ" (John
1:17)—is the basis and the problem of all Catholic and Protestant
speculations on the relation of love to law.

In this debate Catholic thought, both in its classical version, and in
such a modern treatise as Martin D'Arcy's *Mind and Heart of Love*, is
more inclined than the Reformation to interpret love as *pleroma* of
everything intended in nature and in law. But it is also inclined to
interpret love as yet a more rigorous law, thus obscuring the elements
of ecstasy and spontaneity, which are the marks of "grace."

Reformation thought, on the other hand (or at least Lutheran
thought, for Calvin does not deviate essentially from the Catholic
version), is much nearer in its apprehension of a dimension of love
which transcends law and even contradicts it; but it usually fails to
do justice to love as the fulfillment of law and therefore tends to
obscure the intimate relation between love and justice.

Modern liberal Protestantism is inclined to equate law and love by
its effort to comprehend all law within the love commandment. It
does not deny the higher dimensions of love which express themselves in sacrifice, forgiveness, individual sympathy, and universal
love, but it regards them as simple possibilities and thereby obscures
the tensions between love and law, both on the subjective and the
objective side.

THE PUSH OF DUTY AND THE PULL OF GRACE

In terms of the subjective dimension, the problem of love and law is the problem of the "push" of duty and the "pull" of grace. If the law of love comes to us as a "thou shalt," it is obviously a law. We can have a sense of obligation toward the interests of others without a definition of specific obligations. In this case, love is simply the summary of all our obligations. This is why Thomas Aquinas includes love in the "old law," though this inclusion is inconsistent with his definition of the "old law" as the "law of fear" and his confining it to the restraint of actions rather than attitudes, to "restraining the hand rather than the will." On the other hand, love means a perfect accord between duty and inclination in such a way that duty is not felt as duty and "we love the things that thou commandest." This second aspect of love is disregarded in Kant's interpretation of love, for instance. For him, the sense of obligation in its most universal and least specific form is identical with the law of love.

In Luther's exposition of the life of grace, "law" and "conscience" are left behind with sin and self. This freedom from the sense of "ought" is described by him as an ecstatic experience in which the self calculates no advantages, rises above every form of prudence, and feels itself at one with Christ, being motivated purely by a sense of gratitude for the divine forgiveness. Emil Brunner stands in the Lutheran tradition when he also emphasizes this transcendence over the "ought" and declares that "if we feel we ought it is a proof that we cannot." It is a question whether this point of "grace" is understood by Calvin at all. For his ethic is one of obedience to the divine law. Love is a summary of this law, but he is also careful to spell it out in specific detail. The detail is as specific as Catholic "natural law," except that he draws the details not from the intuitions of reason but from "various portions of Scripture." He is convinced that we need this law in specific form to guide our conscience, corrupted by sin; and there is no suggestion that law and conscience do not operate in the state of grace.

This contrast between the conception of an identity of love and the sense of obligation, on the one hand, and a contradiction between them, on the other, is the proof of a complicated relationship between love and law in both the subjective and the objective sphere. What is described by Luther as freedom from law may well conform to momentary heights of spiritual experience in which there is such a "pull" of grace (which may include everything from ecstatic religious experience to the "common grace" of family love) that we are not conscious of any "ought" or any sense of obligation. But it may be questioned whether it can describe anything more than such moments. It certainly does not describe the ongoing experience of even the most consecrated Christian, particularly not if it is true about him, as Luther asserts, that he is *"simul justus et peccator."* For if he remains a sinner, it must be true of him that he feels the tension between his self-interest, anxieties and insecurities, and the obligation to forget himself for the sake of his concern for others. It may well be that everything defined as the "sense of justice" is an expression of the law of love within the limits of law.

There are some aspects of the law of love, objectively considered, which are more clearly in the realm of duty than in the realm of grace. The injunction "If ye love them that love you what thanks have ye?" (Matt. 5:46), for instance, points to the universalistic tendencies in the law of love. It expresses our obligations beyond the boundaries of the natural communities of family, tribe, and nation. But paradoxically the love within the family may be by "grace" rather than law, while the love of "mankind" must be by law. That is, there may be such conjugal or paternal or filial affection as disposes us to seek the good of wife, husband, or child without any sense of duty, "common grace" or "habitual grace" having drawn the self beyond itself and out of itself into the lives of others. But our concern for those beyond our circle, our obligation to the peoples of the world and the community of mankind, comes to us very much with the push of the "ought" against the force of our more parochial habits of grace.

Yet on the other hand, pure obligation, while not so impotent as Brunner suggests, is more impotent than generally recognized, which is why purely moralistic sermons, which always tell us what we ought to do, tend to be boring. The best modern psychiatry, when dealing with the problem of delinquency in children, significantly does not preach to them what they ought to do, not even that they "ought to accept themselves." It insists that they must be accepted, must find security in the love of others, out of which security they gain sufficient freedom from self to "let go" and love others. Common grace, in short, rather than law is offered as a cure for their ills.

It might be added that a good deal of modern Christian teaching about Christian love may be by comparison very loveless. For the preacher chides his congregation endlessly for not meeting the most ultimate possibilities of the law of love, such as sacrifice, forgiveness, and uncalculated freedom from self, as if these were simple possibilities of the will. Thus the law of love becomes the occasion for loveless castigation because it is not recognized that, on the subjective side, love is a curious compound of willing through the strength of the sense of obligation and of willing not by the strength of our will but by the strength which enters the will through grace. This defect in the liberal Protestant attitude toward love is the subjective aspect of its lack of a doctrine of grace. The objective aspect, which must be considered subsequently, is revealed in its lack of distinction between love and justice. In both aspects the basis of the defect lies in the failure to appreciate the force of self-love in life. The consequence of this failure creates the belief that love is a law which can be easily fulfilled if only the preacher will establish its validity and present it persuasively. Grace, whether "common" or "saving," has meaning only when life is measured at the limits of human possibilities, and when it is recognized that there are things we ought to do which we cannot do merely by the strength of our willing, but which may become possible because we are assisted by the help which others give us by their love, by the strength which accrues to our will in moments of crisis, and by the saving grace of the Spirit of God indwelling our spirit.

THE TRANSCENDENCE OF LOVE OVER LAW

Subjectively, we have defined the problem of love and law as the problem of the relation of duty to grace. Materially, the problem is the relation of love as the sum and total of all law, and of love as defining indeterminate possibilities, transcending law. These points of indeterminacy in the law of love correspond to the indeterminate character of human freedom. In so far as man has a determinate structure, it is possible to state the "essential nature" of human existence to which his actions ought to conform and which they should fulfill. But in so far as he has the freedom to transcend structure, standing beyond himself and beyond every particular social situation, every law is subject to indeterminate possibilities which finally exceed the limits of any specific definition of what he "ought" to do. Yet they do not stand completely outside of law, if law is defined in terms of man's essential nature. For this indeterminate freedom is a part of his essential nature.

The points at which the transcendence of love over law are clearest are four, of which one point may really belong to the realm of law:

(1) Love as Universal

The freedom of man over every historic situation means that his obligation to others cannot be limited to partial communities of nature and history, to family, tribe, or nation. ("If ye love them that love you what thanks have ye?" [Matt. 5:46].) Love acknowledges no natural bounds and is universal in scope. ("Whoso loveth father or mother more than me is not worthy of me" [Matt. 10:37].) This first element in the indeterminacy of love has already been described as being, in one respect at least, within the limits of law. For it describes the sum total of all our obligations to our fellow men without specific detail. It is thus the summary of all law. It may come to us subjectively in the force of obligation in opposition to more parochial forms of love which are nourished by common grace.

Yet this universalistic aspect of the law of love is frequently made to bear the whole burden of the idea of love beyond law. In the thought of Augustine, the love of God, as distinguished from the love of any creature, defines the difference between the realm of grace and the realm of nature. Augustine makes the mistake of never being concerned whether, in a relation of love, we rise to the point of loving the other person for his own sake or only for our sake. His concern is always whether we love the person for his own sake or for God's sake. This is to say, he is afraid that love of the other may degenerate into idolatry. He compounds this error by insisting that the love of the neighbor must express itself not so much in meeting his needs as in leading him to God. "So when one . . . is commanded to love his neighbor as himself, what else is he enjoined than that he shall commend him to the love of God?"[1]

In Catholic asceticism, the universalism of the Christian love commandment becomes one basis for celibacy and virginity. (The other basis is its attitude toward sex.) The institution of the family is destroyed in order that there may be no parochial impediment to uni-

---

1. *De Civ. Dei,* 10.3.

versal love. This is one aspect of the Catholic strategy of dealing with the dimension of love which transcends law in its "counsels of perfection." The difference between commandment and counsel, declares Aquinas, is "that a commandment implies obligation whereas a counsel is left to the option of the one to whom it is given."[2] This definition of the universal aspects of the law of love in its universalistic indeterminacy, as a more rigorous law which is too rigorous for the majority of Christians "because their disposition is not inclined" to it but must be kept by the few who have the "fitness" to observe it, is a part of the whole Catholic strategy of creating two grades of Christians: (a) those who live by the law of love within the limits of love as law; and (b) those who live by the law of love beyond the limits of natural law. The difficulty with this strategy is that it removes the element of the indeterminate in the law of love as a resource upon all Christian life, and it reduces the ultimate possibilities of love to the dimension of a yet more rigorous law.

This defect in Catholic thought arises from the incorporation of Stoic natural law into Christian ethics. For Stoic natural law assumes a determinate human freedom and falsely equates the fixed structures of nature and the less fixed structures of human nature. The supposedly fixed structures of human nature are the basis of a law which states those things to be done and not to be done "which follow in an inevitable manner from the fact that man is man" (Maritain). But the indeterminate character of human freedom and the variety and uniqueness of historic occasions produce fewer things than supposed in Catholic natural law theory, about which one may be sure that they must be done or not done. Everything one does stands under more ultimate possibilities of love, which cannot merely be reserved for the celibate who has decided that he will make one extra effort "to be perfect."

In Catholic mysticism (particularly clearly in the mysticism of St. John of the Cross), the love of God is set in complete contradiction to the love of the neighbor in such a way that the love of the creature is merely a stepladder to the love of God, which must be abandoned when the love of God (universal love) is reached. All of these errors arise from adding the biblical conceptions of freedom, sin, and grace to a classical, rationalistic definition of the structure of human

---

2. *Summa* III, qu. 108.3.

nature. In this rationalism there is an inadequate conception of human selfhood, particularly of its indeterminate possibilities of both love and self-love.

But the same error creeps into some Protestant emphases on the universal aspects of the love commandment. Kierkegaard, despite his existentialist understanding of human selfhood, presents a legalistic version of universal love in his *Works of Love*, according to which the love of a person in his uniqueness and in the uniqueness of a particular relation (as wife or husband, for instance) has nothing to do with "Christian" love. Christian love is a universal love which proves itself by regarding the loved self as anonymously as possible. The force of love is lacking in every element of spontaneity and "grace." It is the force of law and of conscience. Kierkegaard, in short, defines Christian love in precisely those terms which Brunner, with contrasting one-sidedness, regards as outside the dimension of Christian love. For Christian love reveals itself for Brunner only in uniquely personal and intimate relations. Kierkegaard writes: "Christianity has not come into the world to teach you how specifically to love your wife or your friend but . . . how in common humanity you shall love all men. . . . Love is a matter of conscience and hence not a matter of impulse or inclination."[3]

The universalistic dimension of the love commandment is, in short, both within and beyond the love commandment as law. It represents the outer circumference of the totality of our obligations to our neighbors and to God. It includes all of them but also goes beyond anything that can be specifically defined.

(2) Love as Sacrificial

The freedom of the self over itself as contingent object in nature and history means that there is a dimension of human existence in which the preservation of the self in history becomes problematic. ("Fear not them which are able to kill the body, but rather those that are able to destroy both soul and body in hell" [Matt. 10:28].) The love commandment promises self-realization through self-giving ("Whosoever loseth his life will find it"), but historic success is not guaranteed in this form of self-realization. The *agape* of Christ, which is the norm of Christian selfhood, is always finally defined as sacrificial

3. *Works of Love*, 116.

love, as the love of the cross. "And walk in love even as Christ loved you and gave himself for you" (Eph. 5:2). Sacrificial love represents the second pinnacle of love which represents both the completion and the annulment of love as law. It is the completion of the law of love because perfect love has no logical limit short of the readiness to sacrifice the self for the other. Yet it is a point which stands beyond all law, because the necessity of sacrificing one's life for another cannot be formulated as an obligation, nor can it be achieved under the whip of the sense of obligation. Law in the determinate sense must stop with distributive justice and mutual love. Yet a sensitive conscience will have conscience pricks if another life has been taken in self-defense or if a common peril has resulted in the loss of another life but not of one's own.

Unprudential love, in which there is no calculation of mutual advantages, obviously stands in a dialectical relation to mutual love and to every scheme of distributive justice as well. In mutual love and in distributive justice, the self regards itself as an equal, but not as a specially privileged, member of a group in which the rational self seeks to apportion the values of life justly or to achieve perfect reciprocity of advantages. The will to do justice is a form of love, for the interests of the neighbor are affirmed. Mutual love (*philia*) is also a form of love, for the life of the other is enhanced. Yet, on the other hand, such expressions of love fall short of love in its ultimate form. For they are mixed with a careful calculation of interest and advantages in which the self always claims an equal share. The final form of love is bereft of such calculation and meets the needs of the other without calculating comparative rights. Sacrificial love is therefore a form of love which transcends the limits of law. It is a form of love which cannot be embodied in any moral code. Nor can it be achieved by the compulsion of a sense of obligation. Yet common sense, not merely in Christian thought but also in the pagan reverence for heroic sacrifice, has, with spiritually shrewd instinct, recognized such heedless love as the final norm of love.

It cannot be separated from the realm of natural love (whether *eros* or *philia*) by a neat line. It transcends the line of natural love. Yet without an element of heedless love, every form of mutual love would degenerate into a calculation of mutual advantages and every calculation of such advantages would finally generate resentment about an absence of perfect reciprocity. Aristotle tries to solve this problem by preferring friendship between equals. In the absence of equality there must be, he thinks, calculation of different types of advantage for the stronger and the weaker member of the friendship: honor for the one and help for the other. This is a nice illustration of the impossibility of finding a logical end for the love commandment within the limits of prudence. The final limits are beyond prudence and calculation; but these final limits are not neatly separated from the whole realm of mutual love and distributive justice. They tend to redeem this realm from degenerating into a competition of calculating egotists.

On the subjective side the line is equally lacking in neatness. For a sense of obligation may prompt men into a hazardous cause, but the final act of sacrifice by which a soldier gives his life for his comrade is, as even the army rightly surmises, "beyond the call of duty." It is possible only by an accretion of strength to the will which is in the realm of grace.

In trying to do justice to this dialectical relation, Catholicism has the advantage of recognizing that sacrificial love is related to natural love as the "perfect to the imperfect." It declares that this perfection is possible only by grace. But it makes grace to mean the "fitness" of man to embrace monastic poverty, in which he cannot call anything his own. Thus, as in the case of the universal dimension of love, the sacrificial dimension is a "counsel of perfection," which means that it is yet another and more rigorous statement of love as law. But the possibilities of ecstatic, heedless, and unprudential completions of the love commandment by "grace" in all kinds of human and historic situations are obscured.

D'Arcy, who rightly insists on the dialectical relation of sacrificial to mutual love in opposition to Nygren, spoils the validity of his exposition by interpreting sacrificial love as the flower of one element in human nature, the element of *anima* as distinguished from *animus*. *Anima* is the feminine principle in human nature, the tendency toward self-giving as opposed to the tendency toward self-assertion. In such a formulation *agape* is too simply the completion of nature, and the contradiction between sacrifice and justice, between heedlessness and prudence, is obscured.

But the error is hardly greater than the one which is made by the Lutheran formulation. In Luther's doctrine of the "two realms," justice is consigned completely to the realm of law. There "nothing is known of Christ," even as in the realm of the kingdom of heaven "nothing is known of law, conscience, or sword." The law, in such a rigorous dualism, does not even contain within it the desire to do justice. It is no more than a coercive arrangement which prevents mutual harm. Love, on the other hand, is only *agape* in its purest and most unadulterated form, which means in a form which is known in human experience only in rare moments of evangelical fervor or crisis heroism. This is why the Lutheran formulation of the relation of love to law is so irrelevant to the broad area of common experience, in which one must balance claims and counterclaims and make discriminate judgments about competing interests.

Nygren's exposition of the contrast between *agape* and natural love is not so much concerned with the contrast between *agape* and the positive law as in Luther. But his idea of an absolute contradiction between *agape* and *eros* contains the same error. It is the error of a too rigorous separation of the realm of grace and the realm of nature. This separation must lead, as D'Arcy rightly observes, to a withering of both *eros* and *agape*. For *eros* has no goal beyond itself, and *agape* has no real relevance to the human situation.

The literature of the Protestant social gospel is filled with references to sacrificial love. Men are constantly challenged to follow the "way of the cross" and to espouse the "Jesus way of life." But there is a curious mixture of bourgeois prudence with this pinnacle of grace. For it is assumed that a rigorous sacrifice will finally prove successful, so that a sufficient cumulation of sacrificial acts will obviate the necessity of sacrifice. Sacrifice really means the abandonment of short-range for long-range advantages. If the enemy is loved he will become a friend. If the conqueror is not resisted he will cease to be a conqueror. If the businessman sacrifices his profits he will gain greater advantages in the end, though not necessarily greater profits. Up to a point all this is true, for the paradox of self-realization through self-giving has a promise for this life also. Only there is always an ultimate tragic possibility in sacrificial love which is obscured in this prudential version.

(3) Love as Forgiveness

Forgiveness has the same relation to punitive justice as sacrificial love to distributive justice. Forgiveness is both a completion and an annulment of punitive justice. It is its completion in the sense that a rigorous analysis of all factors involved in a wrong act will lead to an understanding both of the extenuating circumstances and the causal preconditions of the crime. Thus imaginative justice moves in the direction of forgiveness, or at least to remedial rather than punitive justice.

Yet forgiveness is finally in contradiction to punitive justice. It represents, in the words of Berdyaev, "the morality beyond morality." Jesus justifies the love of the enemy in terms of the imitation of a God whose mercy cuts across every conception of justice as rigorously as the impartialities of nature, in which the rain falls on the just and the unjust and the sun shines upon the evil and the good. In the parable of the laborers in the vineyard (Matt. 20:1–16), the divine mercy is challenged for being unjust and defended because it exceeds justice. The whole doctrine of the atonement in Christian thought contains the paradox of the relation of mercy to judgment. For the mercy of God is in His judgment, and yet it is something which cancels His wrath. There is no nice discrimination of merit and demerit in forgiveness, any more than there is a nice discrimination of interests in sacrificial love. Here law is transcended. Forgiveness seems to be purely in the realm of grace.

Yet even forgiveness comes partially into the category of love as law. For we are warned that if we forgive not men their trespasses neither will our heavenly Father forgive our trespasses (cf. Matt. 7:14–15). This would seem to mean that forgiveness is something we owe the erring brother as a right. Or rather it is something we owe God. But our forgiveness of our brethren is primarily a grateful response to God's forgiveness. ("And be ye kind one to another, tenderhearted, forgiving one another, even as God for Christ's sake hath forgiven you" [Eph. 4:32].) Usually the New Testament presents forgiveness only as a possibility for those who are of contrite heart and whose uneasy conscience has been eased by divine forgiveness. Yet the fact that it is also presented as an obligation, which will incur the punishment of judgment if left undone, proves that even on this pinnacle of grace law is not completely transcended.

On this issue Luther is again clearest in illuminating the element of grace in the experience of forgiveness and least adequate in relating forgiveness to punitive justice. There are no diagonal lines in Luther's thought which relate mercy to punitive justice. There is therefore nothing to inspire the kind of development of punitive justice in the direction of imaginative justice which has in fact taken place in modern criminology and which proves that the "two realms" have more commerce with each other than Luther supposes.

Nygren's version of forgiveness as an aspect of *agape* results in so sharp a distinction between justice and mercy that it leaves no place at all for discriminate judgments about justice. The distinction is so sharp that all moral distinctions in history seem to become invalid.

Modern liberalism, including Christian liberalism, tends to a sentimental version of forgiveness in which mercy has also completely triumphed over justice in such a way that responsibility of sin is denied. Sir Walter Moberly, in his book *Responsibility*, finds the final form of this sentimentality in modern psychiatry.

The Catholic exposition of this pinnacle of grace in the law of love has special significance because it is one ultimate possibility of love which is not bound to the ascetic system. The love of the enemy is a possibility for all Christians but only through the help of supernatural grace. It belongs to the "counsels of perfection" which can be added to ordinary justice; but it has no dialectical relation to the schemes of justice, whereby the injustice in every scheme of justice would come under judgment.

(4) Love as Standing in the Place of the Other

The final pinnacle of grace in the realm of love is the relation between persons in which one individual penetrates imaginatively and sympathetically into the life of another. This pinnacle finds no special place in the Catholic counsels of perfection because it represents the ordinary possibilities of love above the level of justice as defined in natural law. It is the very substance of the realm of love in Buber's exposition of *I and Thou* and in Brunner's *Divine Imperative*. It is, however, wrongly interpreted as the very substance of the realm of love. For in that case love does not include the general spirit of justice, which expresses itself in the structures, laws, social arrangements and economic forms by which men seek to regulate the life of the community and to establish a maximum of harmony and justice.

The love which wills justice must not be excluded from the realm of *agape*. Brunner is in great error when he interprets an act of personal kindness as more "Christian" than a statesmanlike scheme in the interest of justice. Brunner's dictum that love "never seeks great things" is capricious. It separates love too completely from the realm of justice, though in a different way than the thought of Nygren. A modern liberal form of this same error is to be found in such reactionary movements as "Christian Economics," which insist that unemployment insurance is unnecessary because "Christians of sensitive conscience will organize private charity for the needy." The effort to confine *agape* to the love of personal relations, and to place all the structures and artifices of justice outside that realm, makes Christian love irrelevant to the problems of man's common life.

On the other hand, it is true that beyond and above every human relation as ordered by a fixed structure of justice, by custom, tradition, and legal enactment, there remain indeterminate possibilities of love in the individual and personal encounters of those who are in the structure. Whether men meet their fellow men with generosity or with envy, with imagination or with ambitions of dominion, is a question which cannot be fully solved by the structure of justice which binds them to their fellow men. Human actions can, to a degree, corrupt even the highest structure, and they can also partially redeem the worst structure. The fact that slavery was essentially wrong proves the invalidity of regarding structures of justice as irrelevant to love. Yet it did make a difference to a slave whether he was subject to a kind or to a cruel master. The institution was wrong because the disproportions of power in the institution of slavery were such that they could predispose even decent men to unconscious cruelties. But the most adequate institution is still only a bare base upon which the higher experiences of love must be built.

The commandment to love the neighbor as the self must finally culminate in the individual experience in which one self seeks to penetrate deeply into the mystery of the other self and yet stand in reverence before a mystery which he has no right to penetrate. This kind of love is a matter of law in the sense that the essential nature of man, with his indeterminate freedom, requires that human relations should finally achieve such an intimacy. But it is also a matter of grace, because no sense of obligation can provide the imagination and forbearance by which this is accomplished. Such intimacy is of course closely related to sacrificial love, for the intermingling of life with life predisposes to sacrificial abandonment of the claims of the self for the needs of the other.

If the intimacy of personal friendship, in which life is interwoven with life, is one of the pinnacles of *agape*, it must follow that a sexual partnership has a natural basis for such *agape* far beyond other partnerships. The sexual union as a parable, symbol, and basis for *agape* has been little appreciated in Christian thought, partly because of a generally negative attitude toward sex which Christianity absorbed from Greek thought; and partly because the particularity of the sexual union is suspect from the standpoint of Christian universalism. Yet this aspect of the relation of love beyond law to love as law has been explored in Greek Orthodoxy and has been most significantly illumined and also exaggerated by Vladimir Solovyov, who writes:

> Fully admitting . . . the high dignity of other kinds of love . . . we find nevertheless that only sexual love satisfies the two fundamental conditions without which there can be no abolition of selfhood through complete vital union with another. In all other kinds of love there is absent either the homogeneity between lover and beloved, or the all inclusive difference of complementary qualities.[4]

It is significant that despite the ascetic traditions of Roman Catholicism there are also recent efforts in Roman thought to explore this relation between love and sexual love. D'Arcy's *Mind and Heart of Love* sees the relationship not so much as the intimate and mutual self-giving of both partners of the marriage union as in the feminine impulse of self-giving. A more adequate exposition of the significance of the mutual relation in marriage has recently been given in the Catholic treatise *Essay on Human Love*, by Jean Guitton.

Naturally a particular relationship cannot exhaust the meaning of *agape*, particularly not the dimension which expresses itself in its universalistic motif. But if any justice is to be done to particular and intimate relations, the marriage union must receive a more positive appreciation in Christian thought and life. The intimacy of the relation has of course a basis in nature. But it can be endlessly transfigured by grace, so that the possibilities of love as law, and love at

---

4. S. L. Frank, ed., *A Solovyov Anthology*, 160.

the limits of law, and love beyond the limits in this partnership, are identical with the general logic of love as law and love as grace.

THE RELATION OF LOVE TO LAW

This analysis of love as law and love as transcending law is incomplete without consideration of one further problem: the relation of love to law as such. Law as such is composed of norms of conduct prescribed by custom, legal enactment, scriptural injunction, or rational intuition, in which duties and obligations are prescribed without seeming reference to the ultimate spirit of law, namely, love. What is the standing of such law in a Christian scheme of ethics, and how is love related to it? In Catholic thought, this law is drawn from the intuitions or logical deductions of reason, so that even the Decalogue is regarded as normative by Aquinas only in so far as it corresponds to the natural law. In Reformation thought, systematically in Calvin and less systematically in Luther, this law is drawn from Scripture, either from explicit law, such as the Decalogue, or from moral admonitions in various portions of Scripture which are raised to the authority of explicit norms for the Christian life.

All such law will be found to have two characteristics: (a) It states our obligations to our neighbor as minimal and usually in negative terms: "Thou shalt not kill." "Thou shalt not steal." (b) It states our obligations to our neighbors in terms which presuppose the fact of sin and self-interest and the complexity of claims and counterclaims which are arbitrated by some "rule of reason" rather than by the ultimate scruples of the law of love.

Thus the law, however conceived, accepts and regulates self-interest and prohibits only the most excessive forms of it. It does not command that we love the neighbor but only that we do not take his life or property. It does not command that we seek our neighbor's good but only that we respect his rights. Broadly speaking, the end of the law is justice. But we have already seen that justice is related to love. Thus there is a dialectical relation between love and law even as there is between love beyond law and love as law. It might be stated as follows: The law seeks for a tolerable harmony of life with life, sin presupposed. It is, therefore, an approximation of the law of love on the one hand and an instrument of love on the other hand. Consequently the distinction between law and love is less absolute and more dialectical than conceived in either Catholic or Reformation thought.

If this conclusion be correct, it follows that law, however conceived, whether drawn from Scripture (as in Reformation thought) or from rational intuitions (as in Catholicism) or from historical tradition, is less fixed and absolute than all these theories assume. The scriptural authority, below the level of love, is less valid in the realm of law than the Reformation assumes because there is always an element of historical contingency in the allegedly absolute norms of Scriptures which makes its authority questionable in a different historical context. (St. Paul's attitude toward women in the Church is a case in point.) The authority of rational "natural" law is less valid than Catholicism supposes. The whole concept of natural law rests upon a Stoic-Aristotelian rationalism which assumes fixed historical structures and norms which do not in fact exist. Furthermore, it assumes a human participation in a universal reason in which there is no ideological taint. The moral certainties of natural law in Catholic thought are all dubious. Sometimes they rest upon deductive reason. It is assumed that it is impossible to draw logical conclusions in the field of material ethics, from the formal ethical principle that good is to be done and evil avoided. But there is no guide in the formal principle of ethics about the norms of good and evil. Sometimes they rest upon the "intuitions" of reason. While there are some seemingly universal moral judgments such as the prohibition of murder, it must be noted that they are the most universal if they are the most minimal and most negative expressions of the law of love. The more specific they become the more they are suspect as "self-evident" propositions of the natural law.

Sometimes Catholic natural theory sinks to the level of eighteenth-century rationalism, which it ostensibly abhors. It regards the propositions of natural law as propositions of analytic reason. This reason analyzes the structures of nature, including human nature, and arrives at certain conclusions about what nature "intends," as, for instance, that nature intends procreation in sexual union. In this case it forgets that human nature is characterized not only by an indeterminate freedom but by an intimate and organic relation between the impulses of nature and human freedom which permits endless elaborations of human vital capacities for which it is not easy to find a simple descriptive norm.

In short, both Catholic and Reformation theory are too certain about the fixities of the norms of law. All law, whether historical, positive, scriptural, or rational, is more tentative and less independent in its authority than orthodox Christianity, whether Catholic or Protestant, supposes, even as it is more necessary than liberal Protestantism assumes. The final dike against relativism is to be found not in these alleged fixities, but in the law of love itself. This is the only final law, and every other law is an expression of the law of love in minimal or in proximate terms or in terms appropriate to given historical occasions.

12

≡

THE CHILDREN OF LIGHT AND THE CHILDREN OF DARKNESS

Democracy has a more compelling justification and requires a more realistic vindication than is given it by the liberal culture with which it has been associated in modern history. The excessively optimistic estimates of human nature and of human history with which the democratic credo has been historically associated are a source of peril to democratic society; for contemporary experience is refuting this optimism and there is danger that it will seem to refute the democratic ideal as well.

A free society requires some confidence in the ability of men to reach tentative and tolerable adjustments between their competing interests and to arrive at some common notions of justice which transcend all partial interests. A consistent pessimism in regard to man's rational capacity for justice invariably leads to absolutistic political theories; for they prompt the conviction that only preponderant power can coerce the various vitalities of a community into a working harmony. But a too consistent optimism in regard to man's ability and inclination to grant justice to his fellows obscures the perils of chaos which perennially confront every society, including a free society. In one sense a democratic society is particularly exposed to the dangers of confusion. If these perils are not appreciated they may overtake a free society and invite the alternative evil of tyranny.

But modern democracy requires a more realistic philosophical and religious basis, not only in order to anticipate and understand the perils to which it is exposed; but also to give it a more persuasive justification. Man's capacity for justice makes democracy possible; but man's inclination to injustice makes democracy necessary. In all non-democratic political theories the state or the ruler is invested with uncontrolled power for the sake of achieving order and unity in the community. But the pessimism which prompts and justifies this policy is not consistent; for it is not applied, as it should be, to the ruler. If men are inclined to deal unjustly with their fellows, the possession of power aggravates this inclination. That is why irresponsible and uncontrolled power is the greatest source of injustice.

The democratic techniques of a free society place checks upon the power of the ruler and administrator and thus prevent it from becoming vexatious. The perils of uncontrolled power are perennial reminders of the virtues of a democratic society; particularly if a society should become inclined to impatience with the dangers of freedom and should be tempted to choose the advantages of coerced unity at the price of freedom.

The consistent optimisim of our liberal culture has prevented modern democratic societies both from gauging the perils of freedom accurately and from appreciating democracy fully as the only alternative to injustice and oppression. When this optimism is not qualified to accord with the real and complex facts of human nature and history, there is always a danger that sentimentality will give way to despair and that a too consistent optimism will alternate with a too consistent pessimism.

THE COMPLEX ROOTS AND RESOURCES OF THE DEMOCRATIC IDEAL

Democracy, as every other historic ideal and institution, contains both ephemeral and more permanently valid elements. Democracy is on the one hand the characteristic fruit of a bourgeois civilization; on the other hand it is a perennially valuable form of social organization in which freedom and order are made to support, and not to contradict, each other.

Democracy is a "bourgeois ideology" in so far as it expresses the typical viewpoints of the middle classes who have risen to power in European civilization in the past three or four centuries. Most of the democratic ideals, as we know them, were weapons of the commercial classes who engaged in stubborn, and ultimately victorious, conflict with the ecclesiastical and aristocratic rulers of the feudal-medieval world. The ideal of equality, unknown in the democratic life of the Greek city states and derived partly from Christian and partly from Stoic sources, gave the bourgeois classes a sense of self-respect in overcoming the aristocratic pretension and condescension of the feudal overlords of medieval society. The middle classes defeated the combination of economic and political power of mercantilism by stressing economic liberty; and, through the principles of political liberty, they added the political power of suffrage to their growing economic power. The implicit assumptions, as well as the explicit ideals, of democratic civilization were also largely the fruit of middle-class existence. The social and historical optimism of democratic life, for instance, represents the typical illusion of an advancing class which mistook its own progress for the progress of the world.

Since bourgeois civilization, which came to birth in the sixteenth to eighteenth centuries and reached its zenith in the nineteenth century, is now obviously in grave peril, if not actually in rigor mortis in the twentieth century, it must be obvious that democracy, in so far as it is a middle-class ideology, also faces its doom.

This fate of democracy might be viewed with equanimity, but for the fact that it has a deeper dimension and broader validity than its middle-class character. Ideally democracy is a permanently valid form of social and political organization which does justice to two dimensions of human existence: to man's spiritual stature and his social character; to the uniqueness and variety of life, as well as to the common necessities of all men. Bourgeois democracy frequently exalted the individual at the expense of the community; but its emphasis upon liberty contained a valid element, which transcended its excessive individualism. The community requires liberty as much as does the individual; and the individual requires community more than bourgeois thought comprehended. Democracy can therefore not be equated with freedom. An ideal democratic order seeks unity within the conditions of freedom; and maintains freedom within the framework of order.

Man requires freedom in his social organization because he is "essentially" free, which is to say, that he has the capacity for indeterminate transcendence over the processes and limitations of nature. This freedom enables him to make history and to elaborate communal organizations in boundless variety and in endless breadth and extent. But he also requires community because he is by nature social. He cannot fulfill his life within himself but only in responsible and mutual relations with his fellows.

Bourgeois democrats are inclined to believe that freedom is primarily a necessity for the individual, and that community and social order are necessary only because there are many individuals in a small world, so that minimal restrictions are required to prevent confusion. Actually the community requires freedom as much as the individual; and the individual requires order as much as does the community.

Both the individual and the community require freedom so that neither communal nor historical restraints may prematurely arrest the potencies which inhere in man's essential freedom and which express themselves collectively as well as individually. It is true that individuals are usually the initiators of new insights and the proponents of novel methods. Yet there are collective forces at work in society which are not the conscious contrivance of individuals. In any event society is as much the beneficiary of freedom as the individual. In a free society new forces may enter into competition with the old and gradually establish themselves. In a traditional or tyrannical form of social organization new forces are either suppressed, or they establish themselves at the price of social convulsion and upheaval.

The order of a community is, on the other hand, a boon to the individual as well as to the community. The individual cannot be a true self in isolation. Nor can he live within the confines of the community which "nature" establishes in the minimal cohesion of family and herd. His freedom transcends these limits of nature, and therefore makes larger and larger social units both possible and necessary. It is precisely because of the essential freedom of man that he requires a contrived order in his community.

The democratic ideal is thus more valid than the libertarian and individualistic version of it which bourgeois civilization elaborated. Since the bourgeois version has been discredited by the events of contemporary history and since, in any event, bourgeois civilization is in process of disintegration, it becomes important to distinguish and save what is permanently valid from what is ephemeral in the democratic order.

If democracy is to survive it must find a more adequate cultural basis than the philosophy which has informed the building of the bourgeois world. The inadequacy of the presuppositions upon which the democratic experiment rests does not consist merely in the excessive individualism and libertarianism of the bourgeois world view; though it must be noted that this excessive individualism prompted a civil war in the whole Western world in which the rising proletarian classes pitted an excessive collectivism against the false individualism of middle-class life. This civil conflict contributed to the weakness of democratic civilization when faced with the threat of barbarism. Neither the individualism nor the collectivism did justice to all the requirements of man's social life, and the conflict between half-truth and half-truth divided the civilized world in such a way that the barbarians were able to claim first one side and then the other in this civil conflict as their provisional allies.[1]

But there is a more fundamental error in the social philosophy of democratic civilization than the individualism of bourgeois democracy and the collectivism of Marxism. It is the confidence of both bourgeois and proletarian idealists in the possibility of achieving an easy resolution of the tension and conflict between self-interest and the general interest. Modern bourgeois civilization is not, as Catholic philosophers and medievalists generally assert, a rebellion against universal law, or a defiance of universal standards of justice, or a war against the historic institutions which sought to achieve and preserve some general social and international harmony. Modern secularism is not, as religious idealists usually aver, merely a rationalization of self-interest, either individual or collective. Bourgeois individualism may be excessive and it may destroy the individual's organic relation to the community; but it was not intended to destroy either the national or the international order. On the contrary the social idealism which informs our democratic civilization had a touching faith in the possibility of achieving a simple harmony between self-interest and the general welfare on every level.

It is not true that Nazism is the final fruit of a moral cynicism which had its rise in the Renaissance and Reformation, as Catholic apologists aver. Nazi barbarism is the final fruit of a moral cynicism which was only a subordinate note in the cultural life of the modern period, and which remained subordinate until very recently. Modern civilization did indeed seek to give the individual a greater freedom in the national community than the traditional feudal order had given

---

1. The success of Nazi diplomacy and propaganda in claiming the poor in democratic civilization as their allies against the "plutocrats" in one moment, and in the next seeking to ally the privileged classes in their battle against "communism," is a nice indication of the part which the civil war in democratic civilization played in allowing barbarism to come so near to a triumph over civilization.

him; and it did seek to free the nations of restraints placed upon their freedom by the international church. But it never cynically defied the general interest in the name of self-interest, either individual or collective. It came closer to doing this nationally than individually. Machiavelli's amoral "Prince," who knows no law beyond his own will and power, is made to bear the whole burden of the Catholic polemic against the modern world. It must be admitted that Machiavelli is the first of a long line of moral cynics in the field of international relations. But this moral cynicism only qualifies, and does not efface, the general universalistic overtone of modern liberal idealism. In the field of domestic politics the war of uncontrolled interests may have been the consequence, but it was certainly not the intention, of middle-class individualists. Nor was the conflict between nations in our modern world their intention. They did demand a greater degree of freedom for the nations; but they believed that it was possible to achieve an uncontrolled harmony between them, once the allegedly irrelevant restrictions of the old religio-political order were removed. In this they proved to be mistaken. They did not make the mistake, however, of giving simple moral sanction to self-interest. They depended rather upon controls and restraints which proved to be inadequate.

THE "CHILDREN OF LIGHT" AND THE "CHILDREN OF DARKNESS"

In illumining this important distinction more fully, we may well designate the moral cynics, who know no law beyond their will and interest, with a scriptural designation of "children of this world" or "children of darkness."* Those who believe that self-interest should be brought under the discipline of a higher law could then be termed "the children of light." This is no mere arbitrary device; for evil is always the assertion of some self-interest without regard to the whole, whether the whole be conceived as the immediate community, or the total community of mankind, or the total order of the world. The good is, on the other hand, always the harmony of the whole on various levels. Devotion to a subordinate and premature "whole" such as the nation, may of course become evil, viewed from the

* Niebuhr employs a variety of translations in arriving at this comparison; cf. RSV: "The sons of this world are wiser in this generation than the sons of light" (Luke 16:8). — ED.

perspective of a larger whole, such as the community of mankind. The "children of light" may thus be defined as those who seek to bring self-interest under the discipline of a more universal law and in harmony with a more universal good.

According to the scripture, "the children of this world are in their generation wiser than the children of light." This observation fits the modern situation. Our democratic civilization has been built, not by children of darkness but by foolish children of light. It has been under attack by the children of darkness, by the moral cynics, who declare that a strong nation need acknowledge no law beyond its strength. It has come close to complete disaster under this attack, not because it accepted the same creed as the cynics; but because it underestimated the power of self-interest, both individual and collective, in modern society. The children of light have not been as wise as the children of darkness.

The children of darkness are evil because they know no law beyond the self. They are wise, though evil, because they understand the power of self-interest. The children of light are virtuous because they have some conception of a higher law than their own will. They are usually foolish because they do not know the power of self-will. They underestimate the peril of anarchy in both the national and the international community. Modern democratic civilization is, in short, sentimental rather than cynical. It has an easy solution for the problem of anarchy and chaos on both the national and international level of community, because of its fatuous and superficial view of man. It does not know that the same man who is ostensibly devoted to the "common good" may have desires and ambitions, hopes and fears, which set him at variance with his neighbor.

It must be understood that the children of light are foolish not merely because they underestimate the power of self-interest among the children of darkness. They underestimate this power among themselves. The democratic world came so close to disaster not merely because it never believed that Nazism possessed the demonic fury which it avowed. Civilization refused to recognize the power of class interest in its own communities. It also spoke glibly of an international conscience; but the children of darkness meanwhile skilfully set nation against nation. They were thereby enabled to despoil one nation after another, without every civilized nation coming to the defence of each. Moral cynicism had a provisional advantage over moral sentimentality. Its advantage lay not merely in its own lack of moral scruple but also in its shrewd assessment of the power of self-interest, individual and national, among the children of light, despite their moral protestations.

While our modern children of light, the secularized idealists, were particularly foolish and blind, the more "Christian" children of light have been almost equally guilty of this error. Modern liberal Protestantism was probably even more sentimental in its appraisal of the moral realities in our political life than secular idealism, and Catholicism could see nothing but cynical rebellion in the modern secular revolt against Catholic universalism and a Catholic "Christian" civilization. In Catholic thought medieval political universalism is always accepted at face value. Rebellion against medieval culture is therefore invariably regarded as the fruit of moral cynicism. Actually the middle-class revolt against the feudal order was partially prompted by a generous idealism, not unmixed of course with peculiar middle-class interests. The feudal order was not so simply a Christian civilization as Catholic defenders of it aver. It compounded its devotion to a universal order with the special interests of the priestly and aristocratic bearers of effective social power. The rationalization of their unique position in the feudal order may not have been more marked than the subsequent rationalization of bourgeois interests in the liberal world. But it is idle to deny this "ideological taint" in the feudal order and to pretend that rebels against the order were merely rebels against order as such. They were rebels against a particular order which gave an undue advantage to the aristocratic opponents of the middle classes.[2] The blindness of Catholicism to its own ideological taint is typical of the blindness of the children of light.

Our modern civilization, as a middle-class revolt against an aristo-

2. John of Salisbury expresses a quite perfect rationalization of clerical political authority in his *Policraticus* in the twelfth century. He writes: "Those who preside over the practice of religion should be looked up to and venerated as the soul of the body. . . . Furthermore since the soul is, as it were, the prince of the body and has a rule over the whole thereof, so those whom our author calls the prefects of religion preside over the entire body" (bk. 5, ch. 2).

A modern Catholic historian accepts this justification of clerical rule at its face value as he speaks of Machiavelli's politics as a "total assault upon the principles of men like John of Salisbury, preferring to the goodness of Christ, the stamina of Caesar" (Emmet John Hughes, *The Church and the Liberal Society*, 33).

John of Salisbury's political principles were undoubtedly more moral than Machiavelli's. But the simple identification of his justification of clericalism with the "goodness of Christ" is a nice illustration of the blindness of the children of light, whether Christian or secular.

cratic and clerical order, was irreligious partly because a Catholic civilization had so compounded the eternal sanctities with the contingent and relative justice and injustice of an agrarian-feudal order, that the new and dynamic bourgeois social force was compelled to challenge not only the political-economic arrangements of the order but also the eternal sanctities which hallowed it.

If modern civilization represents a bourgeois revolt against feudalism, modern culture represents the revolt of new thought, informed by modern science, against a culture in which religious authority had fixed premature and too narrow limits for the expansion of science and had sought to restrain the curiosity of the human mind from inquiring into "secondary causes." The culture which venerated science in place of religion, worshipped natural causation in place of God, and which regarded the cool prudence of bourgeois man as morally more normative than Christian love, has proved itself to be less profound than it appeared to be in the seventeenth and eighteenth centuries. But these inadequacies, which must be further examined as typical of the foolishness of modern children of light, do not validate the judgment that these modern rebels were really children of darkness, intent upon defying the truth or destroying universal order.

The modern revolt against the feudal order and the medieval culture was occasioned by the assertion of new vitalities in the social order and the discovery of new dimensions in the cultural enterprise of mankind. It was truly democratic in so far as it challenged the premature and tentative unity of a society and the stabilization of a culture, and in so far as it developed new social and cultural possibilities. The conflict between the middle classes and the aristocrats, between the scientists and the priests, was not a conflict between children of darkness and children of light. It was a conflict between pious and less pious children of light, both of whom were unconscious of the corruption of self-interest in all ideal achievements and pretensions of human culture.

THE DOCTRINE OF ORIGINAL SIN

In this conflict the devotees of medieval religion were largely unconscious of the corruption of self-interest in their own position; but it must be admitted that they were not as foolish as their secular successors in their estimate of the force of self-interest in human society. Catholicism did strive for an inner and religious discipline upon inordinate desire; and it had a statesmanlike conception of the necessity of legal and political restraint upon the power of egotism, both individual and collective, in the national and the more universal human community.

Our modern civilization, on the other hand, was ushered in on a wave of boundless social optimism. Modern secularism is divided into many schools. But all the various schools agreed in rejecting the Christian doctrine of original sin. It is not possible to explain the subtleties or to measure the profundity of this doctrine in this connection. But it is necessary to point out that the doctrine makes an important contribution to any adequate social and political theory the lack of which has robbed bourgeois theory of real wisdom; for it emphasizes a fact which every page of human history attests. Through it one may understand that no matter how wide the perspectives which the human mind may reach, how broad the loyalties which the human imagination may conceive, how universal the community which human statecraft may organize, or how pure the aspirations of the saintliest idealists may be, there is no level of human moral or social achievement in which there is not some corruption of inordinate self-love.

This sober and true view of the human situation was neatly rejected by modern culture. That is why it conceived so many fatuous and futile plans for resolving the conflict between the self and the community; and between the national and the world community. Whenever modern idealists are confronted with the divisive and corrosive effects of man's self-love, they look for some immediate cause of this perennial tendency, usually in some specific form of social organization. One school holds that men would be good if only political institutions would not corrupt them; another believes that they would be good if the prior evil of a faulty economic organization could be eliminated. Or another school thinks of this evil as no more than ignorance, and therefore waits for a more perfect educational process to redeem man from his partial and particular loyalties. But no school asks how it is that an essentially good man could have produced corrupting and tyrannical political organizations or exploiting economic organizations, or fanatical and superstitious religious organizations.

The result of this persistent blindness to the obvious and tragic facts of man's social history is that democracy has had to maintain itself precariously against the guile and the malice of the children of darkness, while its statesmen and guides conjured up all sorts of abstract and abortive plans for the creation of perfect national and international communities.

The confidence of modern secular idealism in the possibility of an easy resolution of the tension between individual and community, or between classes, races and nations is derived from a too optimistic view of human nature. This too generous estimate of human virtue is intimately related to an erroneous estimate of the dimensions of the human stature. The conception of human nature which underlies the social and political attitudes of a liberal democratic culture is that of an essentially harmless individual. The survival impulse, which man shares with the animals, is regarded as the normative form of his egoistic drive. If this were a true picture of the human situation man might be, or might become, as harmless as seventeenth- and eighteenth-century thought assumed. Unfortunately for the validity of this picture of man, the most significant distinction between the human and the animal world is that the impulses of the former are "spiritualized" in the human world. Human capacities for evil as well as for good are derived from this spiritualization. There is of course always a natural survival impulse at the core of all human ambition. But this survival impulse cannot be neatly disentangled from two forms of its spiritualization. The one form is the desire to fulfill the potentialities of life and not merely to maintain its existence. Man is the kind of animal who cannot merely live. If he lives at all he is bound to seek the realization of his true nature; and to his true nature belongs his fulfillment in the lives of others. The will to live is thus transmuted into the will to self-realization; and self-realization involves self-giving in relations to others. When this desire for self-realization is fully explored it becomes apparent that it is subject to the paradox that the highest form of self-realization is the consequence of self-giving, but that it cannot be the intended consequence without being prematurely limited. Thus the will to live is finally transmuted into its opposite in the sense that only in self-giving can the self be fulfilled, for: "He that findeth his life shall lose it: and he that loseth his life for my sake shall find it" (Matt. 10:39).

On the other hand the will-to-live is also spiritually transmuted into the will-to-power or into the desire for "power and glory." Man, being more than a natural creature, is not interested merely in physical survival but in prestige and social approval. Having the intelligence to anticipate the perils in which he stands in nature and history, he invariably seeks to gain security against these perils by enhancing his power, individually and collectively. Possessing a darkly unconscious sense of his insignificance in the total scheme of things, he seeks to compensate for his insignificance by pretensions of pride. The conflicts between men are thus never simple conflicts between competing survival impulses. They are conflicts in which each man or group seeks to guard its power and prestige against the peril of competing expressions of power and pride. Since the very possession of power and prestige always involves some encroachment upon the prestige and power of others, this conflict is by its very nature a more stubborn and difficult one than the mere competition between various survival impulses in nature. It remains to be added that this conflict expresses itself even more cruelly in collective than in individual terms. Human behaviour being less individualistic than secular liberalism assumed, the struggle between classes, races and other groups in human society is not as easily resolved by the expedient of dissolving the groups as liberal democratic idealists assumed.

Since the survival impulse in nature is transmuted into two different and contradictory spiritualized forms, which we may briefly designate as the will-to-live-truly and the will-to-power, man is at variance with himself. The power of the second impulse places him more fundamentally in conflict with his fellowman than democratic liberalism realizes. The fact he cannot realize himself, except in organic relation with his fellows, makes the community more important than bourgeois individualism understands. The fact that the two impulses, though standing in contradiction to each other, are also mixed and compounded with each other on every level of human life, makes the simple distinctions between good and evil, between selfishness and altruism, with which liberal idealism has tried to estimate moral and political facts, invalid. The fact that the will-to-power inevitably justifies itself in terms of the morally more acceptable will to realize man's true nature means that the egoistic corruption of universal ideals is a much more persistent fact in human conduct than any moralistic creed is inclined to admit.

If we survey any period of history, and not merely the present tragic era of world catastrophe, it becomes quite apparent that human ambitions, lusts and desires, are more inevitably inordinate, that both human creativity and human evil reach greater heights, and that conflicts in the community between varying conceptions of the good and between competing expressions of vitality are of more tragic proportions than was anticipated in the basic philosophy which underlies democratic civilization.

There is a specially ironic element in the effort of the seventeenth century to confine man to the limits of a harmless "nature" or to bring all his actions under the discipline of a cool prudence. For while democratic social philosophy was elaborating the picture of a harmless individual, moved by no more than a survival impulse, living in a social peace guaranteed by a pre-established harmony of nature, the advancing natural sciences were enabling man to harness the powers of nature, and to give his desires and ambitions a more limitless scope than they previously had. The static inequalities of an agrarian society were transmuted into the dynamic inequalities of an industrial age. The temptation to inordinate expressions of the possessive impulse, created by the new wealth of a technical civilization, stood in curious and ironic contradiction to the picture of essentially moderate and ordinate desires which underlay the social philosophy of the physiocrats and of Adam Smith. Furthermore a technical society developed new and more intensive forms of social cohesion and a greater centralization of economic process in defiance of the individualistic conception of social relations which informed the liberal philosophy.[3]

The demonic fury of fascist politics in which a collective will expresses boundless ambitions and imperial desires and in which the instruments of a technical civilization are used to arm this will with a destructive power, previously unknown in history, represents a melancholy historical refutation of the eighteenth- and nineteenth-century conceptions of a harmless and essentially individual human life. Human desires are expressed more collectively, are less under

3. Thus vast collective forms of "free enterprise," embodied in monopolistic and large-scale financial and industrial institutions, still rationalize their desire for freedom from political control in terms of a social philosophy which Adam Smith elaborated for individuals. Smith was highly critical of the budding large-scale enterprise of his day and thought it ought to be restricted to insurance companies and banks.

the discipline of prudent calculation, and are more the masters of, and less limited by, natural forces than the democratic creed had understood.

While the fury of fascist politics represents a particularly vivid refutation of the democratic view of human nature, the developments within the confines of democratic civilization itself offer almost as telling a refutation. The liberal creed is never an explicit instrument of the children of darkness. But it is surprising to what degree the forces of darkness are able to make covert use of the creed. One must therefore, in analyzing the liberal hope of a simple social and political harmony, be equally aware of the universalistic presuppositions which underlie the hope and of the egoistic corruptions (both individual and collective) which inevitably express themselves in our culture in terms of, and in despite of, the creed. One must understand that it is a creed of children of light; but also that it betrays their blindness to the forces of darkness.

In the social philosophy of Adam Smith there was both a religious guarantee of the preservation of community and a moral demand that the individual consider its claims. The religious guarantee was contained in Smith's secularized version of providence. Smith believed that when a man is guided by self-interest he is also "led by an invisible hand to promote an end which is not his intention."[4] This "invisible hand" is of course the power of a pre-established social harmony, conceived as a harmony of nature, which transmutes conflicts of self-interest into a vast scheme of mutual service.

Despite this determinism Smith does not hesitate to make moral demands upon men to sacrifice their interests to the wider interest. The universalistic presupposition which underlies Smith's thought is clearly indicated for instance in such an observation as this:

> The wise and virtuous man is at all times willing that his own private interests should be sacrificed to the public interest of his own particular order of society—that the interests of this order of society be sacrificed to the greater interest of the state. He should therefore be equally willing that all those inferior interests should be sacrificed to the greater interests of the universe, to the interests of that great society of all sensible and intelligent beings, of which God himself is the immediate administrator and director.[5]

4. *Wealth of Nations*, bk. 4, ch. 7.
5. Ibid., bk. 5, ch. 1, pt. 3.

It must be noted that in Smith's conception the "wider interest" does not stop at the boundary of the national state. His was a real universalism in intent. Laissez faire was intended to establish a world community as well as a natural harmony of interests within each nation. Smith clearly belongs to the children of light. But the children of darkness were able to make good use of his creed. A dogma which was intended to guarantee the economic freedom of the individual became the "ideology" of vast corporate structures of a later period of capitalism, used by them, and still used, to prevent a proper political control of their power. His vision of international harmony was transmuted into the sorry realities of an international capitalism which recognized neither moral scruples nor political restraints in expanding its power over the world. His vision of a democratic harmony of society, founded upon the free play of economic forces, was refuted by the tragic realities of the class conflicts in western society. Individual and collective egotism usually employed the political philosophy of this creed, but always defied the moral idealism which informed it.

The political theory of liberalism, as distinct from the economic theory, based its confidence in the identity of particular and universal interests, not so much upon the natural limits of egotism as upon either the capacity of reason to transmute egotism into a concern for the general welfare, or upon the ability of government to overcome the potential conflict of wills in society. But even when this confidence lies in reason or in government, the actual character of the egotism which must be restrained is frequently measured in the dimension of the natural impulse of survival only. Thus John Locke, who thinks government necessary in order to overcome the "inconvenience of the state of nature," sees self-interest in conflict with the general interest only on the low level where "self-preservation" stands in contrast to the interests of others. He therefore can express the sense of obligation to others in terms which assume no final conflict between egotism and the wider interest: "Everyone," he writes, "as he is bound to preserve himself and not to quit his station willfully, so by the like reason, when his own preservation comes not into competition, ought as much as he can preserve the rest of mankind."[6] This is obviously no creed of a moral cynic; but neither is it a

6. *Two Treatises of Government*, bk. 2, ch. 19, par. 221.

profound expression of the sense of universal obligation. For most of the gigantic conflicts of will in human history, whether between individuals or groups, take place on a level, where "self-preservation" is not immediately but only indirectly involved. They are conflicts of rival lusts and ambitions.

The general confidence of an identity between self-interest and the commonweal, which underlies liberal deomcratic political theory, is succinctly expressed in Thomas Paine's simple creed: "Public good is not a term opposed to the good of the individual; on the contrary it is the good of every individual collected. It is the good of all, because it is the good of every one; for as the public body is every individual collected, so the public good is the collected good of those individuals."[7]

While there is a sense in which this identity between a particular and the general interest is ultimately true, it is never absolutely true in an immediate situation; and such identity as could be validly claimed in an immediate situation is not usually recognized by the proponents of particular interest.[8] Human intelligence is never as pure an instrument of the universal perspective as the liberal democratic theory assumes, though neither is it as purely the instrument of the ego, as is assumed by the anti-democratic theory, derived from the pessimism of such men as Thomas Hobbes and Martin Luther.

The most naïve form of the democratic faith in an identity between the individual and the general interest is developed by the utilitarians of the eighteenth and nineteenth centuries. Their theory manages to extract a covertly expressed sense of obligation toward the "greatest

7. *Dissertations on Government, The Affairs of the Bank, and Paper-Money* (1786).

8. The peril of inflation which faces nations in war-time is a case in point. Each group seeks to secure a larger income, and if all groups succeeded, the gap between increased income and limited consumer goods available to satisfy consumer demand would be widened to the point at which all groups would suffer from higher prices. But this does not deter shortsighted groups from seeking special advantages which threaten the commonweal. Nor would such special advantage threaten the welfare of the whole, if it could be confined to a single group which desires the advantage. The problem is further complicated by the fact that an inflationary peril never develops in a "just" social situation. Some groups therefore have a moral right to demand that their share of the common social fund be increased before the total situation is "frozen." But who is to determine just how much "injustice" can be redressed by a better distribution of the common fund in war-time, before the procedure threatens the whole community?

good of the greatest number" from a hedonistic analysis of morals which really lacks all logical presuppositions for any idea of obligation, and which cannot logically rise above an egoistic view of life. This utilitarianism therefore expresses the stupidity of the children of light in its most vivid form. Traditional moralists may point to any hedonistic doctrine as the creed of the children of darkness, because it has no real escape from egotism. But since it thinks it has, it illustrates the stupidity of the children of light, rather than the malice of the children of darkness. It must be observed of course that the children of darkness are well able to make use of such a creed. Utilitarianism's conception of the wise egotist, who in his prudence manages to serve interests wider than his own, supported exactly the same kind of political philosophy as Adam Smith's conception of the harmless egotist, who did not even have to be wise, since the providential laws of nature held his egotism in check. So Jeremy Bentham's influence was added to that of Adam Smith in support of a laissez-faire political philosophy; and this philosophy encouraged an unrestrained expression of human greed at the precise moment in history when an advancing industrialism required more, rather than less, moral and political restraint upon economic forces.

It must be added that, whenever the democratic idealists were challenged to explain the contrast between the actual behaviour of men and their conception of it, they had recourse to the evolutionary hope; and declared with William Godwin, that human history is moving toward a form of rationality which will finally achieve a perfect identity of self-interest and the public good.[9]

Perhaps the most remarkable proof of the power of this optimistic creed, which underlies democratic thought, is that Marxism, which is ostensibly a revolt against it, manages to express the same optimism in another form. While liberal democrats dreamed of a simple social harmony, to be achieved by a cool prudence and a calculating egotism, the actual facts of social history revealed that the static class struggle of agrarian societies had been fanned into the flames of a dynamic struggle. Marxism was the social creed and the social cry of those classes who knew by their miseries that the creed of the liberal optimists was a snare and a delusion. Marxism insisted that the increasingly overt social conflict in democratic society would have to

9. William Godwin, *Political Justice*, bk. 8, ch. 9.

become even more overt, and would finally be fought to a bitter conclusion.

But Marxism was also convinced that after the triumph of the lower classes of society, a new society would emerge in which exactly that kind of harmony between all social forces would be established, which Adam Smith had regarded as a possibility for any kind of society. The similarities between classical laissez-faire theory and the vision of an anarchistic millennium in Marxism are significant, whatever may be the superficial differences. Thus the provisionally cynical Lenin, who can trace all the complexities of social conflict in contemporary society with penetrating shrewdness, can also express the utopian hope that the revolution will usher in a period of history which will culminate in the Marxist millennium of anarchism. "All need for force will vanish," declared Lenin, "since people will grow accustomed to observing the elementary conditions of social existence without force and without subjection."[10]

The Roman Catholic polemic against Marxism is no more valid than its strictures against democratic liberalism. The charge that this is a creed of moral cynicism cannot be justified. However strong the dose of provisional cynicism, which the creed may contain, it is a sentimental and not a cynical creed. The Marxists, too, are children of light. Their provisional cynicism does not even save them from the usual stupidity, nor from the fate, of other stupid children of light. That fate is to have their creed become the vehicle and instrument of the children of darkness. A new oligarchy is arising in Russia, the spiritual characteristics of which can hardly be distinguished from those of the American "go-getters" of the latter nineteenth and early twentieth centuries. And in the light of history Stalin will probably have the same relation to the early dreamers of the Marxist dreams which Napoleon has to the liberal dreamers of the eighteenth century.

TENSION BETWEEN NATIONAL AND INTERNATIONAL COMMUNITIES

Democratic theory, whether in its liberal or in its more radical form, is just as stupid in analyzing the relation between the national and

10. Lenin, *Toward the Seizure of Power*, 2:214.

the international community as in seeking a too simple harmony between the individual and the national community. Here, too, modern liberal culture exhibits few traces of moral cynicism. The morally autonomous modern national state does indeed arise; and it acknowledges no law beyond its interests. The actual behaviour of the nations is cynical. But the creed of liberal civilization is sentimental. This is true not only of the theorists whose creed was used by the architects of economic imperialism and of the more covert forms of national egotism in the international community, but also of those whose theories were appropriated by the proponents of an explicit national egotism. A straight line runs from Mazzini to Mussolini in the history of Italian nationalism. Yet there was not a touch of moral cynicism in the thought of Mazzini. He was, on the contrary, a pure universalist.[11]

Even the philosophy of German romanticism, which has been accused with some justification of making specific contributions to the creed of German Nazism, reveals the stupidity of the children of light much more than the malice of the children of darkness. There is of course a strong note of moral nihilism in the final fruit of this romantic movement as we have it in Nietzsche; though even Nietzsche was no nationalist. But the earlier romantics usually express the same combination of individualism and universalism which characterizes the theory of the more naturalistic and rationalistic democrats of the Western countries. Fichte resolved the conflict between the individual and the community through the instrumentality of the "just law" almost as easily as the utilitarians resolved it by the calculations of the prudent egotist and as easily as Rousseau resolved it by his conception of a "general will," which would fulfill the best purposes of each individual will. This was no creed of a community, making itself the idolatrous end of human existence. The theory was

---

11. "Your first duty," wrote Mazzini, "first as regards importance, is toward humanity. You are men before you are citizens and fathers. If you do not embrace the whole human family in your affections, if you do not bear witness to the unity of that family, if you are not ready, if able, to aid the unhappy,—you violate your law of life and you comprehend not that religion which will be the guide and blessing of the future."

Mazzini held kings responsible for national egotism: "The first priests of the fatal worship [of self-interest] were the kings, princes and evil governments. They invented the horrible formula: every one for himself. They knew that they would thus create egoism and that between the egoist and the slave there is but one step" (*The Duties of Man*, ch. 12).

actually truer than the more individualistic and naturalistic forms of the democratic creed; for romanticism understood that the individual requires the community for his fulfillment. Thus even Hegel, who is sometimes regarded as the father of state absolutism in modern culture, thought of the national state as providing "for the reasonable will, insofar as it is in the individual only implicitly the universal will coming to a consciousness and an understanding of itself and being found."[12]

This was not the creed of a collective egotism which negated the right of the individual. Rather it was a theory which, unlike the more purely democratic creed, understood the necessity of social fulfillment for the individual, and which, in common with the more liberal theories, regarded this as a much too simple process.

If the theory was not directed toward the annihilation of the individual, as is the creed of modern religious nationalism, to what degree was it directed against the universal community? Was it an expression of the national community's defiance of any interest or law above and beyond itself? This also is not the case. Herder believed that "fatherlands" might "lie peaceably side by side and aid each other as families. It is the grossest barbarity of human speech to speak of fatherlands in bloody battle with each other." Unfortunately this is something more than a barbarity of speech. Herder was a universalist, who thought a nice harmony between various communities could be achieved if only the right would be granted to each to express itself according to its unique and peculiar genius. He thought the false universalism of imperialism, according to which one community makes itself the standard and the governor of others, was merely the consequence of a false philosophy, whereas it is in fact one of the perennial corruptions of man's collective life.

Fichte, too, was a universalist who was fully conscious of moral obligations which transcend the national community. His difficulty, like that of all the children of light, was that he had a too easy resolution of the conflict between the nation and the community of nations. He thought that philosophy, particularly German philosophy, could achieve a synthesis between national and universal interest. "The patriot," he declared, "wishes the purpose of mankind to be reached first of all in that nation of which he is a member. . . . This

12. *Philosophy of Mind,* sec. 2, par. 539.

purpose is the only possible patriotic goal. . . . Cosmopolitanism is the will that the purpose of life and of man be attained in all mankind, Patriotism is the will that this purpose be attained first of all in that nation of which we are members."[13] It is absurd to regard such doctrine as the dogma of national egotism, though Fichte could not express it without insinuating a certain degree of national pride into it. The pride took the form of the complacent assumption that German philosophy enabled the German nation to achieve a more perfect relation to the community of mankind than any other nation. He was, in other words, one of the many stupid children of light, who failed to understand the difficulty of the problem which he was considering; and his blindness included failure to see the significance of the implicit denial of an ideal in the thought and action of the very idealist who propounds it.

Hegel, too, belongs to the children of light. To be sure he saw little possibility of constructing a legal structure of universal proportions which might guard the interests of the universal community and place a check upon the will of nations. He declared "states find themselves in a natural, more than a legal, relation to each other. Therefore there is a continuous struggle between them. . . . They maintain and procure their rights through their own power and must as a matter of necessity plunge into war."[14] It may be observed in passing that this is a more accurate description of the actual realities of international relations than that of any of the theorists thus far considered. But the question is whether Hegel regarded this actual situation as morally normative. Hegel's thought upon this matter was ambiguous. On the one hand he tended to regard the demands of the state as final because he saw no way of achieving a legal or political implementation of the inchoate community which lies beyond the state. But on the other hand he believed that a more ultimate law stood over the nation, that it "had its real content in *Weltgeschichte,* the realm of the world mind which holds the supreme absolute truth."[15] This mind, he believed, "constitutes itself the absolute judge over states." The nation is thus politically, but not morally, autonomous. This is no doctrine of moral cynicism. Rather it is a

13. "Patriotische Dialoge," in *Nachgelassene Werke,* 3:226.
14. *Sämtliche Werke,* 3:74.
15. *Philosophy of Right,* par. 33.

sentimental doctrine. Hegel imagined that the nation, free of political but not of moral inhibitions, could nevertheless, by thinking "in *Weltgeschichte*" (that is, by becoming fully conscious of its relation to mankind), thereby "lay hold of its concrete universality."[16]

The error is very similar to that of Fichte and of all the universalists, whether naturalistic or idealistic, positivist or romantic. It is the error of a too great reliance upon the human capacity for transcendence over self-interest. There is indeed such a capacity. If there were not, any form of social harmony among men would be impossible; and certainly a democratic version of such harmony would be quite unthinkable. But the same man who displays this capacity also reveals varying degrees of the power of self-interest and of the subservience of the mind to these interests. Sometimes this egotism stands in frank contradiction to the professed ideal or sense of obligation to higher and wider values; and sometimes it uses the ideal as its instrument.

It is this fact which a few pessimists in our modern culture have realized, only to draw undemocratic and sometimes completely cynical conclusions from it. The democratic idealists of practically all schools of thought have managed to remain remarkably oblivious to the obvious facts. Democratic theory therefore has not squared with the facts of history. This grave defect in democratic theory was comparatively innocuous in the heyday of the bourgeois period, when the youth and the power of democratic civilization surmounted all errors of judgment and confusions of mind. But in this latter day, when it has become important to save what is valuable in democratic life from the destruction of what is false in bourgeois civilization, it has also become necessary to distinguish what is false in democratic theory from what is true in democratic life.

The preservation of a democratic civilization requires the wisdom of the serpent and the harmlessness of the dove. The children of light must be armed with the wisdom of the children of darkness but remain free from their malice. They must know the power of self-interest in human society without giving it moral justification. They must have this wisdom in order that they may beguile, deflect, harness and restrain self-interest, individual and collective, for the sake of the community.

16. *Philosophy of Mind*, sec. 2, par. 552.

13

THE RELATIONS OF CHRISTIANS AND JEWS IN WESTERN CIVILIZATION

The long and tragic history of the relations of the Christian majority to the Jewish minority in Western Christian civilization should prompt more humility and self-examination among Christians than is their wont. Whether we judge these relations in terms of the terrible excesses of the counter-reformation in Spain or the Nazi terror; or in terms of the normal intolerance of an authoritarian Catholicism of medieval Europe with its Jewish ghettos; or in terms of the frustrated zeal of Protestant pietism, which cannot understand the stubbornness of the Jew in resisting conversion; or in terms of the residual anti-semitism of the most liberal societies, we have conclusive evidence that the Christian faith has not had enough grace to extend genuine community to the Jew, despite the fact (or possibly because of the fact) that the two religions have a common bible and a common historical approach to the ultimate.

The Jews are probably in error in attributing the sad state of affairs to specifically Christian deficiencies; for this history simply proves the perpetual pride of any majority dealing with any minority. But the Christians are certainly too complacent about the failure of their allegedly superior universal faith to inculcate a charity which transcends the religious community. The well-known universalism of Paul, that in Christ "there is neither Jew nor Greek, there is neither slave nor free" (Gal. 3.28), does not help in the problem of the relation of two religious communities to each other.

ETHNIC AND RELIGIOUS DIVERGENCES

There has been considerable debate among both Christians and Jews whether anti-semitism is prompted chiefly by religious or by ethnic prejudices. These debates have been on the whole uninteresting because it is so obvious that the prejudice against the Jew arises from the fact that he is *both* ethnically and religiously peculiar and stubbornly resists assimilation, *both* ethnically and religiously.

It is this two-fold divergence from dominant type which is the Jews' chief offence in the eyes of the majority. Jews ought to admit that we are dealing with a human problem rather than a peculiarly Christian problem. For they could not have preserved their integrity as a people throughout the centuries without enforcing their endogamous rules through the sense of their own superiority. In cases of intermarriage, the opposition from Jewish parents has usually been as persistent as, if not even more stubborn than, that of the Christian parents. We are dealing with the problem of the moral capacity of collective man; and we find that the survival impulse in both minority and majority is bound to make use of all spiritual factors available to it. We cannot live and survive collectively without using group prides as instruments of survival.

In the case of our own nation, which prides itself on being a melting pot assimilating all ethnic groups, there is no question of the survival impulse of the Aryan majority. It refuses to assimilate the Negro because it has the sense of the survival of a pure white majority and fears intermarriage with an ethnic group which diverges so obviously from type. But in the case of the Jew it resents his refusal to be assimilated and fails to understand the peculiar problems of a peculiar people who have miraculously survived for two thousand years without a homeland, living under the hazards of the diaspora in many nations and cultures.

The problem of the Christian majority, particularly in America, is therefore to come to terms with the stubborn will to live of the Jews as a peculiar people, both religiously and ethnically. The problem can be solved only if the Christian and Gentile majority accepts this fact and ceases to practice tolerance provisionally, in the hope that it will encourage assimilation ethnically and conversion religiously.

Such provisional tolerance always produces violent reactions when ultimately disappointed, as in the case of Luther, who thought that the Jews had refused to become Catholic but would undoubtedly accept the purer Protestant version of the Christian faith. The Christian majority can achieve a more genuine tolerance only if it assumes the continued refusal of the Jew to be assimilated, either ethnically or religiously. That recognition involves an appreciation of the resources of Jewish life, morally and religiously, which make Judaism something other than an inferior form of religion such as must ultimately recognize the superiority of the Christian faith; and end its long resistance by capitulation and conversion.

THE MEDIEVAL STEREOTYPE OF DISHONESTY

We must consider the task of achieving this kind of toleration in both the moral and the religious spheres. In the moral sphere, the Christian majority is bound to re-examine its presuppositions, which either encourage or fail to discourage the widespread conviction that Jews tend to be sharp to the point of dishonesty in business; and which fail to note that the Jews have in fact a superior capacity for civic virtue which the Gentile majority rather flagrantly overlooks.

In regard to the charge of dishonesty, a part of the difficulty no doubt derives from the old hazard of collective relations. That hazard is that a dubious action in our own group is not regarded as typical but unique, while the same action by an individual of another group is regarded as typical. Thus, when a very prominent Christian banker was sent to Sing Sing on a serious charge several years ago, no one declared that his defalcation was typical of Christian bankers. A similar offence by a Jewish banker would have invariably become the base for a false syllogism.

But more specific historical sources have contributed to this prejudice about the character of Jewish business life. The sources have their origin in medieval Europe. The Jews were excluded from the professions and the ownership of land. Therefore, only trade was open to them as a means of livelihood. Moreover, they were forced into the profession of banking by a curious irony of legalism. For the prohibition of usury, originally derived from the Old Testament, was enforced upon Christians; but it did not bind the Jews because the prohibition was confined to the Jewish community. The Jews consequently became the money-lenders of the medieval economy and earned the disrespect both of the landed aristocrat and of the lower non-commercial classes. Salo Baron points out that Jewish business men in the Middle Ages frequently achieved a high social status, just below the aristocracy. But the social status could not prevent the prejudice against them, particularly since their success in banking and commerce seemed to validate the charge of dishonesty to non-commercial classes. For since Aristotle, both classical antiquity and medieval Christianity had a prejudice against the "huckster."

The medieval prejudice had a very stubborn life. It was transferred to America by the populist movement, which found the very non-medieval farmer just as prejudiced against the money-lender and trader as the medieval peasant. Thus a very powerful stereotype was generated which outlasted medieval culture and has served as the instrument of the sense of moral superiority of the majority group even in liberal cultures in which Jews gradually acquired political rights. In non-liberal or traditional cultures such as those of Poland and Russia, this prejudice was maintained despite the fact that the ghettos developed an impressively unworldly and unprudential spirituality, in comparison with which Gentile behavior would seem flagrantly worldly and prudential.

As illustrating the power of stereotypes, may I be autobiographical and report an experience of my youth? In the Middle-Western town where I spent my childhood there were two prominent Jews. One was a clothing merchant, respected by everyone and deserving of respect. He was public-spirited, honest and generous, and his approach to his fellow men had something of the old-world courtliness in it. Everybody said how nice he was, and wasn't it remarkable that he was not at all typically Jewish? Not knowing many Jews we did not know in what sense he was atypical or unique. He simply did not conform to the stereotype. The other Jew was a very successful business man who began life as a peddler. He had phenomenal success, and that success was assumed to prove his dishonesty, even though there was no evidence of dishonesty anywhere in his record. But he was inclined to display his wealth and to obscure as much as possible his lowly origin. All these human frailties made him in the mind of our community a "typical" Jew rather than a unique one.

THE JEWISH CAPACITY FOR CIVIC VIRTUE

But the unfavorable judgement upon the business ethics of the Jews, made by most Gentiles, is not as prejudiced as the inability of the Christian community to give the Jew credit for his undoubted capacity for civic virtue which equals, and frequently exceeds, that of the Christian community. My first personal acquaintance with this capacity was occasioned by my experience as a young pastor in Detroit, where I served as the chairman of the Mayor's commission on race and had as my vice-chairman a Jewish lawyer, who combined a sophisticated knowledge of human nature with a broad charity. He was realistic almost to the point of cynicism, yet his realism did not tempt to cynicism. Rather it generated both charity and the spirit of justice in him. If one claims that the Jewish capacity for civic virtue frequently excels that of Christians, the claim rests upon the Jewish capacity for critical devotion to the community which frequently excels the more traditional loyalties of the Gentile community and the typical benevolent goodness of the Christian business man. My judgements may be colored by years of political activity, left of center. Whether the problem was one of challenging a nationalist isolationism or of amending the traditional libertarian attitudes of the business community, Jewish men of wealth were more emancipated from the prejudice of their class than Christian business men. They were more discriminate in their judgements of social policy. They were usually also more generous in the support of communal projects which transcended the loyalties of a particular group.

Two possible causes for this capacity for civic virtue might be given. The one reaches deeply into the past and the other is very contemporary.

(1) The cause deriving from the past may well be what has been defined as the "prophetic" passion for justice. The prophets of Israel did not define justice as neatly as Aristotle did. But they defined it more relevantly. For according to the prophets of Israel, the justice of God was critical of the elders, the judges and the princes because they "turned aside the needy at the gates," because "the spoil of the poor was in their houses"; because they "sold the needy for a pair of shoes"; in short, the prophetic analysis of the problems of the community was the beginning of the realism which knew that power was never completely in the service of justice. Therefore, the powerful would be judged more severely than the poor. Justice was not equal justice but a bias in favor of the poor. Justice always leaned toward mercy for the widows and the orphans. The prophetic sense of justice was, in short, relevant to the perennial problems of the human community, where power is needed to establish order but always exacts too high a price in justice for its services.

If the prophetic sense of justice was more existential than the speculations of Greek philosophers, it may also be true that it was more relevant to the problems of the community than the Christian ideal of love. This may be true despite the fact that the prophets drew no sharp distinction between love and justice and that the double love commandment of Jesus was drawn from Old Testament sources. But the Christian idea of love, being drawn from the example of Jesus' sacrifice, is usually interpreted in terms of such selflessness that it has application purely to individual and not to collective situations. In collective situations, justice is achieved by an equilibrium of power, by a balance of social forces; and Christian idealism has had difficulty in incorporating the discriminations necessary for the achievement of such equilibria into its systems of thought. Both Protestant liberalism with its undue optimism about the moral capacities of men, and Lutheran conservatism, with its undue pessimism about collective possibilities of justice, have failed to solve this problem. Ironically enough, the most profound elaboration of the biblical love doctrine has been made by a contemporary Jewish philosopher, Martin Buber; but he unfortunately exhibits the same difficulties in coming to terms with the ethics of all collective and institutional relations as Protestant doctrine. Thus, Emil Brunner drew upon the thought of Buber in order to establish a typically Lutheran distinction between love and justice, which made love into the moral norm for purely personal and intimate relations. But in this sphere Buber is not typically Jewish. The social ethic of Christianity has always been troubled by the fact that it is difficult to derive a social ethic from the *agape* concept of the gospels. A social ethic demands not unprudential heedlessness but discriminate judgements. From Bernard of Clairvaux to the modern Christian philanthropist, it has been difficult for Christian thought to avoid the danger of making almsgiving or philanthropy into a substitute for discriminate justice.

Perhaps it is necessary to add that a religious ethic, whether Jewish or Christian, has some difficulties with the discriminations which justice requires. This is why a certain amount of secularism was necessary before these problems of justice in a complex technical society could be solved. The more discrimination becomes necessary in the adjudication of rights and interests the less can the original religio-ethical impulse be counted on to establish a brotherly justice. For justice is at once the servant of love and an approximation to love under institutional conditions. The superiority of the Jew's sense of justice may be derived from the fact that his norms were elaborated in a communal situation, while the Christian norms transcend all communities. Ideally a new community, the church, was built to incarnate them. But the community beyond the church has remained an enigma to the Christian conscience.

(2) It would be unfair however to attribute the superiority, if any, of the Jew, to these ancient sources, when more contemporary sources are more obvious. The Jewish superiority in civic virtue, if any, rests, according to the testimony of many objective observers, primarily upon their status as a minority group. They have the same superiority as other minority groups, including women. They may be loyal Americans or citizens of other nations, but they stand slightly on the outside, as a minority, and the critical detachment of their status gives them a resource which saves them from their traditionalism in accepting the standards of their community. That is why they stand slightly left of center in any political spectrum.

That is also why the Jews have been so helpful to the Negroes in achieving the status of equal citizenship in a national community in which the Jew was regarded with suspicion for being too smart and the Negro with condescension as being not smart enough for the American amalgam. The benefactions of the Jewish philanthropist, Julius Rosenwald, in favor of Negro education may be regarded as symbols of this peculiar affinity between two minorities in the national community. The more competent minority felt a kinship with the less competent minority.

In explaining the "liberal" tendencies of Jewish business men in the days of the "New Deal" a Jewish business man explained, "We Jews have a more insistent interest in the health of our society because we know that if the society becomes sick it may become hysterical; and as a minority we do not feel safe in any hysterical society." The sickness in Germany gave point to this observation about the Jew's stake in the health of any community.

A SHARED MONOTHEISM AND VIEW OF HISTORY

An analysis of the prejudices and misconceptions as between the two religions in the moral and political sphere may be in accord with the principle of applying the ultimate test: "By their fruits shall ye know them." But it can only be preliminary to a consideration of the relation of the two biblical faiths, with a view to achieving more charity and understanding between them. The misunderstandings are a scandal not only because the two faiths have a common bible, but because they share the spiritual guidance of Western democracy, more particularly in our own nation. Professor Arnold Toynbee has devoted his Gifford Lectures to the problem of religious toleration. But in that book he illustrates the complexity of our problem. For his primary purpose is to achieve more understanding between Christianity and Mahayana Buddhism. Yet he consistently misinterprets the Jewish faith and culture and exhibits facets of prejudice which make understanding more difficult between two faiths which share a common bible and a common Western civilization. We are not dealing with the problems of world community only, but with our own national community when we strive for a better understanding between Jew and Christian.

It is a commonplace to emphasize the common rigorous monotheism when we seek to enumerate the affinities between the two religions. We would give a more adequate description of the affinities and be introduced to the hazards of the relation between the two religions if we emphasized that the two faiths share not only a common monotheism but a common attitude toward history, toward historic responsibilities and toward our relation to the creator God as a sovereign of history.

This common historical attitude contains one of our deepest perplexities, because both religions accept a particular event in history as the ultimate disclosure of the eternal mystery for us; yet they accept by faith different revelatory events. Both faiths ought probably to admit more readily that their attitude toward historic revelation, which is accepted by faith and cannot be compelled by reason or achieved by mystic experience, contains both the secret of their creativity on the historical scene and the offense both to the Greeks and to modern culture, which tries in its various scientific and philosophic pursuits to reduce the mystery of the divine to rational intelligibility; and in the process it inevitably obscures the depth of the divine mystery and makes the world processes self-explanatory and self-fulfilling.

But both faiths derive not only their ethical creativity and their life-affirming impulse from the acceptance in faith of an historical revelation. They also derive the perils of religious caprice and obscurantism from this reliance on historic revelation. How is the claim to be validated, in the one case that Israel is the chosen people of God, and in the other case that "God was in Christ reconciling the world unto himself"? Professor Toynbee heedlessly derives all religious fanaticism from the Jewish adventure of faith, but does not recognize that the second covenant under which Christians live is just as fruitful of fanatic claims as the first. Both covenants assume that an historic fact is more than a mere fact; it is a disclosure of the mystery which bares history. In both cases, a community of believers is organized on the basis of faith's apprehension of the revelatory depth of the fact. In both cases, the burden of proof is on the covenant community that this exclusively apprehended revelation does not imply an exclusive God; but that we have actually to do with the mysterious creator of the universe and the sovereign of history. In both cases, the only proof of the affirmation of faith must be "witness," the witness of life, which is oriented not to some private and peculiar God, but to the divine sovereign who is equally rigorous in his demands upon believers and upon unbelievers and offers no special security to the elect. Whether or not the believer is subject to this God and responds to him in faithfulness and repentance, in gratitude and hope, can only be proved by the quality of a life. Both covenant faiths must bear witness to their revelation. Both faiths are in danger of neglecting the scientific and metaphysical tests for universal validity, which, incidentally, may eliminate caprice but are always in danger of annulling both the mystery of man, who transcends the coherences of nature and reason; and the mystery of history, which is a realm of both divine and human freedom.

THREE BASIC DIFFERENCES

Thus we see that provisionally both faiths exhibit the same resources and are exposed to the same hazards. They are very similar but also very different. Can we deal with these differences in terms which will enhance understanding and not create misunderstanding? Let us begin, both Christian and Jew, by admitting that the commitment of faith does not permit a completely objective view. The presuppositions on the basis of which we reason, determine the reasoning not only of those who are explicitly religious but of all secular faiths. We who are committed to an historic faith are usually regarded as arbitrary by scientists and philosophers. But these, though having no explicit faith, have their own implicit presuppositions. We cannot climb over our presuppositions but we need not be their prisoners. If we were absolutely prisoners there would be no solution for the problem of fanaticism.

Judaism and Christianity are two covenant faiths, in which a community of believers propagates the shared faith and seeks to bear witness to its validity even to those who do not share it. But the covenants and the faiths are different. Let us try as objectively as possible to analyze these differences. The differences may conveniently be studied in three categories: (1) the problem of Messianism, (2) the problem of grace and law, and (3) the problem of particularity and universality.

(1) The most obvious difference between the two faiths was stated succinctly by Martin Buber. He declared: "To the Christian the Jew is the incomprehensibly obdurate man, who declines to see what has happened: and to the Jew the Christian is the incomprehensibly daring man, who affirms in an unredeemed world that its redemption has been accomplished."[1] This difference would remain, even if we eliminated from the Christian record those passages in the Johannine gospel in which the opposition is stylized and stereotyped in the phrase "the Jews," a phrase which undoubtedly obscures the fact that in the founding of the new covenant community there were Jews in both the opposition and the new community of believers. Incidentally, those Jews are probably in error who would eliminate prejudice by emphasizing that it was the Romans who killed Jesus. For that emphasis would not obscure the fact that we are dealing with a religious drama in the Jewish community. Nothing of this kind will obscure the fact that the Christian community accepted a crucified prophet, who may or may not have been informed by a Messianic consciousness, and regarded the whole drama of his life, death and resurrection (about which as a public historic event there is incidentally some question) as the fulfillment of Messianic prophecy.

We need not take too seriously the charge of Toynbee that the Jews in rejecting Jesus turned their back on the insights of their own prophetic heritage. Jesus was obviously not the Messiah whom the Jews expected. Even if the Messianic claims of the church had not been

1. *Israel and the World*, 40.

elaborated in terms of Greek metaphysics and finally defined in the Nicene Creed, the idea of Jesus as the final revelation of the divine would have been unacceptable to normative Judaism. It would have seemed to violate their rigorous monotheism even without the explicit trinitarian formula of the creeds. The offence lay primarily in the crucified rather than in the triumphant Messiah; and in the assertion that in the drama of his crucifixion, we have a revelation of the divine mercy in which God takes the sins of the world upon himself. This affirmation is freely confessed by Paul as being "to the Jews a stumbling-block" (1 Cor. 1:23). It does not follow with logical necessity from anything predicted in Messianic hopes, though the Christian community (rightly I believe) saw it as a fulfillment of the quasi-Messianic conception in the Second Isaiah of the "suffering servant." If it was actually Israel which the Second Isaiah envisaged in the concept, the appropriation by the church will be the more offensive to the Jew, while being plausible to Christians on the ground that no people, but only a single individual, could possibly correspond to the conception of the suffering servant.

But the heart of the Messianic issue between Judaism and Christianity is in the observation of Buber: "To the Jew the Christian is the incomprehensibly daring man, who affirms in an unredeemed world that its redemption has been accomplished." This indeed is the truth, because the Christological center of the Christian faith lies in the assertion that God has been finally and definitely revealed in the Christ drama, and that the burden of that revelation is the divine mercy and forgiveness, which completes what human striving can never complete, since all human efforts and all historic achievements remain ambiguous to the end of history.

The idea of the second coming of the Son of Man at the end of history in the New Testament places the two faiths in somewhat similar positions with regard to the character of the historical process, though the emphasis on the Anti-Christ at the end of history in the New Testament reinforces the idea that history will never solve the problem of history, since the contradictions will be heightened rather than diminished. The real difference in Messianism in the two faiths is the idea in the New Testament that the meaning of life in history and the relation of history to its divine ground have been fully revealed in Christ, though the meaning will not be fulfilled till the end of history.

From the Christian standpoint, this means a radical rejection of utopianism, and with it the hope of the Kingdom of God on earth. From the Jewish standpoint, it may mean a relaxation of the ethical tension in history. Buber in his *Paths to Utopia* shows that utopianism is in principle more at home in Jewish than in Christian thought, though the sectarian utopians of Cromwellian England show that there must always be in Christian thought a place for the prayer "Thy kingdom come, thy will be done on earth as it is in heaven."

On the other hand, even the earliest forms of Hebraic Messianism, that of the First Isaiah for instance, had guards against utopianism because they did not expect the Kingdom of God except in a transfigured nature-history. The difference is one of emphasis and there is no radical contrast.

The difference in the answer to the problem of history corresponds to the difference in the diagnosis of the human situation. Some Jews have made much of the Christian pessimism implied in the doctrine of "original sin" and have contrasted Jewish optimism with this pessimism. But the weight of evidence is that there is not very much difference between the doctrine of the *yetzer hara* and that of original sin. Jesus, incidentally, held the Jewish doctrine of the *yetzer*, and only Paul propounded the doctrine of original sin, relying on the story of the fall, which, after being recorded in Genesis, had remarkably little currency in Jewish thought until later apocalyptic writings, from which Paul undoubtedly derived it. In short, there are differences in emphasis in both the diagnoses of the human situation and the religious assurances corresponding to the diagnoses. But there is no simple contrast.

(2) The second main issue between Christianity and Judaism concerns the nature of law and the relation of grace to law. As to the former, it is usually assumed by Christians that the law, roughly equated with the decalogue, gives the minimal and negative requirements of righteousness to which the New Testament added the positive norm of love, particularly that reckless love which is characteristic of the Sermon on the Mount. This is the burden of the series of sayings: "It has been said to you of old, but I say unto you . . ." (cf. Matt. 5:21–48).

Actually, the contrast is not as absolute as Christians suppose. For the love commandment is taken from the Old Testament, and the

Rabbis have taught consistently that love is the fulfillment of the law. The Jew when dealing with the problem of moral norms may well question whether the absolute requirements of the Sermon, involving non-resistance and sacrificial love, are guides to ordinary conduct.

Shirley Jackson Case, representing the desperate effort of liberal Protestantism to relate this reckless ethic to the ordinary prudence of a social ethic, came to the conclusion that it grew out of the simplicities of a pastoral economy and that we would have to adjust it to the complexities of an industrial civilization. Karl Barth was certainly nearer to the truth when he defined the ethic as "eschatological" and declared that it was directly relevant to no historic or social situation at all. "Eschatological" may be the wrong word for the definition of the ethic. C. H. Dodd, in *Gospel and Law*, observes that the ethical requirements of the sermon are not eschatological, because the demands to turn the other cheek and go a second mile are not meant for an ideal situation. They are meant for the world in which we encounter evil men. The requirements, declares Dodd, give us the direction in which ethical conduct must move. They define, in short, the ethics in the nth degree. Windisch, in his *Sermon on the Mount*, enumerates many of the teachings of the more rigorous Rabbis which fall into the same category. He suggests, in fact, that Matthew had an ideological interest in establishing Jesus as a new lawgiver who was more rigorous than any of the Jewish interpreters of the law. This tendency is partly responsible for the absolute prohibition of divorce, in contrast to Moses, who allowed divorce "for the hardness of your hearts."

The Christian Church, particularly Catholicism, has involved itself in many absurdities by this rigorous form of legalism. Let us assume that Christianity raises the moral pinnacle more consistently than Judaism. But let us also admit that there is a tendency in both faiths to climb the moral pinnacle to the ultimate degree. And let us further observe that such a rigorous ethic complicates the problem of a social ethic which must incorporate prudence and a rational adjudication of competing rights. The perennial problem of pacifism in Christianity and also in Judaism, and the wider problem of sectarian rigorism and ascetic withdrawal, common to both religions but more pronounced in Christianity, prove that it is not possible to survey the moral possibilities of the individual to the nth degree without sacrificing some responsibilities for the order and justice of the community. It will come as a shock to many Christians that the demand of Jesus "Be ye therefore perfect, even as your Father in heaven is perfect" (Matt. 5:48) has been a source of much moral confusion, of more confusion than the Old Testament demand, "Be ye therefore holy as I am holy" (Lev. 11:44). Some of this confusion can be eliminated if Professor Torrey is correct in his surmise that the actual Aramaic words of Jesus, which were rendered by the Greek "perfection," were "Let your love therefore be all-inclusive as God's love includes all." This would make the demand a part of the consistent love-universalism of Jesus. It is still a part of the ethics in the nth degree, but its emphasis is horizontal and historical rather than vertical and otherworldly. It is therefore more relevant to the problem of communal justice than "perfection," which is usually interpreted in terms of inner purity of motive.

In regard to the law, we therefore arrive at the provisional conclusion that the main outline of the law, as embodied in the decalogue, is accepted by Christians as valid; that the idea of love as the fulfillment of the law is more explicitly stated in the New Testament; but that the heightening of the *agape* norm until it reaches sacrificial and forgiving love is elaborated in the New Testament so that it explores the final ethical possibilities of the individual, but probably to the embarrassment of an adequate social ethic. Here there are differences but no contrasts.

But the real problem arises in regard to the *halakah*, the details of Jewish legalism, including dietary and sabbath laws, which play such a large part in Jewish moral and spiritual life and which concern the Christian not at all. He simply follows the admonition of Paul: "Stand fast therefore in the freedom with which Christ has made you free" (Gal. 5:1). The underlying assumption is that the law is used in Judaism as a guarantee of righteousness but that there is no such guarantee, so that man must rely ultimately upon divine forgiveness. There is, in short, no moral solution for the moral problem of life. The Christian feels himself emancipated from the law. He is probably oblivious to the resources of grace which have been exhibited in Jewish legalism; but he is also bound to observe the embarrassment of many morally sensitive Jews, some secularized, but some, like Buber, genuinely religious, who have difficulty in regarding the *halakah* as morally relevant. One might mention the protest against

this legalism by such an impressive Jewish humanist and human-
itarian as Victor Gollancz in his *Dear Timothy*.

But the problem of the scope of the law is probably but a facet of the
larger problem of the relation of grace to law. Christianity distinguishes itself, in its own mind, from Judaism, as a religion of grace
rather than of law. The Johannine gospel states the distinction, from
the standpoint of the New Testament, rather flatly: "The law was
given by Moses but grace and truth came through Jesus Christ" (John
1:17). The question is what we Christians mean by "grace." Since the
word has been subject to many interpretations, not all of them valid,
let us begin by defining grace as having to do, not with moral norms
but with moral dynamics. The problem of grace looms so large in the
New Testament because the diagnosis of the human situation includes an analysis of what Augustine has defined as the "defect of the
will," a situation of self-contradiction in the self, which Paul describes in the words, "the good that I would I do not do, and the evil
that I would not, that I do" (Rom. 7:19).

This confession of impotence is probably the most significant characteristic of Pauline Christianity. It is from the diagnosis of impotence that the doctrine of grace achieves its significance; for grace is
the answer to the human problem. Grace is consistently both power
and pardon. The Reformation insisted that it was above all pardon
and that it was power insofar as the assurance of forgiveness healed
the anxious soul of man and emancipated him from preoccupation
with self, including preoccupation with his own righteousness. The
Christian must not claim that redemption is unknown in Judaism, or
that there is not a fully elaborated doctrine of the divine mercy in its
relation to the divine justice, even if he believes that this relation,
explicated in the Old Testament, is fully defined in the New Testament doctrine of the atonement. I speak as a Christian, of course,
when I affirm that on this issue many Christians see the most striking difference between Christianity as a religion of redemption and
Judaism as a religion of law.

From the standpoint of the Christian, the doctrine of grace is the
most significant distinction between Christianity and Judaism. But
before we claim superiority as Christians because we regard the
Christian diagnosis of the human situation as more adequate for us,
we must recognize that all Christian conceptions of grace as power,
enabling us to do what is right, are no guarantee that we are in posses-

sion of such a power. Grace is an accretion of power to the will. Saving grace may be the fruit of the soul's intimate relation with the divine source. There is no doctrine which can guarantee such power. Perhaps it would be well as both Christians and Jews to acknowledge that modern psychiatry and the social sciences have validated the efficacy of "common grace" more explicitly than any saving grace which we may claim as religious people. It is a simple observable fact that we have the capacity to love only as we have the security of the love of others. It is this security which is the real source of grace to most people. It is a grace which can be meditated by any one, religious or irreligious, who is capable of love. Religious faith, of course, tends to lift the security of love above and beyond the vicissitudes of our earthly friendships, and thus emancipates us from the failure of our human companions. It is nevertheless true that the most potent form of divine grace is that which is mediated by human love.

It is almost inevitable that we as Christians should claim uniqueness for our faith as a religion of redemption. But we must not claim moral superiority because of this uniqueness. For the efficacy of common grace and the necessity of rational discrimination in all problems of justice do not give a religion of grace that practical superiority over a religion of law which we are inclined to assume. The fact that Jews have been rather more creative than Christians in establishing brotherhood with the Negro, and have done so particularly in a part of the country where the grace of a new life in Christ has been proclaimed in the experience of conversion in the sects of Protestantism, may prove that "saving grace" may be rather too individualistically conceived in Christianity to deal with collective evil. In short, if we measure the two faiths by their moral fruits, the Jewish faith does not fall short, particularly in collective moral achievement, whatever the superior insights of the Christian faith may be in measuring the inner contradictions of the human spirit and in establishing the weakness of his moral will, and the spiritual force to overcome the defect of the will.

(3) The third great complex of issues between Christianity and Judaism centers in the problem of particularity and universality. It is probably this problem which prompted Toynbee to suggest that the Jews, in rejecting Jesus, turned their backs on the insights of their great prophets. Obviously the Jewish faith is not universal in the sense of being missionary and offering its way of life to all people. Yet

it is universal in the sense that it worships a God who is the sovereign of all nations and offers no special security to Israel. One might argue that the Jews have enlisted the divine so little for their own political survival that they have been homeless for two thousand years. They have, of course, been forced to make their piety into an instrument of collective survival in the diaspora. They could in fact not have survived as a purely secular nation. From the Christian standpoint, the Jews seem to be a nation which has tried desperately to be a church throughout the ages. This is involved in the tension of having a potentially universal religion standing on the historic base of a particular nation.

It is this situation which persuaded Franz Rosenzweig to define the relation of Christianity and Judaism as two religions with one center, worshiping the same God, but with Christianity serving the purpose of carrying the prophetic message to the Gentile world. The definition will not satisfy Christians, for it obscures some of the real differences between the two religions; but it is better than almost all alternative definitions of the relation between Jew and Christian, for it does do justice to the fact that Christianity is basically Hebraic in genius and that the Hellenic elements in its amalgam have not seriously changed the Hebraic base.

It is certainly a better definition than those which prompt Christian missionary activity among the Jews. Our analysis assumes that these activities are wrong not only because they are futile and have little fruit to boast for their exertions. They are wrong because the two faiths, despite differences, are sufficiently alike for the Jew to find God more easily in terms of his own religious heritage than by subjecting himself to the hazards of guilt feeling involved in a conversion to a faith, which whatever its excellencies, must appear to him as a symbol of an oppressive majority culture.

Both Jews and Christians will have to accept the hazards of their historic symbols. These symbols may be the bearers of an unconditioned message to the faithful. But to those outside the faith they are defaced by historic taints. Practically nothing can purify the symbol of Christ as the image of God in the imagination of the Jew from the taint with which ages of Christian oppression in the name of Christ tainted it. This is not merely an historic matter. We are reminded daily of the penchant of anti-semitic and semi-fascist groups, claiming the name of Christ for their campaigns of hatred.

Rosenzweig's definition of the relation may do better than any other for the two religions, but it does not solve the problem of the Jews insofar as they are both a religious and an ethnic community. Many Christians are pro-Zionist in the sense that they believe that a homeless people require a homeland; but we feel as embarrassed as anti-Zionist religious Jews when Messianic claims are used to substantiate the right of the Jews to the particular homeland in Palestine; or when it is assumed that this can be done without injury to the Arabs.

History is full of strange configurations. Among them is the thrilling emergence of the State of Israel, as a kind of penance of the world for the awful atrocities committed against the Jews; and as a community in which secular and religious forces have been curiously commingled in such a way that the homeland could not have been established in Palestine except for religious memories and could not be maintained as a workable nation if modern secularism (of which the Prime Minister, Ben-Gurion, is a convenient symbol) had not leavened the lump of Orthodoxy sufficiently to free a modern state from the legal norms which were handed down in tradition from a pastoral community thousands of years ago.

These are complications so great that the indifferent outsider will be tempted to laugh at the anachronisms; and the hostile critic will be unduly critical of the Jewish political will to survive. One of Toynbee's most fantastic judgements upon the Jews is his opinion that in "the Last Judgment," the Nazis will be judged more severely, not for having well nigh exterminated the Jews, but for having "tempted the remnant of Jewry to stumble," that is, to fight for their lives rather than espouse the "way of gentleness" which presumably means, having failed to adopt a pacifism, which neither Christianity nor Judaism ever consistently espoused. The Jewish nation was formed partly by the heroic fight for survival of the Jewish people and partly by the sympathies of the Western nations, possibly absolving their consciences for their involvement in the evil of Nazism. It is a glorious moral and political achievement. But a sympathetic Christian cannot but observe that the Jewish ethic and faith, so impressively universal in the diaspora, so fruitful in leavening Western civilization, is not morally safe when it becomes embodied in a nation like all other nations, and when in fighting for the survival of that nation, it comes in conflict with Arab forces. Significantly, Martin Buber's religious Zionism and his effort to establish a bi-national state with the Arabs must come to nothing. Political choices are always more limited than our moral and religious ideas find convenient. The State of Israel is not a religious state; and if it were, there would be a danger that it might become a sacerdotal state, because the religious forces in it would be heedless of the hundreds of years of Western history which proved even to the devout that politics, particularly in a technical and complex society, must be secular, lest primitive religious loyalties corrupt the character of its justice.

As Christians, we owe the Jew both gratitude for his "prophetic" contribution to our common civilization and understanding of his impulse to build a homeland for a homeless people; and appreciation for the remarkable feat of statemanship which has provided a home for the homeless. But all this cannot obscure the unsolved problem of particularity and universality of the Jewish people. We ought not to demand that the problem be solved. It is in fact insoluble. For a thousand years the Jews have served our common civilization by exploiting the universalistic implications of their faith. If now after the terrible holocaust of the past decades they, or some of them, should function as a nation and not a church, we Christians can appreciate the impulse and the achievements which are the fruits of the impulse. But the "Council of Judaism" is right when it insists that the two achievements in particularity and universality must not be confused or the prestige of the one be made the servant of the other.

A Christian contemplation of the Jewish problem of particularity and universality will tempt to self-righteousness on the part of the Christian, who is informed by a faith in which the problem is solved in principle, if he does not understand that history is full of realities which violate solutions in principle. The history of Christianity abounds in examples of the use of the Christian faith to exalt or to protect a particular community. The Irish struggle is aggravated by the fact that the Scots-Irish of Northern Ireland are Protestant, while the Southern Irish are Catholic. In the Balkans, the Roman and the Orthodox versions of Christianity are intimately merged with national survival impulses. Even in our nation, priding itself on its melting pot, the Protestant faith is undoubtedly an instrument of pride and cohesion for the North European or "Nordic" groups, as distinguished from the Slavs and the Latins. Every Protestant denomination has some particular ethnic or historical particularity.

We are dealing with a universal, rather than a Jewish, problem. Recognizing that fact will dissipate self-righteousness. But still there is the Jewish problem of particularity and universality. We ought to recognize that among the many illogical emergences of history (that is, configurations which do not fit into our logic) there is the strange miracle of the Jewish people, outliving the hazards of the diaspora for two millennia and finally offering their unique and valuable contributions to the common Western civilization, particularly in the final stage of its liberal society. We should not ask that this peculiar historical miracle fit into any kind of logic or conform to some historical analogy. It has no analogy. It must be appreciated for what it is.

V
THE POSSIBILITIES
AND LIMITATIONS
OF OUR KNOWING

14

IDEOLOGY AND THE SCIENTIFIC METHOD

The opinions which men and groups hold of each other and the judgments which they pass upon their common problems are notoriously interested and unobjective. The judgments of the market place and the political arena are biased, not only because they are made in the heat of controversy without a careful weighing of evidence, but also because there is no strong inclination to bring all relevant facts into view. While the ideological taint upon all social judgments is most apparent in the practical conflicts of politics, it is equally discernible, upon close scrutiny, in even the most scientific observations of social scientists. The latter may be free of conscious bias or polemic intent. Yet every observer of the human scene is distinguished from the scientific observer of the sequences of nature by the fact that he is, in some sense, an agent in, as well as an observer of, the drama which he records.

LIMITATIONS OF MARXIST IDEOLOGY

The relation of interest to historical knowledge is so obvious and inevitable that it is somewhat surprising that it came fully into view so late in the history of culture, and that Marxism, a polemic creed, should have been the primary agent of its discovery. The Marxist sponsorship of the theory of ideology was unfortunate, for Marxism discredited itself so quickly by becoming the prisoner of its own ideological presuppositions, that it has seemed unnecessary to deal seriously with the Marxist theory. Yet Marxism stumbled upon an important, and in some respects, an insoluble problem, in the realm of historical knowledge.

Despite its limitations, we may well begin with the Marxist conception of ideology. According to Marx, even the most "objective" interpretations of human life and destiny, of legal and moral norms and ideals, are in fact the rationalization of the interest of the ruling groups of a society, and mirror the economic interests of that group. The charge of the *Communist Manifesto* reads: "You transform into eternal laws of nature and reason the social forms springing from present modes and forms of property. What you see clearly in the case of ancient property, what you admit in the case of feudal property you are of course forbidden to admit in the case of your own form of bourgeois property." The Marxist interpretation of ideology naturally betrays the defects of Marxism as a philosophy and as a polemical political creed. It limits the ideological taint purely to economic interest, whereas it is obvious that any form of interest or passion may color our judgments. There are undoubtedly "male" and "female" ideologies, that is, viewpoints which are peculiar to the man or the woman, as illustrated, for instance, in Aeschylus' tragedy in the conflict between Antigone and Creon, rooted in the irreducible differences between male and female perspectives upon political issues. Every race and class, every generation and age, every particular locus of time and place in history can be the root of an ideology in so far as a parochial situation may color a judgment about facts beyond that situation.

The Marxist thesis implies but does not explicitly illumine the fact that an ideological taint upon a judgment implies a true and untainted judgment. One could go further and insist that false judgments depend upon true judgments for their prestige. There can be no counterfeit money without genuine money. This fact reveals an aspect of the human situation which the Marxist theory does not understand. It is significant that men cannot simply claim some desired object as their own without seeking to prove that it is desirable in terms of some general scheme of value. This is the tribute which self-interest must pay to a wider system of interest. The fact that men are under an inner necessity of paying this tribute proves that, while self-interest may be powerful, it is never so powerful as to be able fully to obscure a person's knowledge of and loyalty to a wider system of values than those which have his own desires at the center.

The Marxist theory of ideology is not only incomplete on several important issues. It is contradictory on one of them: that is the degree of conscious dishonesty which is involved in the ideological taint. In the Marxist psychology and in its theory of knowledge, conscious dishonesty is specifically disavowed. "Ideology is a process," declared Engels, "which is carried on in the consciousness of the so-called thinkers, but with a false consciousness. The real driving force which moves it remains unconscious, otherwise it would not be an ideological process." It works with pure conceptual material which it unwittingly takes over as the product of thought, and therefore does not investigate its relation to a process further removed from and independent of thought.

Thus conscious dishonesty is explicitly denied in the theory of knowledge; but it is explicitly affirmed in the Marxist polemic against the class foes of the proletariat. They are consistently accused of conscious dishonesty.

Thus Trotsky speaks of the patent dishonesties of the landlords in the first Russian constituent assembly:

> They spoke for the rights of idealism, the interests of culture, the prerogatives of a future assembly. The leader of the heavy industries concluded his speech with a hymn in honor of liberty, equality and fraternity. Where were the metallic baritones of profit, the hoarse bass of land rents, where were they hiding? Only the oversweet tenors of disinterestedness filled the hall. But listen for a moment and how much spleen and vinegar there is under this syrup. [They are afraid that the land will be] turned over to the dark, semi-illiterate peasant. If in their struggle with this dark muzhik the landlords happen also to be defending their property, it is not for their own sakes, O no, but only afterwards to lay it upon the altar of freedom.

This biting scorn for the patent dishonesty in ideological pretension would of course be an equally fitting response to the current propaganda in favor of "peoples' democracies," etc., etc.

There are intricacies in the process of self-deception which are not illumined by these contradictory theories. In any event, the tendency to "make the worse appear the better reason," must be regarded as at least quasi-conscious.

The inadequacies of the Marxist theory of ideology are perhaps best revealed by the fact that Marxism could make the theory so completely into a weapon of political struggle and apply it to the foe and not to the self. Having interpreted interest in purely economic terms and having assumed that the corruption of ideas by interest could occur only in a society in which there was a disparity of economic interest, it sought to create a society in which a presumed identity or mutuality of interest would eliminate ideology in human affairs. It was not fortuitous that a tyranny should be generated from these illusions, in which men of absolute power should mistreat weak men; and that their cruelties should be obscured by the theory which insists that powerful and weak men have no difference of interest so long as both are propertyless.

It is also not fortuitous that a theory of ideology, which attributes the taint only to a foe should result in the most monstrous pretensions of purity of reason for the self, in contrast to the ideologically corrupted opinion of the foe. Thus Molotov can draw the contrast: "The diplomacy of capitalist states is based upon mere expediency and opportunism. The foreign policy of the Soviet Union alone, based upon the firm foundation of Marxist-Leninist science, rises above opportunism and is able to estimate the international scene not only in the immediate but in the distant future." These claims of omniscience incidentally reveal the real pathos of the ideological problem. For the greater the pretension of purity and disinterestedness, the greater the impurity.

LIMITATIONS OF THE LIBERAL IDEOLOGY

But the answers of the liberal world to the problem of ideology are hardly more adequate than the Marxist answer, though they are considerably less noxious. Many modern liberal theories derive their defects from the failure to make a sufficiently sharp distinction between the natural and the socio-historical sciences, between *Naturwissenschaft* and *Geisteswissenschaft*. Many think that it is a fairly simple task to apply the "scientific method" first perfected in the natural sciences to the world of historical events and social judgments, thereby eliminating and correcting ideological distortions.

In his *Man and the Modern World*, Julian Huxley recognizes that when man studies man, "he cannot use the same methods by which he investigates external nature" for when "he investigates human motives his own motives are involved." This is not the only difference between the two types of inquiry but it is an important one. Yet Huxley believes that the difficulty will be overcome rather simply, though it will "take generations for the social sciences to work out technics for discounting the errors due to bias."

Karl Mannheim thinks he has already perfected a sociological epistemology which will progressively free the scientist from the bias of interest, of time and place, by a rigorous analysis of the hidden presuppositions which color his judgments. "Whenever we become aware of a determinant which has dominated us," declares Mannheim, "we remove it from the realm of the unconscious motivation into that of the controllable, calculable, and objectified."[1] Presumably a sufficiently rigorous sociology of knowledge will produce social scientists who have achieved a completely transcendent position over the flux of the history in which they are, as mere human beings, involved.

John Dewey believes that the historical sciences are corrupted by the obvious restraints of political and religious authority, which once restricted the freedom of all scientific inquiry. The battle for the freedom of science, he declares, resulted in a compromise in which "the world including man was cut into two parts. One of them was awarded to natural inquiry under the name of physical science. The other was kept in fee simple by a higher authoritative domain of the moral and spiritual (church and state)." This compromise resulted in "dumping our actual human problems into the lap of the most immature of all our modes of knowing: politics and ethics." The result is that this division of science "which is potent in human affairs is not a science at all but an ideological reflection and rationalization of contentious and contending practical politics."[2]

The assumption that historical knowledge is corrupted because it has not yet been freed from authority has gained a certain degree of plausibility by the fact that the only way that the natural sciences can be corrupted is by the imposition of external authority (as, for instance, biology in Russia today). But the social and political judgments of politicians and journalists, and for that matter of the man in the street and of the most scientific social observer, are loaded with ideological presuppositions which are not derived from any ex-

1. *Ideology and Utopia*, 169.
2. *Commentary*, October 1947.

plicit pressure of authority. Modern democracies are, in fact, frequently threatened with anarchy by the clash of conflicting ideologies, which an active social science may be able to mitigate but which it cannot abolish.

NATURAL VERSUS SOCIAL SCIENCES

The question is why the ideological taint should be so much greater in the field of social judgments than in the natural sciences and why the application of the "scientific method" should be so much less efficacious in removing bias. The answer to that question involves a rigorous examination of the difference between the fields of natural and social sciences and also the difference in the status of the observer in each field.

(1) The Correlation of Causes

In his "Plight of the Social Sciences,"[3] Robert MacIver emphasizes the many levels of causation which the social sciences must investigate. Every event in history takes place in a half-dozen or more dimensions—geological, geographic, climatic, psychological, social and personal. This complex causation makes it possible to correlate events plausibly in many different ways, usually tempting the observer to "make the field of one's special interest the inclusive ground in which the causes of all relevant phenomena are to be sought."[4] The infinite variety of causal sequences to which every act and event in history is related makes almost every correlation of causes sufficiently plausible to be immune to compelling challenge.

Any social theory therefore has some kinship with the procedures of a Rorschach test, which is more revealing about the state of the patient's mind who makes it than about the inkspots which his imagination interprets in terms of various configurations. Obviously absurd correlations can be ruled out, and flagrant bias can be discovered. But no one can give a scientifically conclusive account, for instance, of the fall of the Roman Empire, or of the reason for the rise of Nazism in Germany, or for the differences between British and French democracy, which would compel the rejection of a com-

3. In *Social Causation.*
4. Ibid., 77.

peting or contrasting interpretation. The conclusions arrived at are partly determined by the principle of interpretation with which the inquiry is begun.

(2) Uniqueness and Contingency

There are no simple recurrences in history and therefore no analogies between sequences in various periods of history which could compel us to accept a proposition that a given policy in a certain period will have similar effects as a social policy in another period. It is only partly true, as Windelband and Rickert have argued, that history is a realm of unique events, as distinguished from the exact recurrences of the physical world. For there are cycles, recurrences and analogies in history; if there were not, there would be no basis for scientific investigation. But endless contingencies supervene upon the recurrences. In the physical sciences, there can be controlled experiments which may be endlessly repeated until the "right" answer is found, but nothing is exactly repeated in history. Therefore a judgment, for instance, that some New Deal policy in America of the twentieth century will expose our nation to the fate of the Roman Empire, on the ground that the latter was the victim of an analogous policy, can neither be asserted nor refuted with certainty. Every reliance upon analogy can be refuted by emphasis upon variants in the compared historical scenes. Toynbee's analogy between the medieval situation of Eastern and Western Christendom and the present conflict between Russia and the West sheds some illumination upon the scene, but not too much. For there are too many novel factors in the contemporary situation which do not fit into the analogy.

Aristotle had an understanding of the contingent elements in history, and he therefore regarded the analysis of the variables as the domain of *phronesis* rather than *nous*, that is of practical wisdom rather than reason. Yet Aristotle could have a greater degree of confidence than we in the scientific element in historical analysis because he believed in an historical, as well as a natural, cycle of recurrence in which the historical norm was revealed. "Among men at least," he declared,

> though not among the gods, though some things are by nature, all are subject to variation. Yet in spite of their variability we may distinguish between what is natural and what is not. How do we distinguish be-

tween what is by nature and what by agreement only? In the same way as the distinctions are drawn in other spheres. Thus the right hand is naturally stronger but any man may be ambidextrous. Similarly rules of justice which are not natural but human are not everywhere identical but everywhere there is one constitution marked by nature as the best.[5]

Thus, in common with all classical rationalism, he finds normative structures in history analogous to the norms in nature. The modern understanding of the endless possibilities of variation in history makes this basis of historical science invalid. At least it has become obvious that it is not easy to make simple distinctions between the natural and the unnatural, the constant and the variable in historical studies.

(3) Patterns and Novelties

Modern historical and social sciences have sought to gain firm ground under their feet by the strategy of interpreting the emergence of novelty in history as subject to discernible patterns, analogous to evolution in nature. There are undoubtedly patterns of historical development, but the analysis of such patterns is subject to hazardous attributions of particular events as causes of subsequent occurrences. These attributions are hazardous not only because of the complexity of the causal chain but because human agents are themselves causes within the causal nexus. The unpredictability of the action of a human agent's action in a particular situation makes prediction of future events highly speculative, and our lack of knowledge of the inner motives of the agents of past action renders even analyses of past events very uncertain. If we hazard guesses about the unconscious as well as the conscious motives and incentives of the human agents, we make our conclusions even more problematic. Only one historian of the recent past, Burckhardt, predicted anything like the rise of totalitarianism.

It might be claimed that the ability to predict consequences of given events and actions is the real criterion of the adequacy of scientific procedures. Without conclusive predictions, the refutation of ideologically-tainted political policies becomes practically impossible; for every political argument involves and implies a prediction that the desired policy will redound to the general welfare. Refuta-

5. *Nich. Ethics*, V, 7.

tion of such a claim would have to offer indisputable proof that the prediction is false. The proof would have to depend upon exact analogies between past and future events. Such proof is impossible. Thus recently the gas-producing states sought legislation which would have prevented government control of the gas, piped from producer to consumer states. Regulation was thought desirable because ordinary competitive processes would not operate to hold prices down. The oil-producing states argued that competition between various types of fuel would serve the purpose of regulating prices. Economists generally held this thesis to be highly improbable; but it was sufficiently plausible to be the ideological garment by which naked interest could be covered. There was no indisputable evidence on how competition between various types of fuel would affect the market.

If it is difficult, if not impossible, to refute conclusively flagrant forms of ideology which operate in ordinary political polemics, it is even more difficult to come to terms with the subtler ideologies which lie at the basis of the ethos of a whole age or culture. Consider the concept of "economic man" as elaborated in classical economics. Morris Cohen, despite a skeptical attitude toward the scientific elements in the social sciences, thinks that the concept of "economic man" is no more hazardous an abstraction than any generalization in the physical sciences. Yet the concept is clearly an "ideology" of a rising bourgeois class. It embodies the individualistic prejudices and illusions of that class, by underestimating the ethnic, national, traditional and other social ties which might prevent an individual from seeking his economic advantage in complete freedom as an individual. It furthermore overemphasizes the economic motive as the key to the mystery of human incentives and obscures such motives as the desire for security, for social prestige and approval, and the desire for power. Some of these mistakes have been corrected, but not so much by a more astute science as by subsequent history which proved the bourgeois interpretation of human incentives to be inadequate. This subsequent history could not have been anticipated by the most enlightened social analysis, in so far as it was intimately and organically involved in the peculiar prejudices of its age.

(4) Historical Value Judgments

Judgments in the field of history are ultimately value judgments in the sense that they do not intend merely to designate the actions which lead to desired ends but seek to give guidance on the desirability of ends. Since history moves above the level of natural necessity and involves actions which seek ends in a wider realm of meaning, the ultimate question about an action or policy is the ethical one: whether the end is desirable. Even the skeptics who try to reduce the concept of desirability to that of "the desired" must admit that human beings have a remarkable penchant for masking what they desire under the idea of the desirable. Indeed, as we have already had occasion to observe, it is the very nature of ideology to confuse the two, not because they are identical but because the desirability or "value" of an end is necessary to sanction the fact that it is desired.

The question is in what degree the scientific method can unmask precisely this tendency to pretend a wider value for an act than merely its gratification of the desires of the agent. The scientific method is obviously most potent when we limit the question to specific and narrow ends and ask what is desirable to achieve the end of health, or security, or the national interest, or the preservation of civilization. But every specific end is enmeshed in a vast system of ends and means; and we cannot ascertain the desirability of an immediate end without making value judgments about the total schemes of meaning in which such judgments are made or by which they are informed.

We cannot criticize these total schemes of meaning scientifically, for every scientific procedure presupposes them. If metaphysics is, as Collingwood claims, the analysis of the presuppositions of our sciences, we can come to terms with the adequacy of the total structure of meaning by metaphysical analyses. The scientific method may help us in detecting an ideological taint in which some partial and parochial interest is sanctified by the prestige of the whole value scheme.

Let us take the ideological conflict in modern technical society as an illustration. Even where the liberal world is not subject to the Marxist challenge, there is an ideological conflict between the more favored and the less favored members of the community. It is to be noted that in the more healthy societies this conflict does not result in a disruption of the community, because it takes place against the background of value systems which do rough justice to both the individual and social dimension of human existence. But the degree to which individuality and individual initiative is cherished on the one hand, and social solidarity and security on the other, is clearly ideological. The bourgeois community tends to be libertarian, and the industrial workers tend, even when they are not Marxist, to be equalitarian and collectivist. In this situation it is interesting to note what social science can and cannot do. A careful analysis of social sequences and causalities can refute the more extravagant claims of each side. There is, for instance, pretty conclusive evidence that an uncontrolled economy does not automatically make for justice, and that a compounding of political and economic power, according to collectivist programs, will threaten both justice and liberty. Those societies in which there is a relative degree of impartial social observation mitigate the ideological conflict, but they cannot eliminate it. They are powerless to do so because of the existential intimacy between interest and idea. The classes which prefer liberty to security are those which already have a high measure of security through their social and professional skills, and who do not like to have their economic power subjected to political power. The classes which prefer security to liberty, on the other hand, are on the whole devoid of special skills and therefore individual securities; they are exposed to the perils of a highly integrated technical society, and therefore fear insecurity more than they fear the loss of liberty.

There can be no scientific dissolution of these preferences. It is probably true that the health of a democratic society depends more upon the spirit of forbearance with which each side tolerates the irreducible ideological preferences of the other than upon some supposed scientific resolution of them, because the scientific resolution always involves the peril that one side or the other will state its preferences as if they were scientifically validated value judgments.

The field of historical events thus differs radically from the field of natural events in the complexity of the causal chain, and by the fact that human agents intervene unpredictably in the course of events. These two factors prevent any scientific method from leading to absolutely compelling conclusions, because all alternative conclusions can always be plausibly presented.

THE STATUS OF THE OBSERVER

There is, however, an even more marked difference between the status of the observer of the realm of nature and the realm of history. The scientific observer of the realm of nature is in a sense naturally and inevitably disinterested. At least, nothing in the natural scene can arouse his bias. Furthermore, he stands completely outside of the natural so that his mind, whatever his limitations, approximates pure mind.

The observer of the realm of history cannot be disinterested in the same way, for two reasons: first, he must look at history from some locus in history; secondly, he is to a certain degree engaged in its ideological conflicts. This engagement is most obvious in the case of a statesman who is a proponent of a particular interest of class, race, or nation, but it is also obvious in the case of a more impartial social scientist. "Knowledge," declares Professor George Adams, "is the achievement of a spectator who stands outside the scene which he interprets. To achieve this the mind must emancipate itself from the circumstances to which it owes its birth and transcend the limitations of its own bias."[6] If this be the requirement of historical knowledge it is so severe that it can only be approximated. Furthermore, the challenge to transcend the limits of its own bias is in a sense a moral rather than an intellectual one. That is to say, it is addressed to the self rather than to the mind, i.e., to a self or to a will which is able to use intellectual processes to justify its own ends.

Thus we arrive once more at the problem which was obscured rather than illumined by the Marxist theory of ideology, the problem of the conscious element in social and historical bias. "What a man had rather believe," declared Francis Bacon, "he will more readily believe,"[7] thus calling attention to the existential intimacy between idea and interest in human affairs. The observers of history are selves rather than minds, because their interest and their will is more immediately engaged than in the observation of nature. The further they are removed in time or in space from an historical encounter, the more they can become pure mind, that is, the more they can scientifically analyze without the corruption of passion and interest. Thus the field of historical observation presents us with infinite grades of engagement, from the obvious engagement of the practical statesman, through the observations of social scientists who stand upon some contemporary ground of impartiality, to the observations of social and historical scientists of a subsequent age who have gained a

6. *Ethical Principles of the New Civilization*, a symposium edited by Ruth Anshen.
7. *Novum Organum*, 67, 49.

perspective in time upon the scene of conflict between various interests and passions. These various shades of engagement also determine the degree to which selves rather than minds must be appealed
to. If it is a self rather than a mind, no scientific method can compel a
self to cease from engaging in whatever rationalization of interest
may seem plausible to it.

It is for this reason that we must not, on the one hand, ever despair
of an adequate scientific method mitigating ideological conflicts in
history, but must, on the other hand, recognize the limits of its
power. Perhaps an illustration taken from current politics will illustrate both the possibilities and the limits. In a dispute on the wages of
steel workers, it was obviously valuable to have a Wage Stabilization
Board sufficiently impartial to render an opinion of relative impartiality on the dispute, but it was also inevitable that one side should
challenge the impartiality of its findings so that they became again a
part of the dispute. No perfection of method can thus completely
overcome ideological conflict.

The field of historical events is too complex and too lacking in
exact analogies in its recurrences to coerce the mind to a particular
interpretation of the causal sequences, but, even if the mind could be
coerced, the historical observer may always turn out in the end to be
an agent in history rather than an observer of it, with a sufficient
stake in the contests of history to defy conclusions which should
compel the mind but will not compel the interested self.

15

<u>≡≡</u>

COHERENCE, INCOHERENCE, AND
CHRISTIAN FAITH

The whole of reality is characterized by a basic coherence. Things and events are in a vast web of relationships and are known through their relations. Perceptual knowledge is possible only within a framework of conceptual images, which in some sense conform to the structures in which reality is organized. The world is organized or it could not exist; if it is to be known, it must be known through its sequences, coherences, causalities, and essences.

The impulse to understand the world expresses itself naturally in the movement toward metaphysics, rising above physics; in the desire to penetrate behind and above the forms and structures of particular things to the form and structure of being per se. It is natural to test the conformity to the particular coherence in which it seems to belong. We are skeptical about ghosts, for instance, because they do not conform to the characteristics of historical reality as we know it.

THE PERILS OF MAKING COHERENCE THE BASIC
TEST OF TRUTH

We instinctively assume that there is only one world and that it is a cosmos, however veiled and unknown its ultimate coherences, incongruities, and contradictions in life, in history, and even in nature. In the one world there are many worlds, realms of meaning and coherence; and these are not easily brought into a single system. The worlds of mind and matter have been a perennial problem in ontology, as have subject and object in epistemology. There must be a final congruity between these realms, but most of the rational theories of their congruity tend to obscure some truth about each realm in the impulse to establish total coherence. The effort to establish simple coherence may misinterpret specific realities in order to fit them into a system. There are four primary perils to truth in making coherence the basic test of truth.

(1) Things and events may be too unique to fit into any system of meaning; and their uniqueness is destroyed by a premature coordination to a system of meaning, particularly a system which identifies meaning with rationality. Thus there are historical characters and events, concretions and configurations, which the romantic tradition tries to appreciate in their uniqueness, in opposition to simpler and neater systems of meaning which obscure the uniqueness of the particular. There are also unique moral situations which do not fit simply into some general rule of natural law.

(2) Realms of coherence and meaning may stand in rational contradiction to each other; and they are not fully understood if the rational contradiction is prematurely resolved as, for instance, between being and becoming, or eternity and time. Thus the classical metaphysics of being could not appreciate the realities of growth and becoming, the emergence of novelty, or, in short, historical development; and modern metaphysics has equal difficulty in finding a structure of the permanent and the perennial in the flux of becoming (Bergson versus Aristotle). The problem of time and eternity is not easily solved in rational terms. Hegel invented a new logic to comprehend becoming as integral to being; but his system could not do justice to the endless possibilities of novelty and surprise in historical development. He prematurely rationalized time and failed to do justice to genuine novelty.

(3) There are configurations and structures which stand athwart every rationally conceived system of meaning and cannot be appreciated in terms of the alternative efforts to bring the structure completely into one system or the other. The primary example is man himself, who is both in nature and above nature, and who has been alternately misunderstood by idealistic and naturalistic philosophies. Idealism understands his freedom as mind but not his reality as contingent object in nature. It elaborates a history of man as if it were a history of mind, without dealing adequately with man as determined by geography and climate, by interest and passion. Naturalism, on the other hand, tells the history of human culture as if it were a mere variant of natural history. These same philosophies are of course equally unable to solve the problem presented by the in-

congruity of mind and matter in ontology and of subject and object in epistemology. The one tries to reduce mind to matter or to establish a system of psychophysical parallelism. The other seeks to derive the world of objects from the world of mind. The inconclusive debate between them proves the impossibility of moving rationally from mind to matter or matter to mind in ontology, or of resolving the epistemological problem rationally. There is no rational refutation of subjective idealism. It is resolved by what Santayana calls "animal faith." All science rests upon the common-sense faith that the processes of mind and the processes of nature are relevant to each other.

(4) Genuine freedom, with the implied possibility of violating the natural and rational structures of the world, cannot be conceived in any natural or rational scheme of coherence. This furnishes a second reason for the misunderstanding of man and his history in all rational schemes. The whole realm of genuine selfhood, of sin and of grace, is beyond the comprehension of various systems of philosophy. Neither Aristotle nor Kant succeeds in accounting for the concrete human self as free agent.

This mystery of human freedom, including the concomitant mystery of historic evil, plus the previous incongruity of man both as free spirit and as a creature of nature, led Pascal to elaborate his Christian existentialism in opposition to the Cartesian rationalism and Jesuit Thomism of his day. Pascal delved "in mysteries without which man remains a mystery to himself"; and that phrase may be a good introduction to the consideration of the relation of the suprarational affirmations of the Christian faith to the antinomies, contradictions, and mysteries of human existence.

CHRISTIAN SUPRARATIONALISM AND THE ANTINOMIES OF EXISTENCE

The question to be considered is in what way these suprarational affirmations are related to and validated by their capacity to resolve and clarify the antinomies, the aspects of uniqueness and particularity, the obscure meanings and tangents of meaning in human life and history.

Judged by any standard of coherence and compared with other high religions, Christianity seems to be a primitive religion, because all of these are more, rather than less, rigorous than science and philosophy in their effort to present the world and life as a unified whole and to regard all discords and incongruities as provisional or illusory. Of the high religions, only Christianity and Judaism and possibly Zoroastrianism may be defined as historical religions. Perhaps Mohammedanism could be included as a legalistic version of historical religion. All other religions, including the mystic version of Mohammedanism—Sufism—could be defined as culture religions in which a universal principle of meaning is sought either within the structures of the world or within some universal subsistence above and beyond the structures. These culture religions are, to use John Oman's distinction, pantheistic in either the cosmic or the acosmic sense.

Cosmic forms of pantheism are religious versions of various metaphysical systems, idealistic and naturalistic, in which the ultimate religious issue implied in the ontological quest is made explicit. Stoicism is a naturalistic form of pantheism in so far as it presents the world as a vast rational order to which human life must conform. In so far as Stoicism has a "reason within us" to which we may flee from the reason within the world, it tends to an acosmic form of pantheism. Spinozism is a more consistently naturalistic version of pantheism. Modern naturalism is a form of pantheism in which the temporal process needs no longer to be explained but becomes the principle of the explanation of all things. In the thought of Bergson, the religious veneration for time as a source of meaning is explicit. He believes it possible to penetrate to it as a source of the meaning of life by a kind of mystic identification, to be distinguished from conceptual knowledge.

Acosmic forms of pantheism, whether Neo-Platonism, Brahmanism, or Buddhism, are distinguished from cosmic forms by placing the mystery of consciousness outside the rational or natural coherence of the world. Sensing a deeper mystery of spirit than will fit into either the concepts of nature or of mind, they practice a technique of introversion by which the self as subject extricates itself endlessly from the self as contingent object (the mind as well as the physical self being reduced to the level of the temporal world) until the self has achieved the universality of the divine. The divine is significantly an undifferentiated ground and goal, which underlies all things. In such mysticism, the drive toward coherence has taken its most consistent form. From the standpoint of this pure mysticism, the whole temporal world, with all its particular events and objects, including the particular self, is reduced to essential meaninglessness. Buddhism may be regarded as the most consistent form of this drive toward the ultimate in culture religion, ending with a vision of a Nirvana which is at once the fulness of existence and nonexistence. This is the kind of spirituality in which Aldous Huxley seeks a refuge from the twentieth century.

In contrast to this logic of culture religions, the emphasis in the Christian faith upon the unique, the contradictory, the paradoxical, and the unresolved mystery is striking. The temporal world comes into existence through God's creation. The concept of creation defines the mystery beyond both natural and rational causalities, and its suprarational character is underscored when Christian theology is pressed to accept the doctrine of creation ex nihilo. Thereby a realm of freedom and mystery is indicated beyond the capacity of reason to comprehend. This is where reason starts and ends. The final irrationality of the givenness of things is frankly accepted.

On the other end of time is the culmination of the world in a transfigured time. As von Hügel rightly asserts, biblical eschatology must adhere to the rational absurdity that there will be time in eternity, that our partial simultaneity will not be annulled by God's *totum simul*, that the culmination means not the annulment but the fulfilment of the temporal process. In Cullmann's *Christ and Time*, the biblical concept of a new aeon, a new time, is interpreted even more radically but probably too radically. These conceptions of alpha and omega, of beginning and end, are rationally absurd, or at least paradoxical, but they guard the Christian interpretation of life from both an empty heaven and an impossible utopia, from either a meaningless time or a self-fulfilling time. They are, however, only the frame for the more positive content of the Christian message. Every tendency to make the Christian revelation mean primarily the invasion of time by the eternal (as in some doctrines of the Incarnation) obscures this more positive content of the Christian gospel, which has to do with man's and God's freedom, with man's sin and God's grace.

The Christian answer to the human predicament—a divine mercy toward man, revealed in Christ, which is at once a power enabling the self to realize itself truly beyond itself in love, and the forgiveness of God toward the self which even at its best remains in partial contradiction to the divine will—is an answer which grows out of, and which in turn helps to create, the radical Christian concept of human freedom. In the Christian faith, the self in its final freedom does not find its norm in the structures either of nature or of reason. Nor is either able to bind the self's freedom or guarantee its virtue, as the proponents of "natural law" would have it. The principle of rationality, the force of logic, does not secure the virtue of the self, as in the thought of Kant. For the self can make use of logic for its ends. The partial and particular self is not merely a provisional particularity which is overcome in the universal self which develops with increasing rationality. Nor is the evil in the self the provisional confusion and cross-purposes of natural passion before being ordered by mind, as in Aristotle. There is, in other words, no form, structure, or logos in nature to which the self ought to return from its freedom, and no such form within its reason which would guarantee that the self will express itself harmoniously with the total structure of existence above the level of natural necessity. The self is free to defy God. The self does defy God. The Christian conception of the dignity of man and of the misery of man is all of one piece, as Pascal rightly apprehended. All Renaissance and modern emphases upon the dignity of man, to the exclusion of the Christian conception of the sin of man, are lame efforts to reconstruct the Christian doctrine of selfhood without understanding the full implications of the Christian conception of the self's freedom.

But the Christian doctrine of selfhood means that neither the life of the individual self nor the total drama of man's existence upon earth can be conceived in strictly rational terms of coherence. Each is a drama of an engagement between the self and God and between mankind and God, in which all sorts of events may happen. The only certainty from a Christian standpoint is that evil cannot rise to the point of defeating God; that every form of egotism, self-idolatry, and defiance stands under divine judgment; that this judgment is partially executed in actual history, though not in complete conformity with the divine righteousness, so that history remains morally ambiguous to the end; and that a divine redemptive love is always initiating a reconciliation between God and man.

According to this answer, a suffering divine love is the final coherence of life. This love bears within itself the contradictions and cross-purposes made possible by human freedom. To a certain degree, this answer reaches down to cover even the antinomies known as natural evil. There is no possibility of defining the created world as good if the test of goodness is perfect harmony. A too-strict identification of goodness with coherence must always lead to a conception of nature which is on the brink of interpreting nature and the temporal as evil because there is conflict in it.

It must be noted that the Christian answer, adequate for a full understanding of both the good and the evil possibilities of human freedom, involves a definition of God which stands beyond the limits of rationality. God is defined as both just and merciful, with His mercy at once the contradiction to and the fulfilment of His justice. He is defined in trinitarian terms. The almighty creator who transcends history and the redeemer who suffers in history are two and yet one. The Holy Spirit, who is the final bond of unity in the community of the redeemed, represents not the rational harmony of all things in their nature but the ultimate harmony, which includes both the power of the creator and the love of the redeemer. Christian theology has sought through all the ages to make both the doctrine of the atonement and the Trinity rationally explicable. This enterprise can never be completely successful, except in the sense that alternative propositions can be proved to be too simple solutions. Without the atonement, all religious conceptions of justice degenerate into legalism and all conceptions of love into sentimentality. Without the Trinity, the demands of a rigorous logic do not stop short of pantheism.

In short, the situation is that the ultrarational pinnacles of Christian truth, embodying paradox and contradiction and straining at the limits of rationality, are made plausible when understood as the keys which make the drama of human life and history comprehensible, and without which it is either given a too-simple meaning or falls into meaningless. Thus existentialism is a natural revolt against the too-simple meanings of traditional rationalism, and logical positivism expresses a skepticism too radically obscured by idealism.

CHRISTIAN TRUTH AND THE "WISDOM OF THE WORLD"

A Christian apologetic which validates the suprarational affirmations of meaning by proving them to be the source of meaning for the seeming contradictions and antinomies of life runs through the whole of Scripture.

The book of Deuteronomy is full of warnings against a too rational conception of the covenant; for that would lead to the conviction that Israel has been chosen either because of its power or because of its virtue. No reason but God's mysterious grace can be given for the covenant. In the book of Job the attempt to measure God's goodness by human standards of justice is rebuked. The Second Isaiah never tires of reminding Israel of the inscrutable and yet meaningful character of the divine sovereignty over history. Every simple moral conception of it would make the tortuous course of history seem completely meaningless, since it does not conform to a simple moral pattern. It is in searching for the ultimate meaning of the morally intolerable suffering of righteous and comparatively innocent Israel that chapter 53 of Isaiah first establishes the relation between a moral obscurity in history with what becomes, in the New Testament, the final clarification of the moral obscurity of history, a suffering God. Paul rejoices in the fact that what seems foolishness from the standpoint of the world's wisdom, the message of the cross, becomes in the eyes of faith the key which unlocks the mysteries of life and makes sense out of it. It is, furthermore, power as well as wisdom, because the faith to apprehend this true wisdom requires repentance, which is to say a destruction of all false systems of meaning in which the self has exalted itself against the knowledge of God, by idolatrous confidence in its own wisdom or its own power.

The perennial question in Christian apologetics is how these validations of the truths of the Christian faith are to be related to the wisdom of the world, to the cultural disciplines which seek on various levels to find the congruities and coherences, the structures and forms of nature, life, and history.

On the one hand, there is a tradition of Christian theology which glories in the contradiction between the foolishness of God and the wisdom of men. It runs from Tertullian, through Augustine, Occam and Duns Scotus, to the Reformation, Pascal, Kierkegaard, and Barth.

Luther speaks for this tradition in the words: "We know that reason is the devil's harlot and can do nothing but slander all that God says and does. If outside of Christ you wish by your own thoughts to know your relation to God you will break your neck.—Therefore keep to revelation and do not try to understand."

The other tradition runs from Origen through Aquinas, the Christian Platonists, the Renaissance Humanists, to modern liberal Christianity. For this tradition Aquinas speaks: "The natural dictates of reason must certainly be true. It is impossible to think of their being otherwise, nor again is it possible to believe that the tenets of faith are false. Since falsehood alone is contrary to truth it is impossible for the truths of faith to be contrary to the principles known by reason.''

COHERENCE, THOMISM, AND LIBERAL PROTESTANTISM

The inconclusive character of the debate between these two schools may be due to the tendency of one side to make the suprarational affirmations of faith too simply irrational. Being unconcerned with the disciplines of culture and the validity of their search for provisional coherences, this side misses the opportunity to find the point where such coherences reveal their own limits and turn sense into nonsense by seeking to comprehend the incongruous too simply in a system of rational coherence.

The Christian rationalists, on the other hand, equate meaning too simply with rationality and thereby inevitably obscure some of the profoundest incongruities, tragic antinomies, and depth of meaning on the edge of the mysteries in human life and history. There is a certain logic in the rise and fall of theological systems. Thomism achieves its triumph in the stabilities of the thirteenth century, while the Renaissance spirituality, culminating in liberal Protestantism, is victorious in the nineteenth-century heyday of the middle-class world in which this type of spirituality arose. Each becomes irrelevant in the historic disintegrations of the fourteenth and twentieth centuries in which things hidden become revealed. This is not to suggest that the basic problems of human existence are essentially different in ages of tranquility than in ages of tragedy. It is merely to suggest that there are aspects of human existence which are more clearly seen and recognized when the relatively rational harmonies of social existence of a stable period prove themselves less typical of the whole human situation than they appeared to be.

In Thomism, the suprarational truths of faith are not identified with the truths of reason. They illumine a realm of mystery above and beyond the limits of the world which is rationally understood and morally ordered. The existence of God is known by reason, but His character as triune God is apprehended by faith. This means that the finiteness of man's reason and its involvement in the flux of the temporal world is not appreciated. In the realm of morality, the rational man feels secure in the virtue which he may achieve by his reason and the justice which he can define by it. This means that the problematic character of all human virtues and the ideological taint in all reasoning about human affairs are not understood. Therefore, grace becomes merely an addition to natural virtue and in no way stands in contradiction to it. Significantly, man is essentially defined as a rational creature, just as Aristotle would define him. The true dimension of selfhood, with its indeterminate relations to itself, to God, and to its fellow-men, is regarded as an addition, a *donum superadditum*. Wherever one touches the Thomistic scheme, one finds a perfectly coherent world, a perfectly understood self, a perfectly possible virtue and justice. This coherent world has superimposed upon it an aura of mystery and meaning in which the limitless possibilities of man's and God's freedom find expression. It is a two-story world with a classical base and a Christian second story.

The general picture of faith's relation to culture, of the gospel's relation to the wisdom of the world, in the world view of the Renaissance and subsequently in liberal Protestantism, represents one further step toward the acceptance of a rationally coherent world. The mystery of creation is resolved in the evolutionary concept. "Some call it evolution and others call it God." The Bible becomes a library, recording in many books the evolutionary ascent of man to God. Sin becomes the provisional inertia of impulses, inherited from Neanderthal man, against the wider purposes of mind. Christ is the symbol of history itself, as in Hegel. The relation of the Kingdom of God to the moral perplexities and ambiguities of history is resolved in utopia. The strict distinction between justice and love in Catholic thought is marvelously precise and shrewd, compared with the general identification of the *agape* of the New Testament with the "community-building capacities of human sympathy" in the thought of Rauschenbusch. This reduction of the ethical meaning of the scandal of the cross, namely, sacrificial love, to the dimensions of simple mutuality imparts an air of sentimentality to all liberal Protestant social and political theories. Usually nothing is added to the insights of the sociology of Comte or Spencer.

At only one point is modern humanism transcended. The self must pray to express itself fully, but this prayer usually assumes a simple harmony between our highest aspirations and God's will. If Catholic thought represents a layer cake with a base of classical rationalism, this Christian liberalism in its most consistent form is a confection in which the whole cake comes from the modern temporal world view. The icing is Christian; and the debate between the secular and the Christian version is usually on the question of whether the icing is too sweet, or whether the cake would be more wholesome with or without the icing. All the tragic antinomies of history, the inner contradictions of human existence, and the ultimate mysteries of time and eternity are obscured. It is not easy to determine whether the antinomies and contradictions of human life and history have been obscured because the Christian frame of reference through which they could be seen has been disavowed, or whether this faith has been disavowed because it answered questions and resolved contradictions which were no longer felt.

Matthew Arnold illustrates the emphasis on congruity in the confluence of Christian and secular types of modern spirituality. He thought that the coincidence of virtue and happiness was the final proof of the truth of Christianity. The idealist Bradley made sport of this conviction, pointing out that nothing was more dubious than the idea of such a coincidence. He should have noted, however, that the idea of such a coincidence is as foreign to the Christian faith as it is untrue to experience. "This is thankworthy, if a man for conscience toward God endure grief, suffering wrongfully. For what glory is it, if, when ye be buffeted for your faults, ye shall take it patiently? But if ye do well and suffer for it, ye take it patiently, this is acceptable with God" (1 Pet. 2:19).

INCOHERENCE, KIERKEGAARD, AND BARTH

It is obviously perilous both to the content of the Christian faith and to the interpretation of life to place such reliance on the coherences and rationalities, the sequences and harmonies, of nature and reason. But the perils in the other direction are vividly displayed in contemporary as well as older Christian existentialism. The primary peril is that the wisdom of the Gospel is emptied of meaning by setting it into contradiction to the wisdom of the world and denying that the coherences and realms of meaning which the cultural disciplines rightfully analyze and establish have any relation to the gospel.

Kierkegaard's protest against Hegelianism betrays him into a position in which all inquiries into essences and universal forms are discounted in order to emphasize the existing particular. The existing individual is the only particular in history with its own internal history. Others have no internal history, and therefore no integral individuality, which could be known existentially. They must be known by fitting them into genus and species.

Kierkegaard, furthermore, exploits the inner contradiction within man—as free spirit and contingent object—too simply as the basis of faith. According to him, the individual, by embracing this contradiction in passionate subjectivity, rather than by evading it, comes truly to himself, chooses himself in his absolute validity. Though the writings of Kierkegaard contain a genuine expression of the Christian faith and are an exposition of the Pauline statement, "that I might know him, no rather that I might be known of him," there are notes in Kierkegaard's thought according to which the self really saves itself by choosing itself in its absolute validity. Sometimes this means that passionate subjectivity becomes the sole test of truth, in such a way that a disinterested worship of an idol is preferred to the wrong worship of the true God. This allows for a justified condemnation of a false worship of God, but it also lacks any standard by which the true God could be distinguished from a false one. In other words, a passionate Nazi could meet Kierkegaard's test. There are standards of judgment in Renaissance and liberal universalism which make their ethic preferable to this kind of hazardous subjectivity.

Sometimes Kierkegaard does choose a rigorous universalism to express the ethical life of the self in its absolute validity. In his *Works of Love*, Christian love is universal love, expressed as a sense of duty. It is a universalism almost identical with Kant's dictum that we must make our actions the basis of universal law. But there is no grace, no freedom, no release in it. It is full of the sweat of a plodding righteousness, and it hides the fact of the self's continued finiteness.

Both errors, though seemingly contradictory, prove that the problems of life have been solved too simply by embracing the inner contradiction in human existence, and not by a genuine commerce of repentance and faith between finite, sinful man and the grace of God. It is a warning that we cannot simply equate the Christian faith with a philosophy which embodies particularity and contradiction rather than one which obscures the particular and the contradictory.

These perils in Kierkegaard's existentialism may have helped to drive Karl Barth more and more in another direction. He will explore neither the inner contradictions of life nor the coherences and congruities of which philosophy speaks, for apologetic purposes. Ethically, Barth is as relativist as Westermarck and epistemologically as much a positivist as Carnap. Man does not know anything of significance. The Word of God is the only light which shines into his darkness, and its acceptance or nonacceptance is a pure mystery of grace. The sower merely sows upon all sorts of fields without inquiring whether it is this or that kind of ground, or whether a word of hope must be spoken to life in despair or a word of judgment to life caught in conventional complacency.

This means that the whole commerce between the foolishness of the gospel and the wisdom of the world, between faith and culture, is disavowed. The truth of the gospel does not stand at the limits of human wisdom. For there is no real content in this wisdom. One could not, for instance, from this standpoint engage in a debate with psychologists on the question of what level of human selfhood is adequately illumined by psychiatric techniques and what level of the self as subject and free spirit evades these analyses. Nor could one debate with social scientists on the possibilities and the limits of a rational justice in human society.

The exposition of the Christian faith, lacking this commerce with culture, becomes more and more literalistic and allegorical, since its only purpose can be to explain the inner coherence of the Scripture. In this enterprise, the fruits of historical scholarship are dealt with in more and more cavalier fashion, and the Old Testament is finally emptied of its most significant meanings, for these are related to particular points in history. An allegorical relation to Christ must be found in order to establish an immediate contact between the center of the spiritual truth and every word of scripture. This is no longer *Heilsgeschichte* but one vast allegory. The ethical consequences of this lack of dialogue between the disciplines of culture and the Christian faith are equally revealing. Barth declares it to be one of the mysteries of divine providence that a civil society should, despite the ideological taint on all its concepts of justice, yet achieve a measure of justice. This means that, with Thomas Hobbes, he arrives at the false conclusion that natural man has no capacity to consider interests other than his own. In short, he applies a doctrine of total depravity to the political realm, and therefore he cannot deal with the actualities of politics, which represent bewildering mixtures of idealism and self-interest, of the sense of justice and the inclination to injustice. We cannot afford to obscure the rational coherences in man's social life, however imperfect.

In this world, Barth bids the Christian Church to witness to the resurrection; that is, to set up signs and symbols of redemption in the confusion of sin. His signs are all explicitly eschatological. They must have something of the aura of martyrdom upon them. He bids the Church to wait until the issues are clear before it bears this heroic witness, just as he himself waited in witnessing against Hitlerism until the manifest injustices of a tyrannical state revealed their clearly idolatrous religious character. This is a religion, as a Catholic critic rightly observes, which is fashioned for the catacombs and has little relation to the task of transfiguring the natural stuff of politics by the grace and wisdom of the gospel.

In the realm of apologetics, Barth never explores the character of the wisdom of the world in its ambivalence between the idolatrous glorification of some particular center of meaning and the mystical search for an end which is free of idolatry but also empty of meaning. It is in this ambivalence that the true pathos of culture religion is to be found. For Barth, all natural religion represents idolatry, the false worship of the collective self as God. Actually there is, as Paul observed, a yearning for the true, the more ultimate, the unknown God beyond and above all the known gods of idolatry. It was at this point that Paul found a point of contact between the gospel and the religious yearnings of mankind. These religious yearnings do not yield a gospel. But they delineate the dimension of the human situation which makes the message of the gospel relevant.

There is, in short, no possibility of fully validating the truth in the foolishness of the gospel, if every cultural discipline is not taken seriously up to the point where it becomes conscious of its own limits, and the point where the insights of various disciplines stand in contradiction to each other, signifying that the total of reality is more complex than any scheme of rational meaning which may be invented to comprehend it.

BIBLICAL REALISM

These criticisms of the two best-known forms of Christian existentialism imply a third position which would distinguish itself from both by taking the coherences and causalities of life and history more seriously than Kierkegaard, and by rejecting the biblical literalism and negative attitude toward the disciplines of philosophy and the sciences into which Barth is betrayed. We might well define this position as biblical realism. The general outlines of such a position are at least negatively defined in the criticisms which have been made here of both the two forms of Christian rationalism and the two forms of Christian existentialism. One dilemma of such a position must be mentioned in conclusion. It is the one which gives a certain validity to the term "neo-orthodoxy."

If we take the disciplines of the various sciences seriously, as we do, we must depart at one important point from the biblical picture of life and history. The accumulated evidence of the natural sciences convinces us that the realm of natural causation is more closed, and less subject to divine intervention, than the biblical world view assumes. We can be completely biblical in interpreting the drama of human history as an engagement between man and God. We can see it, as neither the rationalists nor the naturalists can, as open to indeterminate possibilities of good and of evil. We can recognize in the course of history particular events which have a special depth and penetrate to the meaning of the whole, that is, revelation.

But meanwhile, this history has a base in nature as man himself has. And the course of nature is more subject to inflexible law than the Bible supposes. In other words, we have given up one kind of miracle, and miracle is the dearest child of faith. We do not have difficulty with all miracles. The healing miracles of Jesus, for instance, are credible because we recognize the depth and height of spirit in the dimension of each personality, and the consequent spiritual dimension of bodily ill. Psychosomatic medicine corroborates such a conception. But we do not believe in the virgin birth, and we have difficulty with the physical resurrection of Christ. We do not believe, in other words, that revelatory events validate themselves by a divine break-through in the natural order. There is a great spiritual gain in this position which is in accord with Christ's own rejection of signs and wonders as validations of his messianic mission: "This wicked generation seeketh a sign" (Matt. 12:39). It leads to an apprehension of the points of revelation by repentance and faith; that is to say, it insists that the truth of revelation must be apprehended by the whole person and cannot merely be accepted as a historical fact, validated by the miraculous character of the fact. The deeper truth must be apprehended by becoming the key which unlocks the mystery of what man is and should be, and of what God is in relations with men.

Yet there is a peril in this way of interpreting the gospel truth. The peril lies in the tendency to reduce Christianity to yet another philosophy, profounder than other philosophies because it embodies heights and depths which are not comprehended in the others. We say we take historical facts seriously but not literally; but that may be on the way of not taking them as historical facts at all. Thus we reject the myth of the fall of man as a historical fact. With that rejection, we can dispose of all nonsense about a biologically inherited corruption of sin. But we also easily interpret human evil as an inevitable condition of human finiteness and stand on the edge of Platonism. Or, by rejecting the end of the world as a literal event, we easily obscure the eternity at the end of time and are left with only an eternity over time, again a movement toward Platonism.

There is no simple solution for this problem. It is to be noted that the great Christian existentialists, Pascal, Luther, Kierkegaard, thought in a world in which modern science had not radically altered or was just beginning to alter the conception of nature. Modern Barthians blithely disregard the evidences of modern science as if they did not exist.

A MORE ADEQUATE APPROACH

If a solution is to be found in modern apologetics it must rest upon two primary propositions:

(1) A radical distinction between the natural world and the world of human history must be made, however much history may have a natural base. The justification for this distinction lies in the unique character of human freedom. Almost all the misinterpretations of human selfhood and the drama of history in the modern day are derived from the effort to reduce human existence to the coherence of nature.

(2) Human history must be understood as containing within it the encounters between man and God, in which God intervenes to reconstruct the rational concepts of meaning which men and cultures construct under the false assumption that they have a mind which

completely transcends the flux of history, when actually it can only construct a realm of meaning from a particular standpoint within the flux.

There are at least three ways in which the true God is encountered in history:

(1) God is encountered in creativities which introduce elements into the historic situation which could not have been anticipated. "God chose what is low and despised in the world, even things that are not, to bring to nothing things that are" (1 Cor. 1:28). In history this creativity appears as grace, as a form of election for which no reason can be given, as in God's covenant with Israel. If a reason is given for such events, they are falsely brought into a premature realm of coherence.

(2) God is encountered in judgment whenever human ideals, values, and historical achievements are discovered to be in contradiction to the divine rather than in simple harmony with the ultimate coherence of things. Included in such historical events are the prophetic testimonies which fathom the contradiction between the human and divine. God speaks to the believer not only in mighty acts but through the testimony of the prophets, the "God who spoke aforetime through the prophets" (cf. Rom. 1:2). The prophet Jeremiah significantly makes the promise of security for a particular historic stability, "Ye shall have assured peace in this place" (Jer. 14:13), into a test of false prophecy. No reason for these prophetic insights can be given. They are not anticipated by the highest culture, but they can by faith be incorporated into a new interpretation of the meaning of history.

(3) God is encountered in events in which the divine judgments lead to a reconstitution of life. These are revelations of redeeming grace in which the old self, including the collective self of false cultures, is destroyed, but the destruction leads to newness of life. The Bible rightly represents the whole drama of Christ as the final point in *Heilsgeschichte* (salvation history), for here every form of human goodness is revealed in its problematic character. But a recognition of that fact makes a new form of goodness possible. If we are baptized into Christ's death, we may rise with him to newness of life.

These historic events come to the believer as given. They can therefore not be anticipated by any philosophy of coherence. They presuppose an existential incoherence between human striving and the divine will. They can be appropriated only by faith, that is, existentially rather than speculatively, because the recognition of their truth requires a repentant attitude toward false completions of life from the human standpoint. Furthermore, they assert a relevance between a divine freedom and a human freedom, across the chasm of the inflexibilities of nature which have no other message but death, to this curious animal, man, who is more than an animal.

These historic revelations can be related speculatively to the various aspects of human existence, and can make sense out of them. Reason can thus follow after faith. It can also precede it, in the sense that a highly sophisticated reason can point to the limits of rational coherence in understanding contradictory aspects of reality, and more particularly to the dimension of the human spirit which cannot be understood without presupposing a dimension of divine freedom above the coherences of nature and mind as its environment. Such a sophisticated reason, in its endless self-transcendence, knows that all judgments passed upon it by history are subject to a more ultimate judgment: "He that judges me is the Lord"; and knows finally that it is abortively involved in overcoming the incongruity of its existence as free spirit and as object in nature, either by denying its freedom (sensuality) or by denying its finiteness (hubris). For this sin, when acknowledged, there is a cure, a humble and a charitable life. That testimony can enter into history as a proof of the Christian faith, which the unbelievers may see. But if it should be true that even the most righteous life remains in some degree of contradiction to the divine, it is hazardous either for individual Christians or the Church to point to their goodness as proofs of the truth of their faith. The final answer to this incoherence between the human and the divine will is the divine suffering mercy; and for this no reason can be given.

It is significant that the negative proofs of the Christian faith are not lost on the most sophisticated moderns who have recognized the inadequacy of the smooth pictures of man and history in modern culture. "It cannot be denied," writes an historian, "that Christian analyses of human conduct and of human history are truer to the facts of experience than alternative analyses." But, he adds, "whether the truth of these analyses can be derived only from presuppositions of the Christian faith remains to be determined."

Thus on the positive side we are where we have always been. Faith is not reason. It is "the substance of things hoped for, the evidence of things not seen" (Heb. 11:1). The situation for faith is only slightly altered by the new picture of a quasi-autonomous nature, created by God but not maintained by His fiat from moment to moment. No sign can be given but that of the prophet Jonah, by which Jesus meant the sign of death and resurrection (see Matt. 16:4). This is to say that whenever the vicissitudes from which the self, either individually or collectively, suffers are appropriated by faith as divine judgments and not as meaningless caprice, they result in the love, joy, and peace of a new life.

This faith in the sovereignty of a divine creator, judge, and redeemer is not subject to rational proof, because it stands beyond and above the rational coherences of the world and can therefore not be proved by an analysis of these coherences. But a scientific and philosophical analysis of these coherences is not incapable of revealing where they point beyond themselves to a freedom which is not in them, to contradictions between each other which suggest a profounder mystery and meaning beyond them. A theology which both holds fast to the mystery and meaning beyond these coherences and also has a decent respect for the order and meaning of the natural world cannot be a queen of the sciences, nor should she be the despised and neglected handmaiden of her present estate. Her proper position is that of the crucified Lord, who promises to come again with great power and glory. The power and glory are not a present possession. That is indicated by the fact that the accusers and crucifiers must always pay inadvertent tribute to the kingdom of truth, which they seek to despise.

16

MYSTERY AND MEANING

For now we see through a glass darkly; but then face to face: now I know in part; but then shall I know even as also I am known.

1 Cor. 13:12

The testimonies of religious faith are confused more greatly by those who claim to know too much about the mystery of life than by those who claim to know too little. Those who disavow all knowledge of the final mystery of life are so impressed by the fact that we see through a glass darkly that they would make no claim of seeing at all. In the history of culture such a position is known as agnosticism. Agnosticism sees no practical value in seeking to solve the mystery of life. But there are not really many agnostics in any age or culture. A much larger number of people forget that they see through a glass darkly. They claim to know too much.

Those who claim to know too much may be divided into two groups, one ostensibly religious and the other irreligious. The irreligious resolve the problem of human existence and the mystery of the created world into systems of easily ascertained meaning. They deny that there is any mystery in life or the world. If they can find a previous cause for any subsequent effect in nature, they are certain that they have arrived at a full understanding of why such and such a thing exists. The natural cause is, for them, an adequate explanation of anything they may perceive.

The religious group, on the other hand, recognizes that the whole of the created world is not self-explanatory. They see that it points beyond itself to a mysterious ground of existence, to an enigmatic power beyond all discernible vitalities, and to a "first cause" beyond all known causes. But they usually claim to know too much about this eternal mystery. Sometimes they sharply define the limits of reason, and the further limits of faith beyond reason, and claim to know exactly how far reason penetrates into the eternal mystery, and how much further faith reaches. Yet though they make a distinction between faith and reason, they straightway so mix and confuse reason and faith that they pretend to be able to give a rational and sharply defined account of the character of God and of the eternal ground of existence. They define the power and knowledge of God precisely, and explain the exact extent of His control and foreknowledge of the course of events. They dissect the mysterious relation between man's intellectual faculties and his vital capacities, and claim to know the exact limits of *phusis, psyche* and *nous*, of body, soul and spirit. They know that man is immortal and why; and just what portion and part of him is mortal and what part immortal. Thus they banish the mystery of the unity of man's spiritual and physical existence. They have no sense of mystery about the problem of immortality. They know the geography of heaven and of hell, and the furniture of the one and the temperature of the other.

CHARACTERISTICS OF GENUINE FAITH

A genuine Christian faith must move between those who claim to know so much about the natural world that it ceases to point to any mystery beyond itself and those who claim to know so much about the mystery of the "unseen" world that all reverence for its secret and hidden character is dissipated. A genuine faith must recognize the fact that it is through a dark glass that we see; though by faith we do penetrate sufficiently to the heart of the mystery not to be overwhelmed by it. A genuine faith resolves the mystery of life by the mystery of God. It recognizes that no aspect of life or existence explains itself, even after all known causes and consequences have been traced. All known existence points beyond itself. To realize that it points beyond itself to God is to assert that the mystery of life does not dissolve life into meaninglessness. Faith in God is faith in some ultimate unity of life, in some final comprehensive purpose which holds all the various, and frequently contradictory, realms of coherence and meaning together. A genuine faith does not mark this mysterious source and end of existence as merely an X, or as an unknown quantity. The Christian faith, at least, is a faith in revelation. It believes that God has made Himself known. It believes that He has spoken through the prophets and finally in His Son. It accepts the revelation in Christ as the ultimate clue to the mystery of God's nature and purpose in the world, particularly the mystery of the relation of His justice to His mercy. But these clues to the mystery do not eliminate the periphery of mystery. God remains *deus absconditus*.

Of the prophets of the Old Testament, Deutero-Isaiah is particularly conscious of the penumbra of mystery which surrounds the eternal and the divine. He insists upon the distance between the divine wisdom and human counsels: "Who hath directed the spirit of the Lord, or being his counsellor hath taught him?" (Isa. 40:13). He emphasizes the transcendence of God's power: "It is he that sitteth upon the circle of the earth, and the inhabitants thereof are as grasshoppers . . . that bringeth the princes to nothing; he maketh the judges of the earth as vanity: (Isa. 40:22–23). The question of the meaning of life must not be pressed too far, according to the prophet: "Woe unto him that striveth with his Maker. . . . Shall the clay say to him that fashioneth it, What makest thou? . . . Woe unto him that saith unto his father, What begettest thou? or to the woman, What hast thou brought forth?" (Isa. 45:9–10). Faith, as the prophet conceives it, discerns the meaning of existence but must not seek to define it too carefully. The divine wisdom and purpose must always be partly hid from human understanding—"For my thoughts are not your thoughts, neither are your ways my ways, saith the Lord. For as the heavens are higher than the earth, so are my ways higher than your ways, and my thoughts than your thoughts" (Isa. 55:8–9).

The sense of both mystery and meaning is perhaps most succinctly expressed in the forty-fifth chapter of Isaiah, where, practically in the same breath, the prophet declares on the one hand, "Verily thou art a God that hidest thyself, O God of Israel, the Saviour" (Isa. 45:15), and on the other, insists that God has made Himself known: "I have not spoken in secret, in a dark place of the earth: I said not unto the seed of Jacob, Seek ye me in vain: I the Lord speak righteousness, I declare things that are right" (Isa. 45:19). This double emphasis is a perfect symbolic expression both of the meaning which faith discerns and of the penumbra of mystery which it recognizes around the core of meaning. The essential character of God, in

His relations to the world, is known. He is the creator, judge and saviour of men. Yet He does not fully disclose Himself, and His thoughts are too high to be comprehended by human thought.

DESTROYING THE PENUMBRA OF MYSTERY

For some centuries the intellectual life of modern man has been dominated by rebellion against medieval faith. The main outlines of modern culture are defined by modern man's faith in science and his defiance of the authority of religion. This conflict between the faith which flowered in the thirteenth century and that which flowered in the seventeenth and eighteenth centuries is a conflict between two forms of faith which in their different ways obscured the penumbra of the mystery of life and made the core of meaning too large. Medieval Catholicism was not completely lacking in a reverent sense of mystery. The rites of the Church frequently excel the more rationalized forms of the Protestant faith by their poetic expression of mystery. There is, for instance, an advantage in chanting rather than saying a creed. The musical and poetical forms of a creed emphasize the salient affirmation of faith which the creed contains, and slightly derogate the exact details of symbolism through which the basic affirmation is expressed. That is a virtue of the liturgical and sacramental Church, which is hardened into a pitiless fundamentalism when every "i" is dotted and every "t" crossed in the soberly recited credo.

On the other hand, the same Catholic faith combined a pretentious rationalism with its sense of poetry. Any careful reading of the works of Thomas Aquinas must impress the thoughtful student with the element of pretension which informs the flowering of the Catholic faith in the "golden" thirteenth century. There seems to be no mystery which is not carefully dissected, no dark depth of evil which is not fully explained, and no height of existence which is not scaled. The various attributes of God are all carefully defined and related to each other. The mysteries of the human soul and spirit are mastered and rationally defined in the most meticulous terms. The exact line which marks justice from injustice is known. Faith and reason are so intermingled that the characteristic certainty of each is compounded with the other. Thus a very imposing structure is created. Yet it ought to have been possible to anticipate the doubts which it would ultimately arouse. Granted its foundation of presuppositions, every beam and joist in the intellectual structure is reared with perfect logical consistency. But the foundation is insecure. It is a foundation of faith in which the timeless affirmations of the Christian belief are compounded with detailed knowledge characteristic of a pre-scientific age. An age of science challenged this whole foundation of presupposition and seemed to invalidate the whole structure.

The new age of science attempted an even more rigorous denial of mystery. The age of science traced the relations of the world of nature, studied the various causes which seemed to be at the root of various effects in every realm of natural coherence; and came to the conclusion that knowledge dissolved mystery. Mystery was simply the darkness of ignorance which the light of knowledge dispelled. Religious faith was, in its opinion, merely the fear of the unknown which could be dissipated by further knowledge. In the one case the "spiritual," the "eternal" and the "supernatural," conceived as a separate and distinct realm of existence (instead of as the final ground and ultimate dimension of the unity of existence), is so exactly defined that the penumbra of mystery is destroyed. In the other case the "natural," the "temporal" and the "material" are supposedly comprehended so fully that they cease to point beyond themselves to a more ultimate mystery. There are significant differences between these two ways of apprehending the world about us and the depth of existence within us; but the differences are no greater than the similarity between them. Both ways contain an element of human pretension. Both fail to recognize that we see through a glass darkly.

THE MYSTERY OF NATURE

We see through a glass darkly when we seek to understand the world about us; because no natural cause is ever a complete and adequate explanation of the subsequent event. The subsequent event is undoubtedly causally related to preceding events; but it is only one of many untold possibilities which might have been actualized. The biblical idea of a divine creator moves on a different level than scientific concepts of causation. The two become mutually exclusive, as they have done in the controversies of recent ages, only if, on the one hand, we deny the mysterious element in creation and regard it as an exact explanation of why things are as they are and become what they become; and if, on the other hand, we deny the mystery which overarches the process of causation in nature. Thus two dimensions of meaning, each too exactly defined, come in conflict with each other. More truly and justly conceived, the realm of coherence, which we call nature, points to a realm of power beyond itself. This realm is discerned by faith, but not fully known. It is a mystery which resolves the mystery of nature. But if mystery is denied in each realm, the meaning which men pretend to apprehend in each becomes too pat and calculated. The depth of meaning is destroyed in the process of charting it exactly. Thus the sense of meaning is deepened, and not annulled, by the sense of mystery.

THE MYSTERY OF HUMAN NATURE

The understanding of ourselves is even more subject to seeing through a glass darkly than the understanding of the world about us. We "are fearfully and wonderfully made" (Ps. 139:14). Man is a creature of nature, subject to its necessities and bound by its limits. Yet he surveys the ages and touches the fringes of the eternal. Despite the limited character of his life, he is constantly under compulsions and responsibilities which reach to the very heart of the eternal.

> Thou hast beset me behind and before,
> And laid thine hand upon me.
> Such knowledge is too wonderful for me;
> It is high, I cannot attain unto it,

confesses the Psalmist in recording the universal human experience of feeling related to a divine lawgiver and judge. He continues:

> Whither shall I go from thy spirit?
> Or whither shall I flee from thy presence?
> If I ascend into heaven, thou art there:
> If I make my bed in hell, behold, thou art there.
> If I take the wings of the morning,
> And dwell in the uttermost parts of the sea;
> Even there shall thy hand lead me,
> And thy right hand shall hold me.

> (Ps. 139:5–10)

Thus the Psalmist continues in describing the boundless character of the human spirit, which rises above and beyond all finite limitations to confront and feel itself confronted by the divine.

The finiteness of human life, contrasted with the limitless quality of the human spirit, presents us with a profound mystery. We are an enigma to ourselves.

There are many forms of modern thought which deny the mystery of our life by reducing the dimension of human existence to the level of nature. We are animals, we are told, with a slightly greater reach of reason and a slightly "more complex central nervous system" than the other brute creatures. But this is a palpable denial of the real stature of man's spirit. We may be only slightly more inventive than the most astute monkey. But there is, as far as we know, no *Weltschmerz* in the soul of any monkey, no anxiety about what he is and ought to be, and no visitation from a divine accuser who "besets him behind and before" and from whose spirit he cannot flee. There is among animals no uneasy conscience and no ambition which tends to transgress all natural bounds and become the source of the highest nobility of spirit and of the most demonic madness.

We are a mystery to ourselves in our weakness and our greatness; and this mystery can be resolved in part only as we reach into the height of the mysterious dimension of the eternal into which the pinnacle of our spiritual freedom seems to rise. The mystery of God resolves the mystery of the self into meaning. By faith we find the source of our life: "It is he that hath made us and not we ourselves" (Ps. 100:3). Here too we find the author of our moral duties: "He that judgeth me is the Lord" (1 Cor. 4:4). And here is the certitude of our fulfillment: "But then shall I know even as also I am known" (1 Cor. 13:12), declares St. Paul. This is to say that despite the height of our vision, no man can complete the structure of meaning in which he is involved except as by faith he discerns that he "is known," though he himself only "knows in part." The human spirit reaches beyond the limit of nature and does not fully comprehend the level of reality into which it reaches. Any interpretation of life which denies this height of reality because it ends in mystery gives a false picture of the stature of man. On the other hand, any interpretation which seeks to comprehend the ultimate dimension by the knowledge and the symbols of the known world also gives a false picture of man. Such theologies obscure the finiteness of human knowledge. We see through a glass darkly when we seek to discern the divine ground and end of human experience; we see only by faith. But by faith we do see.

THE MYSTERY OF SIN

The source of the evil in us is almost as mysterious as the divine source and the end of our spiritual life. "O Lord," cried the prophet, "why hast thou made us to err from thy ways, and hardened our heart from thy fear?" (Isa. 63:17). We desire the good and yet do evil. In the words of St. Paul, "I delight in the law of God after the inward man: but I see another law in my members, warring against the law of my mind" (Rom. 7:22–23). The inclination to evil, which is primarily the inclination to inordinate self-love, runs counter to our conscious desires. We seem to be betrayed into it. "Now if I do that I would not, it is no more I that do it, but sin that dwelleth in me" (Rom. 7:20), declares St. Paul, in trying to explain the powerful drift toward evil in us against our conscious purposes.

There is a deep mystery here which has been simply resolved in modern culture. It has interpreted man as an essentially virtuous creature who is betrayed into evil by ignorance, or by evil economic, political, or religious institutions. These simple theories of historical evil do not explain how virtuous men of another generation created the evil in these inherited institutions, or how mere ignorance could give the evil in man the positive thrust and demonic energy in which it frequently expresses itself. Modern culture's understanding of the evil in man fails to do justice to the tragic and perplexing aspect of the problem.

Orthodox Christianity, on the other hand, has frequently given a dogmatic answer to the problem, which suggests mystery, but which immediately obscures the mystery by a dogmatic formula. Men are evil, Christian orthodoxy declared, because of the "sin of Adam" which has been transmitted to all men. Sometimes the mode of transmission is allowed to remain mysterious; but sometimes it is identified with the concupiscence in the act of procreation. This dogmatic explanation has prompted the justified protest and incredulity of modern man, particularly since it is generally couched in language and symbols taken from a pre-scientific age.

Actually there is a great mystery in the fact that man, who is so created that he cannot fulfill his life except in his fellowmen, and who has some consciousness of this law of love in his very nature, should nevertheless seek so persistently to make his fellowmen the tools of his desires and the objects of his ambitions. If we try to explain this tendency toward self-love, we can find various plausible explanations. We can say it is due to the fact that man exists at the juncture of nature and spirit, of freedom and necessity. Being a weak creature, he is anxious for his life; and being a resourceful creature, armed with the guile of spirit, he seeks to overcome his insecurity by the various instruments which are placed at his disposal by the resources of his freedom. But inevitably, the security which he seeks for himself is bought at the price of other men's security. Being an insignificant creature with suggestions of great significance in the stature of his freedom, man uses his strength to hide his weakness and thus falls into the evil of the lust for power and self-idolatry.

These explanations of man's self-love are plausible enough as far as they go. But they are wrong if they assume that the peculiar amphibious situation of man, being partly immersed in the time process and partly transcending it, must inevitably and necessarily tempt him to an inordinate self-love. The situation does not create evil if it is not falsely interpreted. From whence comes the false interpretation? There is thus great profundity in the biblical myth of the serpent who "tempted" Eve by suggesting that God was jealous of man's strength and sought to limit it. Man's situation tempts to evil, provided man is unwilling to accept the peculiar weakness of his creaturely life, and is unable to find the ultimate source and end of his existence beyond himself. It is man's unbelief and pride which tempt to sin. And every such temptation presupposes a previous "tempter" (of which the serpent is the symbol). Thus before man fell into sin there was, according to Biblical myth, a fall of the devil in heaven. The devil is a fallen angel who refused to accept his rightful place in the scheme of things and sought a position equal to God.

This then is the real mystery of evil; that it presupposes itself. No matter how far back it is traced in the individual or the race, or even preceding the history of the race, a profound scrutiny of the nature of evil reveals that there is an element of sin in the temptation which leads to sin; and that, without this presupposed evil, the consequent sin would not necessarily arise from the situation in which man finds himself. This is what Kierkegaard means by saying that "sin posits itself." This is the mystery of "original sin" about which Pascal truly observes that "without this mystery man remains a mystery to himself."

Purely sociological and historical explanations of the rise of evil do not touch the depth of the mystery at all. Christian dogmatic explanations have some sense of it; but they obscure it as soon as they have revealed it by their pat dogmatic formulae. In dealing with the problem of sin, the sense of meaning is inextricably interwoven with the sense of mystery. We see through a glass darkly when we seek to understand the cause and the nature of evil in our own souls. But we see more profoundly when we know it is through a dark glass that we see than if we pretend to have clear light upon this profound problem.

THE MYSTERY OF DEATH

The final mystery about human life concerns its incompleteness and the method of its completion. Here again modern culture has resolved all mystery into simple meaning. It believes that the historical process is such that it guarantees the ultimate fulfillment of all legitimate human desires. It believes that history, as such, is redemptive. Men may be frustrated today, may live in poverty and in conflict, and may feel that they "bring their years to an end like a tale that is told." But the modern man is certain that there will be a tomorrow in which poverty and war and all injustice will be abolished. Utopia is the simple answer which modern culture offers in various guises to the problem of man's ultimate frustration. History is, according to the most characteristic thought of modern life, a process which gradually closes the hiatus between what man is and what he would be.

The difficulty with this answer is that there is no evidence that history has any such effect. In the collective enterprises of man, the progress of history arms the evil, as well as the good, with greater potency; and the mystery of how history is to be brought to completion, therefore, remains on every level of human achievement. It may in fact express itself more poignantly in the future than in the past.

Furthermore, there is no resolution of the problem of the individual in any collective achievement of mankind. The individual must continue to find the collective life of man his ultimate moral frustration, as well as his fulfillment. For there is no human society, and there can be none, the moral mediocrity of which must not be shocking to the individual's highest moral scruples. Furthermore, the individual dies before any of the promised collective completions of history.

But this is not all. The problem of death is deeply involved with the problem of sin. Men die with an uneasy conscience and must confess with the Psalmist, "for we are consumed by thine anger and by thy wrath are we troubled" (Ps. 90:7). Any honest self-analysis must persuade us that we end our life in frustration not only because "our reach is beyond our grasp," i.e., because we are finite creatures with more than finite conceptions of an ultimate consummation of life, but also because we are sinners who constantly introduce positive evil into the operations of divine providence.

The answer of Christian faith to this problem is belief in "the forgiveness of sin and life everlasting." We believe that only a power greater than our own can complete our incomplete life, and only a divine mercy can heal us of our evil. Significantly St. Paul adds this expression of Christian hope immediately to his confession that we see through a glass darkly. We see through a glass darkly now, "but then" we shall "see face to face." Now we "know in part" but "then" we shall know even as we are known (cf. 1 Cor. 13:12). This Christian hope makes it possible to look at all the perplexities and mysteries of life without too much fear.

In another context St. Paul declares: "We are perplexed, but not unto despair" (2 Cor. 4:8). One might well divide the world into those who are not perplexed, those who are perplexed unto despair, and those who are perplexed but not unto despair. Those who are not perplexed have dissolved all the mysteries and perplexities of life by some simple scheme of meaning. The scheme is always too simple to do justice to the depth of man's problem. When life reveals itself in its full terror, as well as its full beauty, these little schemes break down. Optimism gives way to despair. The Christian faith does not pretend to resolve all perplexities. It confesses the darkness of human sight and the perplexities of faith. It escapes despair nevertheless because it holds fast to the essential goodness of God as revealed in Christ, and is therefore "persuaded that neither life nor death are able to separate us from the love of God, which is in Christ Jesus our Lord" (Rom. 8:38–39).

It can not be denied, however, that this same Christian faith is frequently vulgarized and cheapened to the point where all mystery is banished. The Christian faith in heaven is sometimes as cheap as, and sometimes even more vulgar than, the modern faith in Utopia. It may be even less capable of expressing the final perplexity and the final certainty of faith. On this issue, as on the others we have considered, a faith which measures the final dimension of existence, but dissipates all mystery in that dimension, may be only a little better or worse than a shallow creed which reduces human existence to the level of nature.

Our situation is that, by reason of the freedom of our spirit, we have purposes and ends beyond the limits of the finiteness of our physical existence. Faith may discern the certainty of a final completion of life beyond our power, and a final purging of the evil which we introduce into life by our false efforts to complete it in our own strength. But faith cannot resolve the mystery of how this will be done. When we look into the future we see through a glass darkly. The important issue is whether we will be tempted by the incompleteness and frustration of life to despair; or whether we can, by faith, lay hold on the divine power and wisdom which completes what remains otherwise incomplete. A faith which resolves mystery too much denies the finiteness of all human knowledge, including the knowledge of faith. A faith which is overwhelmed by mystery denies the clues of divine meaning which shine through the perplexities of life. The proper combination of humility and trust is precisely defined when we affirm that we see, but admit that we see through a glass darkly.

MEANING IN THE MIDST OF MYSTERY

Our primary concern in this exposition of the Pauline text has been to understand the fact that the Christian faith is conscious of the penumbra of mystery which surrounds its conception of meaning.

Yet in conclusion it must be emphasized that our faith cannot be identified with poetic forms of religion which worship mystery without any conception of meaning. All such poetic forms of faith might well be placed in the category of the worship of the unknown God, typified in the religion which Paul found in Athens. In contrast to this religion Paul set the faith which is rooted in the certainty that the mysterious God has made Himself known, and that the revelation of His nature and purpose, apprehended by faith, must be declared: "Whom therefore ye ignorantly worship him declare I unto you" (Acts 17:23). This declaration of faith rests upon the belief that the divine is not mere mystery, the heart of it having been disclosed to those who are able to apprehend the divine disclosure in Christ. It is by the certainty of that faith that St. Paul can confidently look toward a future completion of our imperfect knowledge: "Now I know in part, but *then* shall I know" (1 Cor. 13:12). The indication that faith regards the meaning, which has been disclosed, as victorious over the mystery of existence is the expression of a certain hope that "then shall I know." Faith expects that ultimately all mystery will be resolved in the perfect knowledge of God.

Faith in a religion of revelation is thus distinguished on the one side from merely poetic appreciations of mystery, just as on the other side it is distinguished from philosophies of religion which find the idea of revelation meaningless. Revelation is meaningless to all forms of rational religion which approach the mystery of life with the certainty that human reason can at length entirely resolve the mystery. The Christian faith is the right expression of the greatness and the weakness of man in relation to the mystery and the meaning of life. It is an acknowledgment of human weakness, for, unlike "natural religion" and "natural theology," it does not regard the human mind as capable of resolving the enigma of existence, because it knows that human reason is itself involved in the enigma which it tries to comprehend. It is an acknowledgment of the greatness of the human spirit because it assumes that man is capable of apprehending clues to the divine mystery and accepting the disclosure of the purposes of God which He has made to us. It is a confession at once of both weakness and strength, because it recognizes that the disclosures of the divine are given to man, who is capable of apprehending them, when made, but is not capable of anticipating them.

According to the Christian faith there is a light which shineth in darkness; and the darkness is not able to comprehend it (cf. John 1:5). Reason does not light that light; but faith is able to pierce the darkness and apprehend it.

Epilogue: A View of Life From the Sidelines

It may be hazardous to give an account of my experiences, and my changed perspectives and views, following a stroke that lamed my left side in 1952, in the sixtieth year of my life. Perhaps the simile "from the sidelines" is inadequate to describe the contrast between my rather too-hectic activities as a member of the Union Theological Seminary faculty; as weekly circuit rider preaching every Sunday in the colleges of the east; and as a rather polemical journalist who undertook to convert liberal Protestantism from its perfectionist illusions in the interventionist political debates at a time when Hitler threatened the whole of Western culture—and the inactivity and helplessness I experienced after my stroke.

The physical trauma prompted at least three depressions, which my neurologist regarded as normal. He was not, however, averse to my seeking advice from friendly psychiatrists. I learned from them, particularly those who combined clinical experience with wisdom and compassion, that the chief problem was to reconcile myself to this new weakness; I had to live through these depressions. Then, as various ancillary ailments increased, my working day grew shorter and shorter but my depressions ceased—because, I imagine, I had adjusted myself to my increasing weakness. Also, daily therapy prevented spastic limbs from growing worse, and this gave me hope. In 1952, neurologists were not particularly interested in rehabilitation; I had to wait about ten years for these therapies. Then my old friend the late Waldo Frank told me about his daughter, Deborah Caplan, who had been trained by the famous Howard Rusk. She not only gave me weekly treatments but trained a number of young nurses, some of whom happened to be the wives of my students, to give me daily therapy. I owe to them a tremendous debt, as I do also to our old friend, Hannah Burrington of Heath, Massachusetts, who stayed with my wife and me every summer and gave me twice-daily treatments.

My first stroke, which was not too severe, was caused by a cerebral vascular thrombosis. Some of my doctors attributed it to nervous exhaustion, while others said it was caused by defective "plumbing" and might have occurred in the life of a janitor. I lost my speech for two days, and the following two years were rough. I was given sick leave from the seminary, but eventually resumed my academic work until my retirement in 1960. With the help of my wife, I was able to accept visiting professorships at Harvard, Princeton and Columbia. My frustration at the relative inactivity was overcome somewhat in that I could continue writing articles and editorials. I used an electric typewriter but found it impossible to use a dictaphone. The habits of a lifetime ordained that I must see what I write, line by line.

In short, my dismissal from the "playing fields" to the "sidelines" was accomplished gradually; but now, in the seventy-fifth year of my life, suffering from various ills and weaknesses, I am conscious of the contrast between an active and a semidependent status. These fifteen years represent almost a quarter of the years of my ministry.

I must confess my ironic embarrassment as I lived through my depressions, which had the uniform characteristic of an anxious pre-occupation with real or imagined future perils. The embarrassment, particularly, was occasioned by the incessant correspondence about a prayer I had composed years before, which the old Federal Council of Churches had used and which later was printed on small cards to give to soldiers. Subsequently Alcoholics Anonymous adopted it as its official prayer. The prayer reads: "God, give us grace to accept with serenity the things that cannot be changed, courage to change the things that should be changed, and the wisdom to distinguish the one from the other."

Many friendly and inquiring correspondents asked for the original inspiration of the prayer, whether I was really its author, or whether it had been Francis of Assisi, or even an admiral who had used it in a shipboard worship service. I received about two such letters a week, and every answer to an inquiring correspondent embarrassed me because I knew that my present state of anxiety defied the petition of this prayer. I confessed my embarrassment to our family physician, who had a sense of humor touched with gentle cynicism. "Don't worry," he said, "Doctors and preachers are not expected to practice what they preach." I had to be content with this minimal consolation.

Now I must come to a discussion of the view of life from the sidelines as compared with the view of life that active participation encourages. This cannot be adequately presented without a discriminate analysis of two connotations of the word "sidelines." Sidelines are on the one hand filled with athletes who have been injured in the battles of the arena, and on the other hand with spectators. My view of life since my stroke had to be informed by both connotations. I was dismissed from the battle, but I was also a spectator to engagements that had hitherto occupied me. Emancipation from the endless discussions of committee meetings, trying to solve problems in both religious and political communities that had hitherto occupied so much of my time, was a desirable freedom from the chores of a democratic society; but it also meant an emancipation from responsibility—a doubtful boon, because responsibility engages us in the causes of moral, political and religious movements.

I still remain uncertain whether the relaxation of the polemical attitudes of my youthful zest for various causes represents the wisdom of old age, the disengagement of a spectator, or an increasing awareness of the strange mixture of good and evil in all the causes and purposes that once had prompted me to carry the banners of religion against secularism, and of Protestantism against Catholicism. I now hope that the unpolemical attitudes of my old age and dependence may have had their roots in experience, rather than in the irresponsibility of weakness and lack of engagement. My early polemical attitude toward the Catholic Church had been modified when, in the days of the New Deal social revolution, the Catholic Church revealed that it was much more aware of the social substance of human nature, and of the discriminate standards of justice needed in the collective relations of a technical culture, than was our individualistic Protestantism. But my view from the sidelines of illness made me more fully aware of the impressive history of the Catholic faith, and of its sources of grace and justice, which even our Reformation polemics cannot obscure.

There is some advantage in the spectator's view as opposed to the advocate's. One can see all the strange forms of spirit and culture that a common faith may take, without disloyalty to one's inherited beliefs. It can be exciting when one ceases to be a consistent advocate and polemical agent of a belief system. If I feel, at times, that an attitude from the sidelines may betray the irresponsibility of a pure spectator, I console myself with the fact that my current loyalty to causes, while less copious, is also more selective. And on the two main collective moral issues of our day—the civil rights movement that seeks democratic improvements for our black minority, and opposition to the terrible and mistaken war in Vietnam—the thoroughly ecumenical cooperation among the three biblical faiths gives one a reassuring confidence that unpolemical attitudes are not in contrast to moral commitments. My semiretirement has brought me nearer to the common moral commitments of the three faiths.

The physical ills that consigned me to the "sidelines" were productive in furnishing me with insights about human nature that had never occurred to me before. I learned to know the goodness of men and women who went out of their way to help an invalid. Among the persons who impressed me with their helpfulness were my doctors, nurses and therapists, my colleagues and friends in the realms of both politics and religion. I soon learned that some of these people who entered my life professionally, or who served me nonprofessionally with visits and walks, showed an almost charismatic gift of love. And, of course, my chief source of spiritual strength was my wife. She was my nurse, secretary, editor, counselor and friendly critic through all those years of illness and occasional depression. We had been happily married for two decades, but I had never measured the depth and breadth of her devotion until I was stricken. It may be an indication of my male pride that I had only casually relied on her superior sense of style in editing my books and articles. Now I absolutely relied on her editing, and it dealt not only with style but, more and more, with the substance of my thought.

Again and again she assured me that I would do as much for her, were she ill. But I doubted it, because I was inclined to affirm the superior *agape* of woman.

The retrospective view that my illness made inevitable was not reassuring for my ego. I found it embarrassing that my moral teachings, which emphasized the mixture of self-regard and creativity in all human motives, had not been rigorously applied to my own motives. I do not pretend that this new insight made for saintliness.

My experience is that constant illness tends to induce preoccupation with one's ills; the tyranny of invalids is a well-known
phenomenon.

The mixture of motives in all people, incidentally, refutes the
doctrines both of total depravity and of saintliness. In my case, ret-
rospection from the sidelines prompted me to remember many instances in my earlier years when my wife had protested my making
an extra trip or going to yet another conference, despite my weari-
ness; I always pleaded the importance of the cause that engaged me,
and it never occurred to me that I might have been so assiduous in
these engagements because the invitations flattered my vanity.

I now proceed to two more objective insights from the "sidelines." The one concerns my view of the church as a hearer, rather
than a preacher, of sermons. I had only one parish, in Detroit, where
I served as pastor after my graduation from the Yale Divinity School
in 1915 until my appointment to the faculty of Union Seminary in
1928. But in subsequent years I was, as I said, a preacher in the universities and, of course, in our seminary chapel. The life of the local
church was therefore terra incognita to me. After my illness I wor-
shiped in many local churches, particularly in the summer months.

I had always believed that the vitality of religion after the rise of
modern science, which tended to discredit the legends of religious
history, was due to the simple fact that faith in an incomprehensible
divine source of order was an indispensable bearer of the human
trust in life, despite the evils of nature and the incongruities of history. An aura of mystery surrounded every realm of historical meaning. But as I became a pew-worshiper rather than the preacher, I had
some doubts about the ability of us preachers to explicate and sym-
bolize this majesty and mystery. These pulpit-centered churches of
ours, without a prominent altar, seemed insufficient. Moreover, in
the nonliturgical churches the "opening exercises"—with a long
pastoral prayer which the congregation could not anticipate or join
in—seemed inadequate. I came to view the Catholic mass as, in
many religious aspects, more adequate than our Protestant worship.
For the first time I ceased to look at Catholicism as a remnant of
medieval culture. I realized that I envied the popular Catholic mass
because that liturgy, for many, expressed the mystery which makes
sense out of life always threatened by meaninglessness.

The second insight about religious faith that I gained from the years of partial invalidism has to do with the problem of mortality and our seeming disinclination to accept the fact. All human beings face death as an inevitable destiny, but those of us who are crippled by heart disease or cerebral injury or other illness are more conscious of this destiny, particularly as we advance in years. The fear of death was a frequent topic of conversation with my closest friend. We were both in a situation in which death might be imminent. We both agreed that we did not fear death—though I must confess that we did not consider the unconscious, rather than the conscious, fear that might express itself. We believed in both the immortality and the mortality of the person, and acknowledged that the mystery of human selfhood was quite similar to the mystery of the divine. In the Hebraic-Christian faith, God both transcends, and is involved in, the flux of time and history. The human personality has the same transcendence and involvement, but of course the transcendence of mortals over the flux of time is not absolute. We die, as do all creatures. But it is precisely our anxious foreboding of our death that gives us a clue to the dimension of our deathlessness.

The belief in a life after death, held by both primitive and high religions, reveals the human impulse to speculate about our deathlessness, despite the indisputable proofs of our mortality. In the Greek and Hebrew faiths, which converge in the Christian faith, we have a significant contrast of the symbols of this faith. The Hebrews, and of course our New Testament, are confident of the "resurrection of the body," thus emphasizing the integral unity of the person in body and soul.

This symbolic expression of faith is currently almost neglected, despite the biblical references to it in the liturgy of funeral services. We moderns seem to believe that the notion of a disembodied immortal soul is more credible than the idea of resurrection. In fact, we have no empirical experience either of a resurrected body or of a disembodied soul. This confusion of symbols in the religious observance at the time of death, incidentally observed even by families of little religious faith, may indicate that belief in the deathlessness of mortal humans is not taken too seriously in strict dogmatic terms. But it does reveal the faith that most of us have, a presupposition of the residual immortality of our mortal friends. We express it simply in the phrase, "I can't believe he's dead." There are, of course, many forms of social immortality. Political heroes are immortal in the memory of their nations; the great figures in the arts and sciences, or of any discipline of culture, have social immortality in their respective disciplines; we common mortals are, at least, remembered by our dear ones. But there is a dimension of human personality that is not acknowledged in these forms of social immortality.

The very contrast between the two symbols of resurrection and immortality in our Western Christian tradition calls attention to this ambiguity in the dimension of deathlessness in our mortal frame. I am personally content to leave this problem of deathlessness in the frame of mystery, and to console myself with the fact that the mystery of human selfhood is only a degree beneath the mystery of God.

This symbolic expression of faith is currently almost neglected. If we recognize that the human self is not to be equated with its mind, though the logical and analytic faculties of the mind are an instrument of its freedom over nature and history, and if we know that the self is intimately related to its body but cannot be equated with its physical functions, we then are confronted with the final mystery of its capacity of transcendence over nature, history and even its own self; and we will rightly identify the mystery of selfhood with the mystery of its indeterminate freedom.

This freedom is its guarantee of the self's relations with the dimension of the "Eternal." While mortal, it has the capacity to relate itself to the "things that abide." St. Paul enumerates these abiding things as "faith, hope and love." Faith is the capacity to transcend all the changes of history and to project an ultimate source and end of temporal and historical reality. Hope is the capacity to transcend all the confusions of history and project an ultimate end of all historical existence, that which does not annul history but fulfills it. Love is the capacity to recognize the social substance of human existence, and to realize that the unique self is intimately related to all human creatures. These capacities relate the self to the eternal world and are its keys to that world.

In an Hebraic-biblical faith, neither history nor human selfhood is regarded as an illness of the flux of the temporal world from which we must escape. Each is regarded as a creation of the divine which is fulfilled, and not annulled by the source and end of history which is rightly revered as divine. Thus the individual, though mortal, is given, by self-transcendent freedom, the key to immortality. Individual selfhood is not a disaster or an evil. It is subsumed in the counsels of God and enters the mystery of immortality by personal relation to the divine. I could not, in all honesty, claim more for myself and my dear ones, as I face the ultimacy of death in the dimension of history, which is grounded in nature.

Index of Persons

Index of Scriptural References

Index of Subjects

and moral passion, 64–65; in nature and history, 65; misunderstandings of, 65–67; as power and pardon, 103; "common grace," 145, 146, 197; and duty, 144–46; and law in Judaism and Christianity, 193–97

Heresy, 103–05
Hope, 84–85, 156
Humour: and faith, 49–60; and despair, 51. *See also* Laughter

Idealism, 51, 56, 123–24, 127, 219, 221; and "children of light," 165–81
Ideology: and scientific method, 205–17; in Marx, 206–08; limitations of liberal ideology, 208–10
Idolatry, 80, 98, 138
Incoherence, 218–36; in Kierkegaard and Barth, 228–31
Incongruity, 49–51, 55–59
Israel, State of, 199–200

Jews and Judaism, 13, 15, 44, 64; ethnic and religious divergences, 182–84; relation to Christianity, 182–201; capacity for civic virtue, 185–88; beliefs shared with Christianity, 188–90; divergences from Christianity, 192–201
Justice: and mercy, 28–30, 42–43, 72–76

Kingdom of God, 12, 27, 75, 83, 86–89, 92, 96, 104, 107, 110, 113–15, 193; and parable of wheat and tares, 41, 44–48

Laughter, 49–60; of God, 49–50, 95; and human judgments, 51–55; and divine judgment, 53–54; at the self, 54–56; and contrition, 55, 58; and incongruity, 56–57; and evil and death, 57–59; limitations of, 59–60
Law: defined, 142–43; in relation to love, 142–59
Love, 14, 85–86, 89, 91, 96, 99, 102, 104–06, 109, 111, 113–14, 142, 143, 146; as "impossible possibility," 103; of neighbor, 108–09, 136, 155; as principle of indiscriminate criticism, 113–16; as principle of discriminate criticism, 116–18; as sacrificial, 136–37, 149–52, 223; in relation to law, 142–59; varieties of, 144; as universal, 147–49; as forgiveness, 152–54; as "morality beyond morality," 153; as standing in place of other, 155–57; and sexual union, 156, 158. See also *Agape; Eros; Philia*

Marcionism, 130
Marxism, 10–12, 83, 85, 94–95, 129, 164, 176–77, 214–16; secular version of Jewish prophecy, 10; myths of, 10–11; as Messianic, 11; as utopian, 12; limits of, 205–08
Meaning, 34, 39, 59, 67, 85, 97, 234–36; need for a sense of, 3–17; threats to, 4; in relation to mystery, 237–49. See *also* Coherence
Mercy, 34, 63–65, 74–75, 85, 87, 92, 222, 235, 247; and justice, 28–30; and judgment, 98–100; as final resource of gospel, 102–03; tension with righteousness, 111–13
Messianism, 11, 21–22, 26; difference between Jewish and Christian versions of, 189
Middle Ages, 6, 8, 12, 90, 95, 130, 132, 140, 161–64, 167, 168, 184–85
Mystery, 14–16, 42, 138, 220–22, 225, 226, 230, 236, 254; and meaning, 29–30, 237–49; Thomistic dissipation of, 240–41; of nature, 241–42; denials of, 241, 243; of human nature, 242–44; of sin, 244–46; of death, 246–48, 256
Mysticism, 82, 148, 221
Myth, mythology, 7, 15, 62, 64, 66–69, 71

Naturalism, 8, 10, 13, 51, 56, 219–21
Natural law, 7, 8, 129–31, 142, 144, 154, 158, 223
Nature, 7–9, 13–14, 37–39, 61–70, 73; versus history, 205–17; mystery of, 241–42
Nazis, Nazism, 11, 36, 39, 47, 118, 164, 166, 178, 199, 210, 219
Neo-Platonism, 6, 68, 125, 138, 221, 222